Making
Each Other
Laugh

Making Each Other Laugh

Contemporary Arapaho Storytelling

ANDREW COWELL

University of Oklahoma Press : Norman

Publication of this book is made possible in part by a grant from the University Press Language Tutorial Fund.

Library of Congress Control Number: 2024059334
ISBN: 978-0-8061-9600-8 (hardcover)

The paper in this book meets the guidelines for permanence and durability of the Committee on Production Guidelines for Book Longevity of the Council on Library Resources, Inc. ∞

The manufacturer's authorized representative in the EU for product safety is Mare Nostrum Group B.V., Mauritskade 21D, 1091 GC Amsterdam, The Netherlands, email: gpsr@mare-nostrum.co.uk.

*[There's] a lot of stories like that; when they're told
in Arapaho, they're a lot [more] . . . real funny, comical.
So, you can make a little book out of [them], like that,
out of small, short stories. And they're, they're common.
But you know if we, let 'em go, just, we'll lose 'em forever,
the small stories, short stories, these comical ones.*

Alonzo Moss Sr., 2005

*Those Arapahos, when they told stories in Arapaho . . .
that's when they would get together. They made each other
laugh. But in English you can't tell it. The humor is lost.
Yeah, for sure! The humor is lost.*

Joint conversation, 2016 (translated from Arapaho)

Contents

Acknowledgments

The work that led to this book was supported by several grants: a Major Documentation Grant from the Hans Rausing Endangered Language Documentation Programme (ELDP); a National Park Service Historic Preservation Trust Fund grant; a Wyoming Council for the Humanities Language Preservation grant; and NSF/NEH Documenting Endangered Languages Program grant #1360809 for an Arapaho lexical database and dictionary. A number of the audio and video recordings on which the material in this book is based are archived in the digital Endangered Languages Archive (ELAR) as part of the ELDP grant.

This work has also been supported by the generosity of Sara and Steve Wiles, who for many years have provided me with in-kind food and lodging during my work in Wyoming; Sara, in particular, has also provided useful and stimulating conversation about the Northern Arapaho people. Without their generosity, I could have accomplished much less with the grant funding I received.

Thanks as well to my adopted Northern Arapaho family, the Moss family, who have provided crucial insight and support, and also to the C'Hair family for their support. And, of course, thanks to the more than one hundred Arapaho speakers who have contributed to my learning and documentation of the Arapaho language over the years.

Labeling and Conventions Used in This Book

[[ ]]   indicates multimodal features of Arapaho narratives: pauses, gesture, silence, etc.

(( ))   indicates editorial comments or guidance on story content, not part of the original text.

[indicates overlapping speech, as in:

> Speaker 1:   I was saying that [he was happy
> Speaker 2:   [yeah, right

[ ]   indicates additional content added to a transcription or translation for clarity's sake

{ }   indicates elements of speech in the Arapaho transcription that are clearly speaker errors

-    Indicates a break in an Arapaho word between the core "stem" of the word and prefixes and suffixes

=   Indicates a proclitic (a loosely attached prefix, sometimes treated by speakers as a separate word)

XXX   indicates speech that could not be transcribed due to features such as a cough by another speaker, overlaps, background noise, etc.

(?)   indicates either a questionable transcription (in the original Arapaho) or a questionable translation (in the English)

???   indicates speech for which no translation could be proposed

P   indicates a pause or break in a word or an uncompleted word

PSL   indicates a Plains sign language gesture

sec.   second(s) of silence

1

Arapaho Oral Stories
and Story Sequences
of the Reservation Era

Native American verbal narrative traditions are an impressive part of our global cultural heritage. They are also absolutely fundamental to tribal knowledge, language, culture, history and identity. Having learned the Arapaho language and worked with the Arapaho people for more than two decades, I have heard over and over about the importance of stories in Arapaho life, and I have witnessed hundreds of tellings of stories. Older Arapaho people recall with special fondness those times before the arrival of television, when as children they would fall asleep listening to their grandparents tell them stories on a winter's evening. People stress to me that the stories are a virtual dictionary of the Arapaho language, since they contain many rare and complex words whose usage can be learned only from the stories. They are also a virtual encyclopedia of Arapaho wisdom and values: Alonzo Moss Sr., with whom I worked for many years, noted often that "you could teach a whole lesson on every sentence in my dad [Paul's] stories" (see Cowell and Moss 2005 for a collection of Paul's stories). And the stories are often hilarious, as people rarely fail to point out! As much as elders today fondly recall childhood story sessions, they also joyously recall the uproarious laughter that would ensue as their grandparents told *each other* stories, in order to "make each other laugh."

One thing that non–Native Americans often fail to appreciate, however, is that these stories are still around and are still being told, and more importantly, that new ones are still being created to comment on and deal with the ever-changing modern world. Non-Natives tend to think of Native American storytelling as a "traditional" activity, focused on "traditional" topics and themes related to precontact days—a tendency unfortunately reinforced by many widely available anthologies of Native American verbal narratives (more on these later). The Arapaho do indeed have a great variety of traditional narratives (see Cowell, Moss, and C'Hair 2014), and these are well worth increased attention. But the people also have a rich variety of narratives that have been created since their forced settlement on reservations and which engage very specifically with the challenges of modern society, including relationships with Euro-Americans. These "reservation-era" oral narratives have received far less attention than earlier forms such as creation stories, myths and legends, and trickster stories, both for Arapahos and for Native Americans in general. The focus of this anthology and study is therefore on Arapaho reservation-era oral narratives.

Single Stories Versus Story Sequences

As a Euro-American scholar writing about Native American peoples and topics, I increasingly think about the relationship between my own identity and perspectives and those of the peoples I am presenting to readers. Over recent decades, people of all backgrounds have expressed an increasing desire to hear the voices of Native Americans themselves, as opposed to voices filtered through scholarly perspectives. One obvious way to achieve this is to offer stories—or oral narratives, to use a more scholarly term—told by Native Americans in their own voices. Even more obviously, the stories should be presented in the language of the tellers—Arapaho in the case of this book.

Stories alone however can be difficult to appreciate without context, especially across cultural divides. For this reason academic fields such as ethnopoetics (see Tedlock 1972 and Hymes 1981 for classic examples) and performance studies (see Turner 1986 and Bauman 1986 for classic examples) have arisen over the years. These fields attempt to offer stories in Native languages and to provide the context needed for better understanding the stories—both the artistic contexts, such as the genres and performance traditions of the stories, and the social contexts that surround the particular moment of the telling.

Within these fields, the vast majority of articles, chapters, and even books typically present either single narratives or sets of single narratives for appreciation and analysis. Yet, from my own experience I know that a single story is rarely told alone in Arapaho society, or in most Native American or other indigenous societies. When Arapaho people describe the storytelling they heard as children, they consistently note that it would continue story after story, sometimes for hours, until the last child fell asleep. Similarly, when the older people *nih'oonoxoeheti3i'* ('would make each other laugh'), the stories ("comicals" in this case) were told in complex sequences, one after the other, each one responding to a preceding one. Such sessions still occasionally occur today on the Wind River

Reservation, in Arapaho, though with increasing rarity as the number of native speakers declines and many comical stories are forgotten. These sequential storytelling sessions are especially fascinating because the stories often link together in a coherent fashion. Each story is in some sense a response to the previous stories, inspired by some theme or moral or memory they have evoked. Each story is thus both enriched by the previously established story context and retrospectively enriches those previous stories. In addition, each story is also an opportunity for the teller to establish a particular identity in the moment, take a particular stance on some issue, or exhibit narrative virtuosity or range. For me, one of the greatest benefits of learning an indigenous language well and developing strong relationships in the community is the chance to sit in on such storytelling sessions.

The broader scholarly literature on interaction and collaborative narration likewise points to the crucial importance of sequencing (Georgakopoulou 2005; Goodwin and Goodwin 2001). Marjorie and Charles Goodwin argue that "the relevant unit for the analysis of emotion is not the individual or the semantic system of the language, but instead the sequential organization of action" (239). We could extend this statement to make the same argument about storytelling, including in Arapaho. But rather than just replacing "emotion" with "storytelling" in the preceding sentence, we need to focus on the word "action." As the Goodwins argue, the semantic system is not the relevant unit for understanding human action (and, by extension, interaction). Yet, clearly the semantic system is the basic tool that humans use for interaction. The more nuanced point the Goodwins are making is that the system is always used *sequentially.* Furthermore, social actions and accomplishments are the true goals of all human interaction. And these actions occur within and across the sequences of semantic expression. They are not directly recoverable outcomes of the semantic system or expressions devoid of sequential context. In this study, I take the same approach to Arapaho stories. These stories are also a semantic system, and as such, are a necessary basis for Arapaho human action and interaction. Whatever "meaning" the stories may have as individual units, their role is often not just—or even primarily— to convey meaning, but rather to serve as a crucial resource and tool for social interaction. And that action cannot be fully understood outside the context of the story sequences.

Therefore, if scholars want to present the narrative voices and understand the social actions of Native peoples as accurately and richly as possible, it follows that we need to present not just a story and an account of that story's context, but entire chains of stories—including any comments that may occur between the stories.[1] I want to briefly clarify that I am not talking about "sequences" of stories in the sense of abstract or potential sequences, in the way that Paul Radin (1956) presents trickster stories as being part of a single long, underlying sequence. This view of Native American narrative genres has been rightly critiqued (see Ballinger 2004, 14). Rather, I am talking about actual, "live" sequences of stories, occurring in a single place during a single stretch of time. Such sequences are especially characteristic of Native American oral traditions, and if we fail to recognize and document them as such, we are engaging in another form of what Dell Hymes would call "narrative inequality" by failing to respect the dynamics of the Native practice (Hymes 1996; see also Hymes 1987, 41–84, and Kroskrity and Webster 2015, 3, for a critique of the practice of anthologizing). Only by engaging with the full sequences do we have the best chance to understand why a specific story in a syntagmatic sequence was told and what its teller sought to accomplish by telling it in that moment. More fundamentally, only then can we understand such story sequences as collaborative artistic accomplishments of the highest order, which must be understood as wholes, not just as sequences of individual texts.[2] A key goal of this book is to present and comment on such story sequences from the Northern Arapaho of Wyoming.

Ideally, my goal here is to turn the anthology over to the Arapaho storytellers themselves by respecting their story sequences, as well as including their surrounding comments on the stories. Chadwick Allen, writing about the need to decolonize indigenous studies—and literary studies in particular—notes that the problem these days is often not one of exclusion, "but rather an insidious inclusion within the dominant academy's dominant paradigms" (2014, 377). Wesley Leonard (2021) echoes this point even more strongly in relation to linguistic anthropology. In the worst cases, including Arapaho stories in an anthology risks performing a very real as well as a symbolic act of "insidious inclusion" that removes the stories from their context and utility and, of course, risks "limit[ing] indigenous authority and control" (Allen 2014, 378). This has indeed been a key function—or at least secondary result—of anthologies in many cases, and I will return to this point later.

Paradigmatics and Syntagmatics

Stories do not just function syntagmatically however, but also paradigmatically. In other words, Native tellers and listeners evaluate a given story not only in relation to what precedes and follows it in the sequence, but also in relation to their broader knowledge of the genre of the story in question, as well as alternate versions and tellings. They recall similar stories, and appreciate the version they are hearing in the context of those other versions and examples of the genre. It is therefore inadequate to present just a series of stories to readers: they also need additional examples of each type of story, so as to have a better paradigmatic appreciation of each link in the chain. As Dell Hymes says, "The one lesson that seems difficult to learn is that myths are performed, and thereby shaped, both in performance and in reflection between performances" (1987, 79), and the same is certainly true of the stories here. Therefore, the other main goal of this book is to provide examples of this phenomenon for a few common story genres. In particular, this study provides four examples of naturally occurring (unelicited) story chains that I happened to record at various times during my work with the Northern Arapaho, combined with four chapters which illustrate the variety of stories that can occur within four different contemporary genres of Arapaho oral narrative: tall tales (or "believe-it-or-not") stories, folk hero stories, "old couple/old folks" stories, and stories about people noted as "characters" in Arapaho society, which can be called "crazy guy" stories. Each of these types of stories appears in the story chains, often repeatedly. Also included are ethnopoetic and ethnographic commentary from Northern Arapaho storytellers themselves.

My interest in the syntagmatics and paradigmatics of narrative goes beyond simple methodology, however. My approach has an obvious grounding in Jakobsonian structuralism, but can also be viewed from the perspective of literary approaches such as poststructuralism. As Arnold Krupat has written on the search for "meaning" in oral narratives, "What is curious to note is that from an historical point of view, such concern for fixed meanings seems not to have been typical of oral cultures at all; rather it appears to arrive only with the shift to literacy and chirographic means of information storage" (1987, 118).

While I have my doubts about such a strict dichotomy between oral and literate cultures, I find the remark interesting. It occurs in a broader discussion of the way that "meaning" is always a product of difference and deferral within poststructuralist theory, and of how this may resonate with Native American views of oral storytelling (1987, 113–28). Certainly, one key point of this study and anthology is that "meanings" (and even genre identity) lie less in individual Arapaho stories than in how they resonate with and are constantly redefined by their place in both syntagmatic sequences and paradigmatic models, as well as by their social performance contexts. Another point that will become evident is that the stories are used as a means of sociality and solidarity, as well as performance of individual virtuosity in narration, and that the "content" of the story may sometimes be important only to the extent that it matches up with the genre and themes of a preceding narrative. In other words, narrators may simply be saying, "Hey, look, I know a story about the exact same thing too." The stories are as much resources for interpersonal interaction as they are units of meaning. For this reason, narrators often play with content, meaning, form, and genre. More fundamentally, the stories' value can be found "in relation to the health of the living *sgadug* [community]," as Christopher Teuton argues (2014, 173). I will return in detail to the notion of health throughout this study. Teuton points out that the narratives are not to be valued primarily for themselves, as relics or records of some past event, but for "the relationships they forge" (2014, 173). This makes Native narratives difficult if not impossible to anthologize, and indeed the process of anthologizing could be seen as turning the narratives into self-contained pieces of "meaning" and "value." This anthology, on the other hand, attempts to present the narratives as processes of relationship. As such, it is part of a larger movement within Indigenous language documentation and reclamation that focuses on indigenous community and relationships, and the modeling and documentation of those relationships (see Henne-Ochoa et al. 2020).

The Issue of Genre

Here I should add a word about the concept of genre, which was referred to several times in the previous paragraphs. Briggs and Bauman (1992) provide a useful survey of genre as the concept was used in linguistic anthropology up to that time and point the way toward productive uses of the concept for helping to understand social action. My goal in this book is certainly not to rigidly classify stories into single genres, or to claim that Arapaho storytellers do this. On the contrary, we will see that old folks stories and crazy guy stories can overlap, and that the latter share elements in common with trickster stories—which themselves can include both very traditional trickster tales and what could be called "neo-trickster" stories, in which the trickster engages with Euro-Americans and their practices and technologies. Folk hero stories likewise can be transitional to legendary hero stories and, more generally, all the narratives examined in this book could be grouped broadly as "comicals." Tellers may also manipulate the generic expectations around a story in the moment of performance, especially in the context of story sequences: they adjust content or evaluative comments and frames in order to make the story fit more smoothly into the overall story sequence, and into the expectations and conditions created by the previous story told. Still, Arapaho story-tellers do, in fact, classify their own stories—based primarily on content, but taking into account structural and ontological differences as well. And in both open-ended elicitation settings and actual natural discourse, they tend to tell stories in groups that focus on a single character or a single kind of thematic action (the tall tale, for example)—or to explicitly acknowledge that they are not doing so and provide some kind of explanation for this dispreferred move.

An additional point of this book is thus to show that it is impossible to understand the structure of Arapaho story sequences without recognizing that Arapaho storytellers operate with an indigenous understanding of genre and genres. This understanding is based on what Jauss and Benzinger (1970) call "horizons of expectations" for the content, structure, and ontological status of a narrative. As such, the Arapaho sequences can be compared to Mexicano *chiste* cycles, which focus on some particular lead character (Briggs 1988). Briggs notes that chiste cycles are especially prominent in chiste-telling sessions (which closely resemble the Arapaho sequences examined here in some ways) because "the emergence of a successful session depends on the ready availability of a substantial number of *chistes* and on the ability of the participants to string them together with minimal interruption" (Briggs 1988, 217). He further adds "invoking the name of the principal figure in a chiste cycle immediately indexes a large collection of chistes . . . [the] cycles also lend a great deal of cohesion to the discourse" (Briggs 1988, 217).

Contemporary versus Traditional Oral Narrative

It is very rare to find anthologies or studies of actual story sequences for Native American languages and cultures. It is also relatively rare to find examples of the particular genres I present here, at least in high-visibility general anthologies. These tend to be dominated by narratives and genres representing precontact Native American society and culture, even if the actual tellings occur post-contact. While it is certainly true that Native American oral traditions in general have often been viewed dismissively in the past and present (see Kroskrity 2012, 6–7), this is even more the case for oral narratives focused on contemporary events. If one reads much written (English-language) Native American contemporary literature, the realities of contact, the colonial situation, and Native American resistance are inescapable. In contrast, we can read many general anthologies of Native American verbal arts—especially those with a broad continental focus and those that are not bilingual—and almost come away with the sense that Columbus never landed, or that few oral narratives have been composed since Euro-American contact.[3] Tribe- or language-specific anthologies, especially those of a bilingual nature, are notably more diverse, but still are often dominated by traditional verbal art genres and themes or, secondarily, by historical accounts of Euro-American encounters in pre-reservation times. Only recently have scholars—mostly Native American scholars—begun to produce anthologies that truly capture the vitality and diversity of living oral traditions in Native America.[4] The story sequences and genres presented in this collection are heavily engaged with the realities of contact and especially with the reservation world. As already noted, a key goal of this book is to provide a rich sample of *contemporary* Native American oral narrative from one language. I will show that these oral narratives are equally as engaged with themes of current life as the written literature so widely known and appreciated.

I want to stress that the preceding remarks are not meant to disparage the value of traditional genres such as creation stories, myths and legends, etiological origins stories, trickster stories, and so forth. Nor do I want to suggest that those genres cannot adapt to contemporary lifeways and perform socially relevant commentary. Although there is certainly much that is problematic about many anthologies of Native American verbal narrative (see Clements 1996, 179–98; Hymes 1987), I also do not want to suggest that the documenting and anthologizing of these genres per se is problematic. The act of preserving traditional oral narratives and continuing to use them in socially relevant ways in the present is an act of cultural affirmation and resistance to Euro-American society on the part of the tellers themselves, the collectors of the narratives, and the editors of the anthologies. I myself have published such material, and I am wholeheartedly in favor of this kind of documentation and publication. It is clear that for Native American communities themselves, traditional genres and stories not only form the core of collective tribal knowledge and identity, but also can continue to evolve to meet present needs (Simpson 2011). From an aesthetic perspective, narrative forms and genres that have developed and been enriched by countless tellers over many decades, or often centuries, are typically the most highly elaborated and intricately developed expressions of verbal artistry: the talent of generations of verbal artists has been brought to bear on these narratives, leading to rich and complex traditions that also show great flexibility in responding to different interactive and performative contexts.

All of that said, there are reasons to be concerned about the relative dearth of documentation of more contemporary oral narrative traditions and genres. First, the largely Euro-American-controlled process of collecting and publishing them may make Native American oral narrative look like a static product purely of the past that is unable to integrate new themes and topics. This sends false messages to non-Native audiences, and to some Native Americans as well. Native Americans have fought for generations against the notion that tribes and languages are doomed to disappear, and that Native American culture is not a viable option for the present and the future. Yet the image of oral narrative in Native America often implies that anyone who wants to engage explicitly with the colonial experience and postcolonial resistance must use exclusively English and write in traditionally Euro-American genres such poetry, short stories, and novels. The valorization of traditional Native American verbal art traditions can ironically turn into a simultaneous devaluation of contemporary Native languages and oral traditions and imply that the *only* mechanism of resistance is the language and genres of the colonizer.

This dynamic is part of a much deeper devaluing of the oral as "primitive" and the written as a sign of evolutionary advancement, as Christopher Teuton has shown convincingly (Teuton 2014, 167–74). He also has shown how the erasure of contemporary themes and engagements from oral narratives, both in anthologies and in ethnographic sources, has a long history, with Franz Boas in particular being a founding practitioner of the effort to make the oral appear deeply historical and noncontemporary in its engagements (169–71). We could think of anthologies in this regard as mechanisms for policing orality, part of "technique[s] for regulating the production, circulation, and reception of discourse" (171) and thus as key components of the reproduction of narrative inequality. In this sense, at their most extreme, the prevailing practice of anthologies (especially large-scale ones) in linguistic anthropology could be seen as participating in practices of white supremacy, often perhaps despite the best intentions of their compilers (see Leonard 2021 for a critique of linguistic anthropology along these lines). From this perspective, the exclusions and gaps in the coverage of narratives begin to look much more problematic.

This false impression of the non-engagement of oral traditions with the present is certainly not the fault of Native Americans. As this anthology and study will show, there is an extremely rich body of modern Arapaho oral narrative that deals explicitly with the themes of Euro-American culture, values, and technologies and the ways in which Arapaho people interact with, resist, and often profit from them. Reservation-era Arapaho oral narrative expresses a quite thorough consideration of the colonial condition, as Arapahos experienced it during the twentieth century. The same is true for other Native American oral traditions as well: Sandra

Isaac's (2019) work on Eastern Cherokee traditions is an excellent example.[5] Traces of the same kind of oral narrative can be found in other collections for other tribes and languages. The stories are out there, but (largely Euro-American) academic collectors, editors, and publishers mostly seem to have ignored them in favor of the more "different" or "exotic" oral narratives of "traditional" verbal arts. Leo Killsback (speaking about Cheyenne history) puts it very straightforwardly: "the oral tradition was the means for organizing and explaining any change, from within and without" (2020, 8). It continues to be so, and it is perhaps the new material of the type presented in this book that is at the forefront of engaging with change in a critical manner for Arapaho and other Native peoples. In this sense, the material exposes "the adaptive mechanism embedded in the traditional art of story-telling" and "keeps the oral tradition alive and able to adapt" (Killsback 2020, xxxii).

Emergence

Despite the criticisms I just elaborated, there is one factor that perhaps partially explains the Euro-American tendency to undervalue contemporary oral narratives and genres. The fact is that in comparison to more traditional genres and stories, they are typically less valued by Native communities themselves and are less culturally salient. Many are what are broadly called "comicals" in American Indian English (by both the Arapaho and other tribes), though certainly not all of them fit this label. As the term implies, comicals are typically taken less seriously than a traditional narrative such as a creation story or a myth about a culture hero. For example, among the Arapaho, traditional stories and genres are known as *heeteetoono* and in the past were only told during the winter. On the other hand comicals are known as *hoo3itoono* (a general word for "stories") and can be told at any time of the year.

Precisely because they are less salient and more casual however, and because they can be told at any time, less traditional stories and genres such as comicals are what most people *actually* tell, most of the time, when they tell each other stories at the Wind River Reservation. They are in fact a key mechanism of adult interaction. Because of their relatively lower social saliency compared to traditional narratives, they are much more likely to emerge from ongoing casual conversations. In many cases long sequences do not result, and the conclusion of the story is followed by a return to the give-and-take of conversation, but when sequences do occur, each story can be seen as what is called an "extended turn" in the field of conversation analysis. Conversation analysis, narrative studies, and interactional linguistics more generally all focus on narrative as a mode of social interaction (see Mandelbaum 2013; Rorrick 2000; Rühlemann 2013). The types of narratives most commonly emerging from conversation and used in this way are often called "small stories." They are typically closely tied to issues of everyday life, personal identity, interpersonal affiliation, and social action. They are normally brief, often ephemeral, and may not ever be told more than once. Wagner (2021) has thoroughly investigated the ways that small stories emerge in everyday Arapaho conversation.

The narratives I present in this volume, however, are definitely somewhat "bigger" stories, less personal and ephemeral, and are known within broader Arapaho society as culturally shared narratives. But they show similar patterns of casual emergence from conversation and extended turn-taking among the tellers. As we will see in later chapters, the comicals often do not follow immediately one after the other, but instead occur within a matrix of surrounding commentary, and sometimes of negotiation as to who will tell the next story or what that story will be about. Some stories are cut short or fall flat, while others are greeted enthusiastically and show more elaboration. In contrast, a traditional narrative is typically proposed by a teller in a very formal manner or requested by an audience member and, once begun, is never interrupted. Such a story virtually never simply emerges from casual conversation. A key subsidiary goal of this book is to provide insight into casual narrative interaction in a Native American community, along with an appreciation of the process of story emergence.

"Stories" versus Stories

Many readers may be saying to themselves at this point, in response to my comments, that there is in fact a rich tradition of collecting and publishing Native American oral histories, ethnographic accounts, and personal histories and accounts, all of which deal intimately with the reality of older as well as more recent Native American colonial experience and efforts at decolonization. This is certainly true, and Native American ethnohistory is a flourishing field. But I am interested here specifically in "oral literature" in the sense of "stories"—the modern equivalent of the origin stories, creation stories, legends, myths, trickster stories, accounts of more-than-human power, narratives of hunting, battle, or horse theft, and other genres that dominate traditional narratives. Put another way, I am interested in narratives that are performed in the sense that the word "performance" is used in performance theory.

As such, the stories presented here fall midway between the small stories and anecdotes of everyday life that so often emerge in conversation and the highly salient and often elaborately signaled and keyed traditional narratives. As I noted earlier, I have published a bilingual anthology of traditional narratives (Cowell, Moss, and C'Hair 2014), as well as a volume of historically based narratives from the nineteenth century (Cowell and Moss 2005). The narratives in both these collections are clearly examples of traditional organization, style, and performance. The present volume constitutes the last of a trilogy of bilingual anthologies. Together, the three volumes provide a reasonably comprehensive introduction to Arapaho oral narrative. I hope ambitious readers will examine all three collections to gain a better appreciation of the continuity as well as the variety and transformation that have occurred, so as to appreciate the narratives in this third volume as the continuing expression of a long tradition of verbal art. The anthologies are further supported by a comprehensive grammar of the language (Cowell and Moss 2008), a very large online lexical database (www.colorado.edu/verbs/Arapaho/main), an ethnography of Northern Arapaho language practices and ideologies (Cowell 2018), and a video-based conversational database (ELAR). The last may be of special interest to serious learners and researchers who want to examine the relationship between everyday conversation and the story sequences in this volume. Highly valuable in this regard is Wagner (2021), which focuses on the emergence of true "small stories" within Arapaho conversation.

What Is a Modern Arapaho Story?

Before concluding this introduction, I must define more clearly what exactly I mean by a full-fledged "story" in the sense I am using the term. We will begin the exploration with the following points of departure, recognizing of course that there is no clear-cut boundary between emergent everyday stories about personal experience, history, news, and events on the one hand and "stories" on the other, and also recognizing that some genres of narrative contained in this anthology are closer than others to the full understanding of a "story."

1. A story can be told by multiple people with more or less equal rights to tellership. It is not seen as linked to one living person's individual experience.
2. A story is thus a form of general cultural property, circulating in the community and likely already heard, told, and known by

some other members of the community in some form. It thus does not count as news or information.

3. As a corollary to the preceding, a story can often simply be referenced to achieve one's goals; it need not be fully told.[6]

4. As another corollary, stories are highly subject to decontextualization and recontextualization via later retellings.

5. A story is often presented as a degree removed from the narrator. It is reported as something someone *else* told the narrator, not something the narrator was personally involved in. Conversely, the story may be presented in the first person—but then the same story will be told on another occasion by another person, again in the first person (see point 1). There is a tacit understanding that the story is not truly a narrative of a first-person experience.

6. The teller of the story does not typically engage epistemically to verify the truth of the story and is not at risk of being accused of lying with regard to the content. This is an important distinction between stories and community oral history or ethnography.

7. Certain genres of stories lack specificity with regard to time or place or named individuals. (Others, however, can be classified by genre based on reference to a single named individual.)

8. Stories often are subject to evaluations of the performance quality of the storytelling, as well as to comparisons with other previous tellings and contexts of telling.

9. These stories are often not considered appropriate to tell when individuals are formally invited to tell stories for educational or cultural purposes. Arapaho language, ceremonies, and traditional myths might all be called sacred, but these stories would not be.

10. Structurally, these stories often lack highly elaborated framing devices such as openings like "long ago" or closings like "and that's how it was."[7] They are typically fairly short and lack highly elaborate internal structure.

One other criterion worth mentioning, in relation to point 6, is that speakers may in fact jokingly describe themselves as "lying" when telling these types of stories—something Arapaho individuals do not do in either true first-person accounts or in telling traditional narratives. For example, in regard to these types of storytelling sessions and sequences speakers will often say something like *beebeet nihneenentooyeini'* 'we just told a bunch of lies' or *heetwoneenentooyeini'* 'we're going to go tell lies.' This does not mean that the speakers actually consider themselves to be lying or don't take the stories seriously. Instead, they're indicating that the story is the primary focus, with a special emphasis on group enjoyment. The reference often indicates a shift back and forth between the personal and anecdotal—with expectations of embellishment—and the types of stories presented in this collection. William C'Hair describes these kinds of stories as "Arapaho comic books" (field notes, May 2018). The usage can be compared to that of the "Turtle Island Liars' Club" described by Christopher Teuton (2012) among the Cherokee. There as well, use of the term "lying" indexes a certain type of story, storytelling setting, and relationship between teller and audience (2012, 7, 23, 33–34, 150). A similar dynamic occurs in an Ojibwe context; see Lois Beardslee's book entitled *Lies to Live By.*

We will return to this question of what exactly constitutes a "story" in the conclusion for further nuancing. It is often the case that stories do arise from actual events, anecdotes, or personal experiences. These are then transformed, embellished, or amalgamated around a specific character. Much of the storytelling in this book, especially in relation to Strong Bear, John Plume, or Henry Snake represents a "proto-story" progression, more or less advanced depending on the character and genre in question, toward full-fledged oral literature. A parallel can be found in what Cunningham (1992, 153) calls "manufactured jokes" among the Navajo. He says that these "in the 1990s are a major genre of Navajo oral tradition, recognized as such by audience and performers. Indeed, they represent a major verbal art form, and the people prize their skilled performance" (153).

Presentation of the Texts

Finally, I should review the transcription conventions used in this book. I produced the translations from Arapaho in consultation with native speakers. In general, the translations lean toward a close representation of what is actually said in Arapaho, as opposed to free and colloquial English. After careful consideration, I did not use reservation-style Arapaho English in the translations, though consultants often provided it. That local style of English can be quite different from standard English in its semantics, and even deceptive in meaning for a reader with a more general English-language perspective. In addition, the forms that consultants provided in Arapaho English sometimes constituted more of a retelling of the passage than a close translation. My goal in this collection is to focus on the Arapaho language of the original texts.

Guided by this philosophy, I have intervened strongly in the presentation of the original texts. On a linguistic level, all prefixes and suffixes are separated from main noun and verb stems by dashes to facilitate inter-action between the texts, the grammar of the language, dictionaries, and the lexical database. I have also included a number of footnotes providing analysis and commentary on interesting or complex words and phrases, and the appendix provides information on the most common prefixes, suffixes, and function words in Arapaho, along with a close linguistic analysis of one brief story.

Formal Arapaho narrative style makes use of specific word order and grammatical forms. One feature is the narrative past prefix *he'ih-* (versus normal past tense *nih-*), which requires non-affirmative verb inflections; others are the narrative sequential prefix *he'ne'-* 'then, next' (versus nor-mal *ne'-*) and the dubitative *he'=* with nouns (versus no marking nor-mally). It also has special citational verbs *heeh-* 'said' and *hee3-* 'said to someone,' which occur with subjunctive inflections (*heeh-ehk* 's/he said,', *hee3-oohok* 's/he said to him/her/them,' etc.). I have underlined these each time they occur in a text, since they are good indicators of the relative stylistic formality of a story, and secondarily they help indicate the ontological status of a narration as a "story" and signal its particu-lar type. When they occur pervasively, I have not reflected them in the translations, but where they occur sporadically, I have translated them as 'I guess. . . .' For *he'ih-* in particular, speakers will often drop the prefix itself but maintain the non-affirmative inflections that the prefix requires. In that case, I have added the prefix in square brackets ([*he'ih*]).

Arapaho narratives can also be segmented into sections. A variety of particles are used to do this—most commonly *wohei* 'okay, so then, so now,' with *woow* 'now,' and occasionally *wo'ooto'* 'just then, right then,' used as well. I have underlined these whenever they seem to serve such a purpose, as their presence is a useful indicator of the degree of elabora-tion (and secondarily, formality) of a narrative.

There are also a variety of story-initiation devices in Arapaho, some relatively formal, others much more conversational in style. These include (1) explicitly asking or telling someone to tell a story or saying that it is "their turn"; (2) mentioning storytelling or proposing to tell a story (using the verbs *hoo3itee-* 'tell a story,' *hoo3itoot-* 'tell the story of . . . ,' *hoo-3itoon-* 'tell someone a story,' and the noun *hoo3itoo*); (3) using topic-initiation particles such as *wohei, ci'(ceese')* 'and also (another one)' and *howoo* 'also, and also'; (4) using the hesitation particle *nihii* 'well . . . , uh . . . '; (5) using the particles *wooce'* 'remember?' or *hi3oowo'* 'remem-ber!' (often with a brief evocation of the story); (6) asking someone if they know of or know about some particular person or topic; (7) using tense particles *teecxo'* 'long ago' or *ceesey* 'one time'; and (8) using definiteness markers *nehe'* and *nuhu'* 'this, the, these' with a noun even when the referent is new to the discourse, as a way of signaling the future relevance of the referent. I have underlined these devices in the text as well and discuss them more fully where they occur.

There are also various summational ('and that's how Strong Bear helped the Arapahos') and closing formulas for narratives. Their use indicates the degree to which something is a story as well as the relative formalness in style. Most formal is *nee'ei'ise' nuhu' hoo3itoo* 'that is as far as the story goes.' Others include *nee'eesoo'* 'that's how it is' and *nohuusoho'* 'that's it, that's all,' among a number of other possible variations. In some cases, a speaker concludes (or initiates) a narrative with a specific reference to the genre of a text. Similarly, speakers (or listeners) sometimes open or conclude a narrative by specifically mentioning the person who told them the story originally. I have underlined all of these features.

I have also indicated multimodal features of the texts, especially pauses and pause lengths, occurrence of laughter, and gestures. Short of using hundreds of photos in the book, it is extremely difficult to capture the components that gesture adds to the narratives. Sandoval (2016) covers the way that gesture is used in Arapaho conversational storytelling in great detail, including distinctions between iconic, conventionalized (Plains sign language), deictic, and metaphorical gestures. I do not seek to make such classifications in this book—I simply label the meaning of each gesture.

Since story sequences are by definition interactional, I have labeled the different speakers in the interactional sequences. Single open square brackets ([. . . .) are used to show where two speakers' utterances overlap, and the overlaps of the two speakers are aligned on the page as follows:

Speaker A: I was going [to go and . . .
Speaker B: [were you going to . . ? .

The original language of the texts is presented in a plain font, while translations appear on the next line in a distinct italicized font. Even where the original language is English due to code-switching, I include another version of the English on the following line (in italics) for clarity and consistency. Double square brackets [[. . .]] are used to indicate all multimodal features of the texts—laughter, pauses, gesture, and so on. Meanwhile, double parentheses ((. . .)) are used to indicate my editorial commentary on the texts.

In contrast to the presentation of the story sequences just described, where texts were elicited or extracted from sequences and lack strong interactional features, they are presented with the entire Arapaho text followed by the entire English translation. Where occasional Arapaho words occur in otherwise English-dominant sequences, I have put a gloss of the Arapaho word immediately following, in single square brackets, in italics [*as such*].

Finally, certain individual texts make one-time, special uses of various features—creative use of reduplication for example, or heavy usage of certain words or certain semantic fields of words and so forth. I note these instances in relation to the particular text and use underlining or italicizing to call out these features.

A Word about the Author

I am not Arapaho or indigenous, though I am adopted into the Northern Arapaho Tribe by a family. My Arapaho name is *Co'ouu3ii'eihii* 'high eagle'. I have spent nearly twenty-five years working with the Northern Arapaho people, and I consider myself a very good though not completely fluent speaker of the language, which I began learning as soon as I began visiting the Wind River Reservation. My work there has included language documentation and revitalization efforts; assistance with teacher training, curriculum development, second-language learner development and teaching; and generally whatever anyone has asked me to do. In return, I get to sit around and listen to some very funny stories.

Names of Arapaho Storytellers

I often do not use the actual names of the storytellers and other individuals referred to (except where noted as "real name"). I very much wanted to link the tellers to their stories. All participants signed consent forms approving this, and when they were alive, many of them stressed to me a desire to receive credit for their contributions. However, they are almost all deceased now, and I could not do one final check of their thoughts. I asked William C'Hair, head of the Northern Arapaho Language and Culture Commission, for his opinion, especially as some stories include risqué material. He knew all the tellers, most of them very well, and said that they themselves would not have a problem with their names being shared publicly. He was concerned however that their children or younger relatives might be offended. Therefore, I agreed to use pseudonyms with the individual stories, except in cases where versions of the stories have been previously published, so that the tellers are publicly known (Joe Goggles, Ralph Grasshopper, Paul Moss, Richard Moss). William agreed however that it would be appropriate to acknowledge the tellers by name here in the first chapter. So I want to very gratefully thank the following: Richard Antelope, Wayne C'Hair, William C'Hair, Joe Goggles, John Goggles, Rupert Goggles, Alonzo Moss Sr., Richard Moss, Charles Piper, Ed Underwood, Clyde Wallowing Bull, and Edward Willow. *Hohou*!

2

Strong Bear Stories, the Folk Hero and the "Man of Power"; and a Story Sequence (c. 1990)

This chapter focuses on a cycle of Arapaho stories about an individual known as "Strong Bear." Strong Bear (real name) is reported to have been a real person who lived in early reservation times.[1] The majority of his adventures involve heroic deeds in confrontations with Euro-Americans, set in the very early reservation era. He stands up for other Arapaho people and protects them, typically at the expense of Euro-American aggressors. He is not a chief, but simply a physically strong and courageous individual who comes to the aid of other Arapahos in times of need. His resistance is always restrained and highly symbolic—he does not kill people or fight battles, but instead uses his combined wisdom and strength to defuse situations and put white people "in their place" while simultaneously restoring dignity to Arapaho people. There are no accounts of him in academic histories about this time period (Trenholm 1970; Fowler 1986), so he lives only in Arapaho oral history so far as I can tell.

Before examining the individual stories in detail, I want to address the figure of the "folk hero" because I believe the genre of folk-hero stories is a useful way of understanding Strong Bear stories. A folk hero is often defined as an individual whose exploits are a strong part of the folk or ethnic or national consciousness of a culture. This definition underlines the extra-literary or supra-literary quality of folk heroes: their exploits are transmitted by various means, only one of which may be writing or "literature," and many people know about the folk heroes without having ever read about them. Moreover, rarely is a folk hero linked to a single named, authored "text" in the way that a literary character is, although they may be linked to one particular cycle or genre of oral literature (Brunvand 1976, 50–51; Georges and Jones 1995, xxiv; Toelken 1996, 183–84; Seal and White 2016, xix).

A second component of the definition involves ideology rather than modes of transmission. The folk hero is understood to represent the values of the "folk"—the working class, peasant class, lower classes, and the like. Thus, the folk hero is often understood as a figure of resistance to wealth, power, and authority; is often engaged in conflict or confrontation; and not uncommonly has an outlaw status (Georges and Jones 1995, xxi–xxvi; Seal and White 2016).

A third component of the definition involves the ontological status of the folk hero. Normally, folk heroes are understood by scholars to be mythical figures, though their origin may lie in some actual individual. The folk hero undergoes a process of development in which his or her exploits grow ever greater in number or ever more amazing in quality. Additionally, various deeds and sayings of other individuals may be accreted onto the legend of the folk hero over time (Brunvand 1976, 64–65).

Folk heroes have elements in common with epic or mythic heroes. The fundamental way in which they differ is that they are normally understood to be "one of us" within the group consciousness (Seal and White 2016, xix) or "ordinariness amplified" and "still like us in so many ways" (Georges and Jones 1995, xxi, xxii). Thus, they must be seen as human, albeit perhaps as an "extra-special human," rather than as mythical or superhuman.

In the context of Native North America, the category of folk hero is not often invoked, and this type of character does not really occur in traditional oral narratives, at least certainly not on the Great Plains. Indeed, I believe the term "folklore" is an entirely inappropriate form of analysis for Native American traditional oral narrative, as there were no "folk" (with all that concept implies) in Native American society, especially not on the Great Plains. Within the traditional corpus of Plains Indian narrative, mythological heroes are quite common, as are culture heroes, who are often associated with the origins of a particular tribal culture, ceremonies, and social practices and who often serve symbolically to maintain harmony or restore order within their own culture (Georges and Jones 1995, xxvi, xxxii). And, of course, all groups have a historical consciousness as well, which finds expression in narrative, and often real historical individuals have a heroic status in their tribe's oral history. In contrast, the extra-historical, sub-mythical character of the folk hero in European and Euro-American contexts most often pertains to peasant or working class or underclass groups within large-scale, hierarchical societies. This particular niche simply did not exist within Plains Indian tribal societies of the nineteenth century and earlier, because they were relatively small-scale, egalitarian societies that lacked any clear folk or subaltern component internal to their organization. There are, however, certainly antecedents to folk-hero-like characters in fairly traditional oral literature. The most notable is the medicine man, whose wondrous deeds are recounted throughout the group, sometimes for generations after the historical person has passed on (see Parks 1996, 177–262, for many Arikara examples; Horse Capture and Gone 1980 for Gros Ventre examples; and Barnouw 1977, 161–78, for Wisconsin Chippewa examples). On the other hand, it is notable that medicine men were often viewed with as much suspicion or fear as admiration, and many stories tell about "bad" medicine men, which is not the case with later folk heroes.

With the beginning of the era of intensive cultural contact between Euro-Americans and Native Americans, especially in the reservation era, Native American tribal societies found themselves to be a newly constituted colonial underclass within larger-scale American society. In this context, it was possible for something approaching a folk hero to develop. The folk hero was imbued with elements emblematic of Native American—specifically Arapaho in this case—identity, which now constituted a specific low-prestige, dominated identity within broader Euro-American society. Thus, the character and genre of the folk hero in Native American oral literature must be understood as a product of conquest, colonialism, and partial assimilation into Euro-American society, but also as a key mechanism of continued resistance and cultural specificity. This type of narrative is rarely documented in contemporary collections of oral narratives, though one notable exception is the stories about "the legendary Tom Laporte" from the Maliseet tradition (LeSourd 2004, 2007).[2] In our examination of the Arapaho folk hero Strong Bear we will see that stories in this genre explicitly incorporate the Euro-American view of the Arapaho as weak, marginalized, abused, and incapable of helping themselves—only to provide an Arapaho-specific response in the person of Strong Bear, who rejects these categorizations and demonstrates their illegitimacy. As such, the character of Strong Bear represents a fascinating "articulation" (Clifford 2013, 44–49) with the perspectives of Euro-American society, in that those perspectives must first be acknowledged in order to be resisted or refuted.

The Stories and Their Author

This chapter differs from all the others in this book in that it begins with a chain of stories dominated by a single teller and all in the single genre of Strong Bear stories. Following the chain, a few additional stories will be presented. This chain was told primarily by Paul Moss (real name) (1911–95) around 1990 to a group of listening elders of roughly his own age or somewhat younger, including his son. The occasion was simply an informal get-together at Paul's home on the Wind River Reservation, in the Ethete area. It was apparently not intended as a recording session, as his son turned on the tape recorder mid-session and mid-story. Note that this is the only chain in this book where no non-Arapaho outsiders were present. When I asked his son fifteen to twenty years later who else had been present, he could not remember exactly but stated all were close friends or relatives of Paul's. Many more of Paul's stories can be found in Cowell and Moss (2005), along with discussions of their narrative content and style. Arapaho was Paul's dominant language, though he was a good second-language speaker of English as well. He was noted for his extensive traditional knowledge and highly developed storytelling ability, especially in the more formal stories documented in Cowell and Moss (2005). But according to his son, the stories he normally told his children as they were growing up were more modern reservation-era stories of the type documented in this book, as well as historical narratives (documented in Cowell and Moss 2005). The son said that Paul rarely told classical traditional narratives, though he certainly knew this material. The son also noted that his father was a Christian who for a number of years traveled around Indian Country as a preacher. Paul was someone who seems to have viewed deep-historical Arapaho narrative traditions as having been largely superseded by more modern reservation life. He was a strong believer in the "Arapaho way of life," but was also very interested in how that way of life could adapt to twentieth-century circumstances, a view that is reflected in the types and genres of stories he preferred to tell.

((Recording begins during the middle of a conversation. The lead speaker, Paul Moss, is just completing telling a story about Strong Bear. A second speaker picks up on this genre.))
((ELAR 4, 00:00))

PM: Wohei hinee hiisiihi'.
   Well, like that.

#2:   Keih-niitowoo3-oo?[3]
   Have you heard of Strong Bear?

#3:   Hee.
   Yes.

Story 2: Raising the Ridgepole for a House or Barn

((Note in the following story the repeated use of *coon-* 'not able to do something' and *ho3on-* 'fail to do something' (*hoo3on-* in imperfective form) in describing the people that Strong Bear helps. The same two prefixes occur in several of the other stories as well.))

#2: Heet-noh'P, hi'in . . . hini'iit tih'iini . . .
They will raise, that . . . that one they use when they are . . .

PM: Wohei. . . hee . . .
Well . . . yes . . .

#2: Nih-'o'oobei'i-3i' beh'eihoho'.
Some old men were building a house.

PM: Hee.
Yes.

#2: Hini'iit ridgepole, <u>he'ih</u>-'ii-<u>coon</u>-noh'en-eeno'.
That ridgepole, they couldn't raise it.

PM: Hee.
Yes.

#2: <u>He'ih</u>-'oo3onoxuuheti-no'.[4]
They weren't getting anywhere with all their efforts.

PM: Hee.
Yes.

#2: <u>Woow</u> Tei'ox <u>he'ne'</u>-no'usee-t;
Now then Strong Bear arrived;

#3: Yeah.
Yeah.

#2: Hee, nii-<u>coon</u>-noh'en-eet nehe', <u>he'ih</u>-'ii3-eeno' Tei'P Tei'ox.
"Yeah, we can't lift it up," they said to Strong Bear.

'osteihoowun!⁵
"You should be able to do that!" he said to them.

Nuhu' he'ih-'eeneiten-ee.
Then he got a good hold on it.

Ne'-bi'-tees-tou'u-t.
Then he just tossed it up there.

[[laughter]]
'osteihoo, hi-ihoowu-uhei3.
"Gee whiz, it's not heavy!"

Nih-'oo3onoxuuheti-nee, he'ih-'ii3-ee.
"You guys weren't getting anywhere with your efforts," he said to them.

[[laughter]]
[[1.5 sec.]]

Story 3: Horse Stuck in Quicksand on the Way to Casper

PM: he'ih-tei'eih Tei'ox, nih-'ii3-oo3i'.
Well, Strong Bear was strong, they said about him.

nih'iiP, he'ih-niihobei.
He was, he was going along with some people.

NoP nootoonoo3-oo3i' Casper.
They were going to buy coal in Casper.

hii3e' he'ih-niihobei.
He was going along with them over there.

hiit he'iitnei'i, huut he'ih-ko3ecise3ei-no' woxhooxebii.
Here somewhere, the horses got stuck in the mud.

he'=quick[sand.
I guess quicksand.

#2:   [yeah.
                    yeah.

PM: Uh-huh.
      uh-huh.

      he'ih-<u>coon</u>iini. . . .
      They could not get them out. . . .

      Sii=sii=P, 'oh <u>he'ih-'oon</u>-oo3oniini . . .
      They really tried, but they failed to . . .

      Beet-nouutP
      They want to get them out of . . .

      'oh <u>he'ih-'oo3on</u>ih-eeno'.
      But they failed to manage it with them.

      wohei, teetee-hek Tei'ox?
      "Well, where is Tei'ox?" they asked.

      Nih-co'on-teexokut hini'iit buckskin, wohei hi'in nihii . . .
      He always sat on that buckskin for a saddle, well that uh . . .

      [[chuckles]]
      Nih-cih-'oowo3eeen-ooni3i, he'ii3ou'u.
      They unloaded whatever was on the horses.

      Wohei, nih-'ii-3i', nii-<u>coon</u>-noh'oen-oono'[6] nehe' woxhoox.
      "Well," they said, "we can't get this horse out of the mud."

      'osteihoo!
      "You should be able to do that!" he told them.

      Ne'P ne'i-iten-oot nuhu' hitihiinin,
      Then, then he took its tail,

      <u>He'</u>=nee'eene3kuu3-oot.
      Then he ripped it out of the mud.

[[laughter]]
Nih-kohtowu-niitouuhu-t, tih-'e3kuu3-oot huut.
The horse made a funny hollering sound when it was ripped out here.

Nih-kohtobeinooni-'.
It sounded funny.

[[laughter]]
Wootii suction, nih-nee-'; nih-nee-', nih-kohtobeinooni-'.
Like suction, that was what it sounded like, it sounded funny.

[[laughter]]
Hiixowuh-ko'oetee-'.
It sounded like a gunshot went off or something.

[[laughter]]
Ceese' nih-'ii-t, koo-he-e'in . . .
One of them said, you know . . .

Nuhu' he'=tee-tei'yooniini, he'ih-'ii-ko3ecise3ei-no', 'oh hei'ii3ei'. . . .
Like this time when kids, they would get things stuck in the mud, and no matter how hard they tried to get out. . . .

Nenee-nee-'.
That's how that all goes.

[[0.5 sec.]]

Story 4: Stands Up for Arapahos Thrown Out of the Casino

((Note that these stories become more developed as the sequence is added to, and in particular, they show more internal segmentation. Key markers of this segmentation are the particles *wohei* 'so now, then, okay, next,' *wo'ooto'* 'right then,' and *woow* 'now.'))

PM: Nee'ei'-ce'-no'uuhu-3i' hinee hooxono'o.

That was, that's when they moved camp back over there to Riverton.

#2: Uhm.
Uhm.

PM: 'oh hinee 3owo3neniteeno', 'oh hinit cebiihetiino'oowu' hii'ootee-'.
And those Indians, right there where the 789 casino is near there . . .

Tents. 'oh hoono' hoowe-entou' ho'oowu'.
There were tents there. But there was not a building there yet.

#2: [Uhm-hmm.
Uhm-hmm

PM: [Beexo'P freight tents.
Only freight tents.

Ne'=nih-'eeneit-cebiihetiitooni-'.
That's where there was gambling.

Nuhu' hinono'eino', he'ihP he'ih-'eentoo-no' huut.
These Arapahos, they would hang around there.

Hi'in nihii nih'oo3ou'u, hini' nih-'ii-tei'eihi-3i' ci', hini'iit nihii be'nih'oo3ou'u, he'=Swedes.
Those, uh, whites, the ones that were strong too, those, uh, red-haired whites, I guess Swedes.

#2: Yeah.
Yeah.

PM: Hinee, neneenit.
That one, that's who he was.

HeesP niine'eeno' nuhu' 3owo3neniini, nih-'ii-beet-o3i'eew-oo3i' nih'oo3ousei-[no] wo'ei3 he'ii3ou'u.

Here are these Indian guys, who wanted to have a white woman
[sexually] or something like that.

Ne'=nii'-ce'-nouukuu3-ei3i' nuhu'.
That's when they threw them back out of this saloon.

he'ih'iiP. . . .
They were. . . .

#2:   Hmm.
Hmm.

PM: <u>Wo'ooto'</u> [<u>he'ih</u>]-he3eb-nou'uukoh-e' nehe' Tei'ox.
Right then he rode up to there, this Strong Bear

#2:   Uhm-hmm.
Uhm-hmm.

PM: <u>Wohei</u> hini'iit Tei'ox, "nii-noo-nonoxoo3ih-eino' niine'eeno'
nih'oo3ou'u."
Well, when that Strong Bear got there, they said to him, "These
white people are treating us badly."

'oh henee'ee-no'? heeh-ehk.
"Who?" Strong Bear said.

Nih'e3ebiini. . . .
It was over there . . .

3ih, cih'wonsehP, 'oh 3iwoo, sooxoenin hini', hini' niiyou hini'
cebiihetiino'oowu'.
"Well, let's see, let's go over there to where the gambling is,"
Strong Bear said.

<u>Woow</u> he'ih-cebiihinee nuhu'.
The one Swede was gambling.

Sii=hootonP, koox=nooxeihi' hesinih-oot;
Once again maybe Strong Bear made him mad;

Woow he'ih-'i3kuu3-ei'i nooxeihi'.
Now all the whites grabbed Strong Bear maybe.

'oh hi-h-'oowu-noh'oowP hoowu-noh'oowkuu3-e'.
But they couldn't even budge him.

Wohei, nih-'ii-t.
"Okay," Strong Bear said.

Niixoo heetn-iinokotii-noo, hee3-oohok.
"I'm going to play too," he said to them.

He'P hih'oowu-niiton-e' nuhu' toh-'unono'eiti3-oot.
The [whites] didn't understand him because he spoke Arapaho to them.

[[laughter]]
Nih-'eenei3kuu3-oot.
He grabbed hold of them real quick.

Wohei ne'-konkuu3-oot.
Well, then he shook them like rag dolls.

[[laughter]]
Hoowuhneniini ceese'.
He threw the whole bunch of them out of the tent at once.

[[laughter]]
Hoowe-e3eih,⁷ nih-'ii-3i';
The Swede is not heavy apparently, the Arapahos said;

Wootii nee'eesP nee'ee3esohoe-3i', nih-'ii-3i'.
I guess they were indicating like this with their hands, they said. [i.e., showing him shaking like a rag doll]

Heet-ciinoxuuh-eino', nih-'ii-3i'.
"They will have to quit bothering us," the Arapahos said.

[1.5 sec.]]

Story 5: Angry Swede Leads a Mob to Try and Get Strong Bear

PM: <u>Wohei</u> ne'-no'eeckoohu-t hi-teexokuut-on.

Well, then Strong Bear came home from the saloon on his saddle horse.

'oh hinee nih'oo3oo hi-teexokuut-on, nih-nonsih'ebi-t.

But that one white man on his own saddle horse, he was drunk.

Noh he'ihP. . . .

And he [came after Strong Bear].

((Strong Bear saw him coming.))

Woow nih-'iis-ciinooxebei-noo, XXX, ce'iihi'.

"Now, I've already let my horse loose and can't get it again," Strong Bear said.

<u>Wo'ooto'</u> nih-cih-nou'uukoh-ei3i'.

Right then the white men arrived there on their horses.

Koo-kooteeyei'i-3i' hi'in nih'oo3ou'u.

Those white men were cursing.

[[laughter]]
All right, chief, I'm gonna . . . the Swede said.
All right chief, I'm gonna . . . the Swede said.

howoh'oe!

"Now, hold on!" Strong Bear said.

Nih-'esinih-einoo, hinee hee3-einoo, nih-'ii-t nehe'.

"He made me mad with those things he said to me," the Swede said.

Hinee neh'ei-noo, nih'ii3ou'u.(?)

"I'm going to murder that one," the Swede said to his companions.

Kookon nee'ee3tone3eih-ei3i'.[8]
But Strong Bear was bashing in their heads when they tried to grab him.

[[laughter]]
Hoonii, nih-'iten-o' nuhu' niiteinoxonee', nuhu'.
After a long time of this fighting, the Swede got his repeating rifle, this one.

XXX nih-'iten-o', ne'iini ciitoh-o'.
??? he got it, and then he loaded it.

<u>Woow</u> ne'i-itenebeen-oot.
Then Strong Bear took it from him.

Nih-beeyooneenebeen-oot.[9]
He bent the barrel of his gun into a curve.

[[laughter]]
Shoot, nih-'ii3-oot.
"Go ahead and shoot," Strong Bear said to him.

[[laughter]]
Ne'iini, beebeet ne'iineeP ne'iini hiineekuu3ei'i-t.
Then the Swede just turned his horse back around real quick.

Nih-'ii-tone'eisiiton-ou'u.[10]
"I was bashing in their horses' heads," Strong Bear said later.

Nih-to'ow-ou'u hitonih'oo[ninoo].
"I hit their horses."

[[laughter]]
Noxobe3eihowuun-o'.[11]
"I really smashed the Swede's horse's head."

[[laughter]]

No, no, no, no, chief, heehehk(?).
"No, no, no, no, chief," he was saying.

[[laughter]]
#2:   Tou3ei'einoon!
"What a huge sound it made."

[[laughter]]
PM: Nih-'ii-noxone'eih-o' hiisoho'uusiihi'.
"I was pounding his head like this."

"Heetne-ihoow-hesiiniih," nih-'ii-t, "kokiyono3-ii."
"You aren't going to hurt me," Strong Bear said, "with bullets."

[[laughter]]
#2:   He'ih-no'oteih.
He was tough.

PM: Hee, ne'=nih-'ii3eih-ehk nuhu' Tei'ox.
Yeah, that's what they say Strong Bear was like.

#2:   Uhm-uhm, [Tei'ox.
Uhm-hmm, Strong Bear.

PM: [He'ih-no'oteih.
                [He was tough.

[[laughter]]
[[1 sec.]]

Story 6: Strong Bear Shakes Hands

((The following story, while quite elaborated in narrative detail, is told much more informally than the preceding ones. In particular, it lacks any of the markers of formal narrative (underlined in the preceding stories).))

PM: Wohei konoo'hoowuP nih-'oowuniihkoh-einoo, nih-'ii-t, beexuuni, sosoni'.

"Well, anyway, I was riding downstream," he said, "a little toward Shoshoni."

<u>Wohei</u> hii3e' neito'eino' koox=noo-noxoo3iheihi-3i', nih-'ii-3i', hinee sosoni'.
"Well, over there my relatives were being treated harshly yet again," they said, "at Shoshoni."

Benoheino'oowuu' niit-cee-cebiiheti-3i' nuhu'.
It was at the bar, where they gamble.

<u>He'ih</u>-'entoo nih'oo3oo, heebe3iihi' nih'oo3oo.
A white man was there, a real big white man.

Nihoone'ei-t.
He had blond hair.

Nehe' Swede,
This Swede,

#2:   Uhm!
Uhm!

PM: Nihi'neeP heeneebe3i3ee3ei-t nuhu' nihoone'ei-t.
Really . . . he had big hands, this Swede.

Nih-nouxon-ou'u neiteh'eiho-ho'.
"I met my friends," Strong Bear said.

Nih-bii-biiwoohu-3i', nih'iit.
"They were all crying," he said.

'ehte, heeyou?
"No way, what's going on?" Strong Bear said.

Hii3e' nih'oo3oo nii-neniniixoo3-ei'eet.
"That white man over there shakes our hands."

Nii-chief-nii3-eino', honoot nii-noxowu-3oo-3o'en-o'
neecetiin-inoo.

" 'Chief,' he says to us, until he has completely crushed our hands."

[[laughter]]

Nih-'iistii-t, nih-no'oteihI-t.

"The way he was doing that, he was tough!"

[[laughter]]

3iwoo, heehehk(?), nih-nee-necenoon-eino'.

"Look at this," they(?) said, "he has paralyzed our hands," the relatives said.

[[laughter]]

'oh 3ih sooxoenin, heetniini heet-won-neniniix{ooh}ouh-u'
heiteh'eihehin, nih-'ii-t, heetih-chief-hiih-einoo.

"Well, maybe, let's go over there, we'll go shake hands with our friend," he said, "so he can chief me."

[[laughter]]

He'ee3eeP, heh=neene'ee-hek.

I guess that's why, "there he is."

Hi3oobei-3i'.

They were right.

Xonouu ceciito'on-einoo.

Right away he came to greet me face-to-face.

Hello chief, howoh'oe, nih-'eihi-t, nih-'ii-t.

"Hello chief, wait a second," he said.

Wohei ne'=nii'-chief-hiih-einoo.

Well, that's when he called me 'chief.'

[[laughter]]

Hee, chief, 'oh ne'i-itenP.
"Hello chief," and then he took my hand.

Wohee'enoun, 'oh kookon nih-3i'eeP 3oo-3o'en-o' neecet.
On and on, he just kept [trying to] crush my hand.

[[laughter]]
Woow heihii nih-'eeneisiwo'oo-t,[12] toh-beet-3oo-3o'en-o' neecet.
Now, soon, he was going down on his knees to the ground because he wanted to crush it.

[[laughter]]
Wohei be, nih-'ii3-o', niixoo heet-chief-hiih-e3en,[13] hee3-o'.
"Well, friend," I said to him, "I'm going to 'chief' you too," I said to him.

3o'enebeen-o' hiicet.[14]
I crushed his hand.

[[laughter]]
Weii,[15] hiisoho' heeneihi-3i',
"Aie!!" he said, like the Indians had said,

keet-cih-tei3-XXX.
"Don't you want to???" I said to him.

[[laughter]]
Nih-woo-woteinooni-'.
There was a lot of noise from the hand breaking.

[[laughter]]
Ciinih-o'.
I let him go.

Hee, biiwoohu-t.
Yeah, he was crying.

[[laughter]]
Heh=tou3ei'oteib nuhu'!
What a lot of crying he was doing!

[[laughter]]
Hiniiteh'eihoho nih-'iixoxo'on-eit.
His friends came and surrounded him.

[[laughter]]
Hetne-ihoow-beetoh-'ooh-chief-iih.[16]
"He won't want to 'chief' anyone else," I said.

[[laughter]]
Ne'=nih-'eeneisiini.
That's how it was.

Howoh-'iinikotiih-ou'u nih'oo3ou'u, nih-'ii-t.
"I had fun playing around with white people," he said.

[[laughter]]
[[1 sec.]]
Nee'P ne'=nih-'ii3eihi-t nehe' Tei'ox.
That's how Strong Bear was.

[[6 sec.]]

Brief Story/Anecdote 7: The Wagon in the Mud

PM: Tih'ini hootoonoo3-oot, tih'iiP Casper ho3o'uunsitee, he'ih-cihkoxcis hotiiwo'.

When they bought coal at Casper, the wagon wheels got stuck in the mud on the way back.

he'ih-bi'-noh'en-ee hinee hotiiw.

Strong Bear just lifted that wagon up out of the mud.

[[2 sec.]]

he'ih'ini tei'eih hi'in Tei'ox.
That Strong Bear was strong.

[[3 sec.]]

Anecdote 8: Strong Bear Carries His Own Horse

PM: He'ih-nii-niihoniini,
He had been traveling for a long time on his horse,

Neetikotii-ni3 woxhoox.
His horse was tired out from walking.

Bi'P he'ih-3ei'iiwoonouh.
He just put it on his back and carried it.

[[laughter]]
[[4.5 sec.]]
Nih-no'oteihi-t nih-'ii3-oo3i'.
He was tough, they said about him.

[[1 sec.]]

Anecdote 9: Strong Bear Uses Rocks Like Bullets Shot from a Gun

#2:   Tih-'ii-ciikokiyon-ohkoni', kokiyono.
When they didn't have guns, guns when they were hunting one time,

hii3e', he'ih-i'-noo-noxowuh-oe hoh'onookeeno, [cese'eihiiho.
Over there, he just killed them with rocks, game animals.

PM: [Hee.
Yes.

PM: Yeah.
Yeah.

[[laughter]]

PM: Nih-tee-teeseyei'ih-oo3i'.
There were so many killed that people were stepping on them.

#2:   He'=tei'eihi-ni3, he'ih-noh'-oe.
No matter how strong the animal was, he would kill it.

PM: Wootii kokiyono3ii, hini' nih-'iis-eh-'etei'oo-3i' hii3e'.
Like bullets, that's how those rocks whizzed by over there.

[[laughter]]
[[3 sec.]]

General Description of Strong Bear

PM: [He'ih]-hi3oow-no'oteih nih-'eenees-sei'ikuu3-oo3i'.
He was truly tough the way he would lay those white guys out flat with a punch.

[[2 sec.]]
Nee'ei'P . . .
That's how strong. . . .

#2:   Tei'ox . . .
Strong Bear . . .

[[2 sec.]]
PM: He'ne'=nih-'iisP he'ne'=nih-'iis-no'oteihi-t hinono'ei.
That how strong he was, that Arapaho.

[[2 sec.]]
Noo-noxoo3ih-oot nih'oo3ou'u.
He would really treat those whites harshly.

[[laughter]]
[[2 sec.]]
Wohei ne'=nih-'iis-iine'etii-t, nuhu' Tei'ox.
Well that's how he lived, this Strong Bear.

Nenee'eeteihi-n.
That's where you are from [i.e., you are related to him].

PM: Heavy, just like iron,
He was heavy, just like iron,

#2:   Yeah.
Yeah.

[[5 sec.]]

PM: Hinee nihii, he'=nee'eeteihi-3i' hinee hinenitee-no', nuhu' Hanaways, Paul Hanaway.
Those uh, that's where those people are from, these Hanaways, Paul Hanaway is related to them.

[[5 sec.]]
3eboosei3iihi', hini' tei'eihi-t, Paul Hanaway.
A long time ago, that strong one, Paul Hanaway is related to him.

Beex-nee'eesiiseihi-t ci'.
Paul's voice is a little like Strong Bear's voice too.

#2:   Beex-woteiseihi-t.
A little gravel-voiced.

PM: Yeah, wooteiseihi-t nuhu'.
Yeah, Paul is gravel-voiced.

Wo'ei3, gravel voice hini', he'niiP he'ih-niibei'i.
Or, with that gravel voice, he sang.

Wo'uuceeceno'oo[17] hini' he'ih-nenih'ohei'i.
His voice would resound so loudly it would drown everyone out!

[[Laughter]]
[[7 sec.]]
Wohei hinee nenee'eesoo-' hini' 3eboosei3iihi'.
Well, that's how it was in those olden times.

Hinee nenitee, nih-'eeneis-iine'etii-t.

That's how that person lived.

Nih-'eenei3oohobeihi-3i', wonoo3ee-' nih-cee-ce'eseihi-3i' neniteeno'.

The ways they were seen, there were a lot of different kinds of people then.

Nih-'e-e'inoneihi-3i' nih-'eeneis-iine'etii-3i'.

They were known for the particular ways each of them lived.

He'ne'=nih-'iis-e'eenebeihi-3i' toon-hiis-nii3nowoo-3i'

That's how they were each depended on for whatever they had as their own special skill.

((At this point the narrator talks about an old man who had special skills to call game. He recounts the story of "The Forks," a fuller version of which is in Cowell and Moss (2005).))

Additional Strong Bear Stories

Strong Bear and the Boxer

((All three of the following stories were told by Richard Moss (real name), Paul's son, in 2002. They are available at the Center for the Study of Indigenous Languages, University of Colorado, Boulder, Audio mp3–16. Note the relatively extensive moral commentary included in the story immediately following, with multiple summational statements from the narrator (underlined below) and multiple citations from Strong Bear himself reinforcing those statements.))

ARAPAHO VERSION
Howoo he'ih-'ii3-eeno' nehe' tei'ox, heetou-' boo3eti-3i';
　　Nihii ko'einoxoeyoon-e' ni'iit-ou'u;
　　Wootii hiikokoyoxoeni-', cii3iihi' niit-iine3eiheti-3i'.
　　Wohei nih-tesiini no'oteihi-t, niiseihi-t nih'oo3oo.
　　He'=neen niitobeekuu-t nuhu' boo'oet.
　　Wohei, nii3-oohkoni', hei-beexu-neyei3ih-oo, hei-beexu-boo3-oo.
　　Hoowuuni, heeh-ehk.
　　Hoowuuni.
　　Ne-ebeh-'esiiniih-oo, wo'ei3 he-ebehP howoo ne-ebeh-noh'-oo.

Ne-ihoow-beet-nee'eestoo.

Noh nih-to'ob-einoohok, wootii ho'nookeen heet-to'ow-oot;

Noh to'ow-oohok, noh sii=ne-ihoowo-e'in heetn-iiP wohoe'et-wonoo3-iine'etii, he'ih-'ii.[18]

Noh ne'=nih-'iis-cii-ni'oow-oo3i'.

Ne-ebeh-'esiiniih-oo.

Hoow-nee'ee3ee-noo nuhu' heesP nuhu' hees-no'oteihi-noo, hetn-i'-eenesiinii3ei-noo.

Hoowuuni, honoot niiP nii-notoonoo3ou'u neito'ei-no', wo'ei3 howoo niiheniihi', neneeni-noo, he'ih-'ii.

Wohei ne'=nih-'iisiini, nihii . . . ;

Hoowuuhu' toh-biinee-noo nuhu' no'otehiit;

'oh niiheyoo nohk-uusiii'oo-noo.

Nohk-cebii'oo-noo.

Hi'in nenee': nee'ees-no'oteihi-noo.

'oh ne-ihoow-beet-i'-eenesiiniih-oo nenitee.

Ne-ihoow-beet-i'-kocoo'o3ih-ee nenitee honoot ni'-eeneecihi'woon-ou'u neito'eino', wo'ei3 howoo niiheniihi' neneeni-noo.

Noh nuhu' nenee' he'ih-'ii-cii-ni'oob-eeno'.

Hoowuuni, he'ih-'ii.

To'ob-einoohok wootii hoh'onookeen heet-to'ow-oot;

Noh hinee to'ow-oohok, 'oh ne-ihoowo-e'in wohoe'et-wonoo3-iine'etii.

Noh nuhu' nenee' ne-ihoow-beet-i'P kookon hi'-kocoo'o3ih-oo.

Nuhu' no'oteiheihii neenih-no'oteihi-t.

Neenihiini.

Ne-ihoow-beet-tooto'oeP ne-ihoow-beet-itenowuun-oo no'otehiit.

Wohei ne'=nih-'iisi-nihii-t;

Noh ne'=nih-'ii3ee-cii-ni'oow-oo3i'.

Nohuusoho'.

ENGLISH VERSION

And they also told Strong Bear where the boxing was going on;

Well, in the boxing ring, they call it;

I guess it was inside a fenced square area where they boxed with each other.

Well, he was very powerful, this one white boxer.

I guess he was the world champion.

"Wohei," they said to Strong Bear, "you should try him, you should fight him."

"No," he said.

"No."

"I might injure him, or I might kill him."

"I don't want to do that."

"And if he hit me it would be like he hit a rock;"

"And if I hit him and I really don't know whether he would live very long," he said.

And that's how come he didn't agree to their request.

"I might injure him."

"That is not the purpose of my strength, to go around hurting people."

"No, I don't use it until I have to stick up for my relatives or for myself," he said.

Wohei that is how it was, well . . . ;

"That's not why I was given this power;"

"I grew up with it on my own."

"I was created with it." [i.e., "I didn't acquire it through my own efforts"]

"That's it: that's how I come to be so powerful."

"But I don't want to hurt anyone with it."

"I don't want to kill a person, unless I have to use it to protect my relatives or myself."

And this is the reason he didn't agree to their request.

"No," he said.

"If he hit me it would be like hitting rock;"

"And if I hit him, I don't know if he would live very long."

"And I don't want to kill him with it for no reason."

"This powerful one, let him be, that powerful one."

"Let it be."

"I don't want to, because I don't want it to take his power from him."

Wohei that's what he said;

That's why he didn't agree to their request.

That's the way it was.

Strong Bear Shakes Hands

((This is the second story from Richard Moss, c. 2002. Of special note is the narrator's use of reduplication (italicized and underlined in this story). Initially, the reduplication refers to the many Arapahos who are suffering mistreatment from the white man. But as the story progresses, the reduplication shifts focus to the extreme suffering that the white man himself undergoes as his hand is crushed completely, further reinforcing the irony that dominates the story.))

ARAPAHO VERSION

Hinee hooxono'o, hinit 3ebiihi', noobe'einiihi', hooxono'o
he'ih-3ebii3iikoh-e'.

[he'ih]-3eboowuniihiikoh-e'.

He'ih-'ii-won-niistoo-3i hinee sosoni'.

He'ih-'e3ebiikoh-e'.

[He'ih]-yiisiikoh-e'.

Hinenno he'ih-'ii-nouxon-ee.

He'ih-'ii-cei3iikoh-ei'i.

He'ih-'ii-toun-owuu hiicet-ino.

Wohei he-ih-toustoo-be?

Heeyou?

Hi'in nono'oteihi-t bee'e'ei-t nih'oo3oo, hinit benoheino'oowuu.

3oo-3o'ohoen-ei'eet.

Nii-neniniixouhu-t xonou nonoohow-oo3i 3owo3neniteeno;

Noh nee3eb-ciiteini-3i xonou nii-yihoon-oot.

Nii-nouxon-oot, niitohoen-oot, niixoo nii-*3oo*-3o'ohoen-eit.

Hee, hohkonee heetn-eh-nou'uukoh-einoo, nih-'ii-t.

He'ih-nouxon-ee;

Ci'=he'ih-'ii-toun-owuu hitiicet-ino.

Yeh, he-ih-toustoo-be?

Hinit bee'e'ei-t nih'oo3oo;

Ciinoo'on-beesei3e-',

3oo-3o'ohoen-ei'eet.

Nii-neniniixouhu-t,

Nii-*3oo*-3o'ohoen-ei'eet.

Hee, hohkonee heetn-eh-no'uukoh-einoo.

He'ih-yiisiikoh-e',

Nee'eh-no'uukoh-eit.

Ceee3i' nii-toukutooxowootiini-', he'ih-touku3-ee hitoniho';

Nee'eh-ciitei-t.

'oh xonouu he'ih-noohob-e' hi'in bee'e'ei-ni3;

He'ne'-ceciito'on-eit.

Wohei, heneeyeih-no'usee-n, heneeyeih-no'usee-n.

Heet-neniniixoo3-e3en.

Heneeyeih-noohob-e3en, he'ih-'ii3-e'.

Hii3eti-' toh-noohob-e3en; heet-neniniixooP . . .

Hee, noh ci'=heet-neniniixoo3-e3en, hee3-oohok.

Ne'i-itohoen-eit.

Ne'iiP hoowP heniix-oohok nehe' nihii tei'oxuho'.

Hee hoowP he'ih-'ii-cooniini he'ih-'ii-coon-3o'en-owun[19] hiicet.

Wohei nuhu' heecis-neyei-3o'ohoen-eit, ne'=nii'-ho'wohoe-t[20] nehe' tei'ox.

Heihii he'ih-co'oekuu nehe' nih'oo3oo.

He'ih-beex-*bii*-biiwoo.

Koo-koseinooni-'i hixono nuhu' hiicetin-e'.

Sii=honoot he'ih-tes-3o'en;

He'ih-beex-*bee*-be'einin.

HoowP he'ih-'eeneiP.

Nehe' tei'ox, me glad to see you, nih-'ii3-oohok,

HoowP hoowP hoowP honoot, hei'-tes-ni'ee3o'ohoen-oot nuhu'.

He'ne'=nih-'iisiini heet-*noo*-noxon-3o'en-o' nuhu' hiicet.

Bii-biiwoohu-t nehe' nih'oo3oo.

Noh ne'=nih-'iisiini ho3ton-oot nuhu' nii-*3oo*-3o'ohoen-ee hiniito'ei-no, hei'-neniniixouhu-t nuhu' nehe' nih'oo3oo.

He'ih'iiP heenoo heeyow-ciiteini-3i 3owo3neniteeno he'ih-'ii-yihoon-ee,

he'ih-'ii-*3oo*-3o'ohoen-ee.

Hohkonee [he'ih]-seh-no'uukoh-e' nehe' tei'ox, sii=ne'-3o'ohoen-eit.

Noh nee'eesise-' nuhu' hoo3itoo.

ENGLISH VERSION

That Riverton there downstream, to Riverton, he rode toward over there.

He rode downstream.

He was going to do something or other at Shoshoni.

He rode over there.

He rode over in that direction.

He was meeting men on the way.

They were riding back toward here.

They were holding their hands.

"Wohei, what did you do?" he asked them.

"What?"

"There is a very strong red-haired white man over there in the saloon."

"He is crushing our hands."

"He shakes someone's hand right away whenever he sees Indians;"

"The ones who go in there, right away he goes to them."

"He meets them, he takes their hand, and he crushes their hand."

"Okay, I guess I will have to, I will ride over to there," he said.

He met more men;

Also they were holding their hands.

"Well, what did you all do?"

"Over there is a red-haired white man;"

"He's pretty big,"

"He's crushing our hands."

"He shakes someone's hand,"

"He crushes our hands."

"Yes, I guess I'll have to ride over there."

He rode away over in that direction,

Then he arrived there.

Outside, where people tie up their horses, he tied up his horse;

Then he went inside there.

And right away that one saw him, the one with red hair;

Then the white man came to greet him.

"Well, it's good that you've come, it's good that you've come."

"I'm going to shake your hand."

"It's good to see you," that Swede said to him.

"It is good to see you I am going to shake . . ."

"Yes, and I'm going to shake *your* hand," Strong Bear said to him.[21]

Then the white man took his hand.

Then he got scared of Strong Bear.

He couldn't, he couldn't crush his hand.

Well, while the white man was trying to crush his hand, then that's when Strong Bear closed his hand.

Soon he was scrunched down, this white man.

He was just whimpering and crying pitifully;

The bones in his hand were crackling.

until Strong Bear completed crushed it;

His hand was just a little bloody pulp.

That was how it was.

Strong Bear, "me glad to see you," he said to him.

Once he had completely crushed this white man's hand.

That was how he brutally crushed his hand.

He was just crying and whimpering, this white man.

And that's how he paid him back for crushing his relatives' hands, once he shook hands with this, this white man.

Normally every Indian who entered, the Swede went up to them [and] he would crush their hands.

But then Strong Bear rode back over there, and he really crushed his hand.

And that's as far as the story goes.

Strong Bear and the Wagon

((Told by Richard Moss, c. 2002))

ARAPAHO VERSION

Teecxo' he'ih-'ii-noo3-eeno' ho3o'uunesiteen hinee bei'i'einiiciihehe'
ni'iitou'u.

Huut niiyou nuhu' cee'iyeino'oowu-u' he'ih-'iiP;

He'ne'=niit-no'uxoh-oo3i' ho3o'uunesiteen tohuu-wottonouhu-3i'
hinee.

Wohei he'ih-noo3-eeno' hinee bei'i'einiiciihehe'.

Ho3o'uunesiteehotiiwo nii-ciinoo'on-beesei3ei-'i.

Wohei ne'iini 3ebiis-nou'usee-3i' hi'in bei'i'einiiciiheh-e'.

Wohei ne'-teexoono3ei-3i', neeneisiini.

Wohei ne'i-cih-ce'P ce'-ce3i3ou'usee-3i' cih-noxuuteiniihi' cei3iihi'.

Noh hinit he'iitnei'i, hinit he'iitnei'i he'ih-neei'iin.

He'ne'iini hinowunoo'oo-t ceese' hotii.

He'ih-koxcis.

'oh nuhu' woxhooxebii he'ih-'ii-coonih-eeno'.

He'ih-'oo3oniini hoo3onci3-eeno'.

Wohei, heeh-ehk nehe' tei'ox, he'ii3P he'ii3P heebeh-nii3P nii3in-
oobe bei'ci3eiseenookuu.

Cih-ceesih-e' hinee woxhooxebii!

Heet-neeciini huut noko3P, heeteh-3i'ookuuh-oonee.

Heetne-e3itoo3iw-o' hinee hotii.

'oh hiihei3e-', heniixoxonee-t nuhu' ho3o'uunesitee.

Niihei3e-' nehe' ho3o'uunesitee.

Hiikoot beesei3ei-'i nuhu' hotiiwo.

Wohei ne'-cih-'iis-ceesiton-oo3i'.

Wo'eii3ow he'iiteihi3i he'ih-nii3in-ee nuhu' bei'ci3eineeseenookuu.

Ne'-oonooten-o', hoonooten-ou'u.

Ne'i-biin-oo3i' hi'in seenookuu.

Nih-i'-biP hi-ce'eenoo ne'-koxu3kuu3-oot.

Sii=heniiP he'ih-'e3itoo3ib-ee.

Sii=he'ih-nohk-ce3ei'oo.[22]

'oh neeneinowusi-'i nuhu' ko'eino'ohtoo-no'.

NiiP noh ne'-nih-'ii3ei'nee-tei'eihi-t, ni'ii3-oo3i' hini' tei'oxuhu'.

He'ih-'iise-e3itoo3ib-ee nuhu' hotiiw.

Noh ne'=nih-'iisi-nihii-3i'.

Ne'=nih-'iis-noohow-oo3i' nih-'ii3ei'nee-tei'eihi-t nehe' tei'ox.

Nih-'een-ei'in-ou'u nuhu', nooxeihi' nih-'ii-beex-cii3oowot-ou'u tih-'ee3nee-tei'eih-ehk.

Wohei ne'iini nuhu' tei'ehiit he'ih-'ii-ni'P hi'-nii-niiteheiw-oot.

Hi'in nenee'.

He'ih-niihen-noohob-eeno' he3itoo3iw-oot hotiiw-un.

He'ih-beex-eeneinowusP heeneinowusi-n neeneinowusi-no' ko'eino'ohtoo-no' neei'in-e'.

Noh ne'=nih-'iisiini.

He'inon-oo3i' hee3ei'nee-tei'eihi-ni3 nehe' Tei'ox.

Nohuusoho'.

ENGLISH VERSION

Long ago they used to go and fetch coal in Casper, as they call it.

Here to Fort Washakie they would . . . ;

That is where they would bring the coals, so they could use them for heating.

Wohei they were fetching some over there in Casper.

Coal wagons are pretty big.

Wohei then they arrived over there at Casper.

Wohei they loaded them on like they always did.

Wohei then they headed back by wagon, back up the river to here.

And right here somewhere, right there somewhere, it was very sandy.

Then one wheel sank out of sight.

It was mired in the sand.

And these horses, they couldn't manage to get it out.

They failed, they failed to pull it out.

"Wohei," Strong Bear said, "do you have any sort of chain?"

"Bring the horses here for me!"

"They will stay here off to the side for a while, you will make them stand away over there."

"I am going to drag out that wheel."

"But it is heavy, it is full, this coal wagon," they said.

"It is heavy, this coal wagon."

"Also they're big, these wagons."

Wohei then they had gotten the chain for him.

It just so happened that somehow they had a chain with them there.

Then he hooked it up to the wagon, they hooked it up.

Then they gave him that chain.

He just . . . then he threw it over his shoulder.

He just dragged the darn thing right out of there.

He just started right on off with it.
Even though they were completely buried, these wheel rims.
And that's how strong he was, they say about that Strong Bear.
He just somehow dragged the wheel right out.
And that's what they said.
That's what they saw him do, that's how strong this Strong Bear was.
They knew it, but maybe they kind of didn't believe it entirely, that he was so strong.
Wohei then with this strength, he would always help people with it.
That's it.
They saw him themselves, he dragged the wagon out of there.
It was kind of out of sight, the wheel rims, in the sand.
And that's how it was.
They learned just how strong this Strong Bear was.
That's how it was.

Synopses of Other Strong Bear Narratives

Another story of Strong Bear, provided by William C'Hair (real name) of the Saint Stephens area of Wind River Reservation, reports that he once lifted the side of a log cabin completely off the ground, at the Saint Michael's Mission in the Ethete area—a story similar to the one Paul Moss told about raising the ridgepole during construction activity.[23] In addition to the characteristics of being very strong and having a deep, gravelly voice, Strong Bear is also reported to have been very large physically and very heavy—it took twelve men to carry his coffin at his funeral. A quite different and very long story about Strong Bear, also told by Richard Moss (Moss and Cowell 2006), recounts how the Arapaho were starving in camp in winter, buried in their tipis by a blizzard. Strong Bear crawls out the top of a tipi and goes in search of food. He obtains game, but while he is cooking some for himself before starting back to help the people, a ghost appears at his campsite. Rather than being scared, however, Strong Bear casually engages the ghost in conversation, until he suddenly throws burning fat on it and reduces it to charred bones, which he takes back to show the other Arapahos. This story is the only Strong Bear story in which he encounters a supernatural foe—and also the only story seemingly set in pre-reservation times. Finally, William C'Hair offered a vision quest story related to Strong Bear, reporting that he was visited by a bear and a mountain lion. These visits accounted for his strength (the bear) and also his cunning (the mountain lion).[24] It is notable, however, that no other Strong Bear stories make reference to the way he obtained his power, nor do they mention him praying, going on vision quests, or doing any kind of ceremonial preparation before using his powers. Instead, the powers are presented as purely prosaic and human. In this sense, Strong Bear is presented as completely different from Arapaho historical, legendary, or mythical figures who make use of more-than-human powers of a sacred type, following more or less elaborate ceremonial protocols (see Cowell and Moss 2005 and Cowell, Moss, and C'Hair 2014 for many examples). On the other hand, C'Hair's unique vision-quest account of Strong Bear links him back to more traditional "powerful ones" who also acted heroically and spectacularly on behalf of the tribe, but using very different sorts of powers. Arapaho examples of these types of narratives are stories about a man known as Beaver Dodge.

Beaver Dodge Stories

Beaver Dodge (real name) definitely was a real person who lived into the 1940s. He was closely involved with ceremony, especially the Sun Dance, and many of his exploits occur in that context; he had the power to bring on rain or hail during the Sun Dance, for example, to cool off the temperature. Examples such as this make Beaver Dodge closer to a shamanic figure than a folk hero. He is also representative of a number of revered Arapaho men who were the last bearers of pre-reservation culture and whose more-than-human powers are often reported—men such as Goes-in-Lodge (real name), Sherman Sage (real name), and Yellow Calf (real name). Such powers are often reported as having been lost when the last of that generation passed away.

I place the term "powerful ones," used to describe Beaver Dodge, in scare quotes because of its complexity. The term is a direct translation of the Arapaho *nono'oteihit* 's/he is powerful,' but has no direct equivalent in English. The closest English term might be 'medicine man,' but this term is really too poorly defined—and too tied to racist stereotypes of Native Americans—to be useful. The Arapaho verb *no'oteihi-*, in the usage translated here, refers to a possessor of more-than-human power. This person therefore has the capacity to do more-than-human things, at least in relation to the typical Arapaho person. The power is understood as coming from sacred, spiritual, or holy sources. Thus, the person can also be described as *beeteet* 's/he is holy.' One use of this power is for healing, and traditional doctors (*notoniheihiiho'*) can be described using this verb. But the power can also be used for a much wider range of practices related to ceremony, hunting, warfare, or other endeavors. Paul Moss's historical narratives (Cowell and Moss 2005) are largely concerned with the acquisition, management, and proper use of this *no'otehiit* ('power'). Beaver Dodge was a very "powerful" person in this sense, and 'Man of Power' would be an appropriate term.

Some of Beaver Dodge's exploits do resemble those of Strong Bear however. In particular, they occur outside of ceremonial contexts and at least partially in relation to Euro-Americans. The following example includes two stories, one involving sacred use of power, the other secular in orientation.[25] This passage is drawn from a conversation between two good friends, which happened after work at the language immersion school in Arapahoe, Wyoming, where both were teachers. The conversation was wide-ranging and had been going on for around fifteen minutes when the following passage occurred. Immediately preceding this passage was a discussion of people who claim to know things, but actually don't (especially regarding ceremonial or medicine power), or try to take on roles they're not suited for.

((ELAR 22b, 12:21; following a discussion of medicine power))

Tom: Wo'ei3 heeneistoo-3i', nii-notonihei-3i' wo'ei3 . . .
Or what they do, they doctor, or . . .

'oh hoowP hoow-tee-teeko'-owuu howoh? [[gesture: fitting things into place]]
But they don't fit that role, you know?

Don: Hoowu-[teeko'-owuu.
They don't fit that role.

Tom: [Yeah hoowu-teeko'-owuu, yeah.
Yeah, they don't fit that role, yeah.

Yeah, xonouu nii-beet-bis-notP bis-nee-3i' notoniheihiiho' you know. [[gesture: wear regalia, put on clothing]]
Yeah, right away they all want to be doctors, you know.

Don: Nii-bis-beet-niistii-3i', 'oh hoowu-nii3in-owuu . . .
They all want to do it, but they don't have . . .

Tom: Yeah, hinee woxu'uu-wo. 'oh nii-beet-bis-nii3inou'u woxu'uu-wo. [[gesture: medicine held in front of oneself, then put in one's mouth]]

Yeah, those medicines. But they all want to have all those medicines.

Don: Hoo3P hoo3oo'o' nii3in-ou'u.
Others really do have medicines [medicine power].

Tom: Yeah, beenhehe' nii3in-ou'u, hee, yeah. [[gesture: a little bit]]
Yeah, a few have it, yes, yeah.

Don: 'oh hoowP, hoowP . . .
But they don't, don't . . .

[[1 sec.]]

Beaver Dodge Cools Off the Sun Dance

Don: <u>Teecxo'</u> nih-beteee-3i'.
Long ago they were dancing in the Sun Dance.

Tom: Yeah, beteee-3i'.[26]
Yeah, they were dancing.

Don: Noh <u>nehe'</u> Beaver Dodge, Beaver Dodge, <u>nih-niitowoo3-o'</u>.
And this Beaver Dodge, Beaver Dodge, I heard about him.

Tom: Yeah.
Yeah.

Don: Beetee-t, nih-'ii3-oo3i'.
"He is holy," they said about him.

Tom: Yeah.
Yeah.

Don: Hoseihoowu' hoonoxone-esitee-' [nih-'ii-3i'.
The Sun Dance was extremely hot that year, they said.

Tom: [Yeah.
                                     Yeah.

Don: Keet-ciiP
"Could you possibly . . . ,"

[[8 sec.]]
Uhh, nih-notton-oo3i' . . .
Uh, they asked him . . .

Don: [Hees-ii-tousi-nihiitoon 'to cool it off?'
How do you say 'cool it off'?

Tom: [Yeah.
Yeah.

[[2 sec.]]
Don: "Koo-he-etP Keet-cii-ni'-beex-toyooben?" [nih-'ii-3i'. [[PSL gesture: "question"]
"Could you cool it off a little?" they said.

Tom: [Yeah.
                                             Yeah.

Don: Ne'-notton-oo3i'.
Well, then they asked him.

Ne'neeP nee'ees-niistoo-t nehe' Beaver Dodge.
Then that's what Beaver Dodge did.

Noh uh . . .
And uh . . .

Tom: Weather medicine. Yeah hini'iit . . .
Weather medicine. Yeah, that . . .

Don: Ne'-nih-beex-oosooninoo'oo-', nih-'ii-3i'. [Wohei hini' uhh,
Then it was suddenly raining a little," they said. Well those, uh

Tom: [Yeah.
                                             Yeah.

Tom: Nih-i'-too'oo-'.
  It was cooled off, thanks to his power.

Don: Wo'wu3oo-no' nih-cih'ini.
  Hailstones came.

Tom: Yeah.
  Yeah.

Don: Noh toads was coming out of his mouth, nih-'ii3-oo3i'.
  [[gesture: something coming out of a person's mouth
  repeatedly]]
  "And toads were coming out of his mouth," they said of him.

Tom: Yeah.
  Yeah.

Don: [[gesture: something up high descends down low]]
Don: Noh toyooben-o'.
  And he cooled it down.

Tom: Yeah. Toyooben-o' yeah.
  Yeah. He cooled it down, yeah.

  Hi3oP hi3oowuuni.
  That's true.

  Nih-nee'eesoo-'. [Hi3oowuuni.
  It was like that. That's true.

Don: [Yeah.
                    Yeah.

Tom: Yeah.
  Yeah.

  [[1 sec.]]

Beaver Dodge Makes Money from Grass

Don: <u>Noh huut</u>, <u>he'ihP he'ih</u>-ben nehe' Beaver Dodge huut huut
hooxono'o. [[gesture: points toward Riverton]]
*And here, I guess this Beaver Dodge was drinking here in
Riverton.*

Tom: Yeah.
Yeah.

Don: Noh <u>he'ih</u>-nii3ih'ebiib-ee nehe' uhh, John Plume.
And I guess he was drinking with this, uh, John Plume.

Tom: Yeah.
Yeah.

Don: Nehe' Beaver Dodge, 'oh hoowo-e'inon-e' tih-betee-t.
And this Beaver Dodge, John didn't know that he was powerful.

Tom: Yeah.
Yeah.

Don: You know, tih-betee-t nehe' Beaver Dodge.
You know, that Beaver Dodge was holy.

John Plume, <u>he'ih</u>-nii3ih'ebiib-ee hini'. [[gesture: one's elbow
touches the person next to one]]
I guess he was drinking with that John Plume.

Tom: Yeah.
Yeah.

Don: He-'otoonoot-ou'u noh nooxeihi', [[gesture: reaching out to get
a glass]]
I guess they were buying drinks,

[<u>He'ih</u>]-hotoobih'eb hini' hih-beneetiin-inoo. [[gesture:
drinking]]
John Plume. finished drinking what they were drinking.

Tom: Yeah.
    Yeah.

Don: [He'ih]-hotoobih'eb. [[gesture: points at "them"]]
    He finished his drink.

Tom: Yeah.
    Yeah.

Don: John Plume. ne'-notton-oot Beaver Dodge, [[gesture: speaker
    points at self, as if he is Beaver Dodge]]
    Then John Plume. asked Beaver Dodge,

    HeP he-et-tousi-itookohei'i-n? He-et-tous-ce'-bene-n, nih-'ii3-oot.[27]
    "How are we going to get a drink now? How are we going to
    get more to drink?" he said to him.

Tom: Yeah.
    Yeah.

Don: Wohei howoh'oe, he'ih-'ii3-ee.
    "Well, just wait," Beaver Dodge said to him.

    Just, noosou-bene-no', you know.
    Just, "we've still got something to drink," you know.

    Wo'ei3 [he'ih]-noon-oo3itoohu-no' wo'ei3 neen-ei'towuun-
    e3en, nih-'ii-3i'.
    Or they were telling each other stories, or I'll tell you about
    something, they were saying to each other.

    'oh hu'un ne'P nee'ee-noxuhu!
    And that one, then he says to Beaver Dodge "hurry up!"

    [Nii-beet-ce'-bene-'.
    He wants to drink some more.

Tom: [Yeah, yeah, [yeah
    Yeah, yeah, yeah

Don: [John Plume., yeah.
                       John Plume, yeah.

        Howoh'oe! nih-'ii-t.
        "Wait!" he said.

Tom: Nii-si'ih'ebi-t hini'.[28]
        He is craving a drink, that one.

Don: Yeah.
        Yeah.

Tom: Yeah.
        Yeah.

Don: Noh ne'-hotoobei-'i hini' hi-beneetiin-inoo. [[gesture: drinking
        something]]
        And then they finished their drinks.

        Noh beneetP no'otii-3i' nuhu'. [[gesture: drinking something]]
        And they finished, they finished it all up.

Tom: Yeah, hoowoohP, [hoowooh'uni.
        Yeah, there's no more.

Don: [Wohei heetP heetP keet-ce'-noot, nih-'ii3-
                       oot John Plume.
                       *"Well you will, you will, are you going to fetch
                       some more?" he said to John Plume.*

        Nuhu' Beaver Dodge nih-'ii3-oot nuhu' John Plume: [[gesture:
        points at self as if he is Beaver Dodge]] [[gesture: points at John
        Plume "over there"]]
        Beaver Dodge said this to John Plume:

        Wohei, heet-ce'-noote-noo.
        "Okay, I'll get some more."

Hoowo-e'inon-e' [hoowo-e'inon-e' toh-betee-t.
John doesn't know, doesn't know that he's holy.

Tom: [Yeah.
                                         Yeah.

      Yeah.
      Yeah.

Don: Nuhu' woxu'u-no heeneiten-o'. [[gesture: repeatedly pulling up
      bits of grass]]
      Beaver Dodge took some grass.

Tom: Yeah woxu'u-no.
      Yeah, grass.

Don: [[gesture: rubbing hands together as if mixing something
      between them]]
      Greenbacks, he'ih-'ii3-ee. [[gesture: presenting money to
      someone]]
      "Greenbacks," I guess Beaver Dodge said to John.

      Wohei be, cih-nootookohei'i.[29] [[gesture: points at bar over there]]
      "Well, friend, fetch us some drinks," Beaver Dodge said to him.

      Senii=ce'ixotii-t nehe' uhh, John Plume. [[gesture: bringing
      something here]]
      Darned if this John Plume didn't bring back some more drinks.

Tom: Yeah, yeah.
      Yeah, yeah.

Don: He'ih-ben about two or three times. [[gesture: drinking
      something]]
      I guess John drank about two or three sips.

      Ne'-tokohu-t. [[gesture: off that way]]
      Then he fled in fear.

Tom: [Yeah.
        Yeah.

Don: [Hih-'oowo-e'inon-e' [tih-betee-t. [[gesture: points at
        someone]]
        He didn't know that Beaver Dodge was holy.

Tom: [Yeah.
                                Yeah.

        Hi3ooP hii3oobei-t yeah.
        He's right yeah.

Don: Got scared of him.
        Got scared of him.

Tom: Heni'hooxouuneeP, nihi'hooxouuneenoo' nih'ii3eihit, 'innit?[30]
        It was ??? by that means, they said about him, right?

Don: Yeah.
        Yeah.

Tom: Yeah.
        Yeah.

Don: Yeah.
        Yeah.

        [[1 sec.]]
        Yeah, he got scared of him, nihi'nee-tokohu-t John Plume.
        [[gesture: off that way]]
        Yeah, John got scared of him, he took off real quick.

        [[1 sec.]]

Follow-Up Discussion

Tom: Niitowoot-owoo hini'iit hoo3itoo.
        I've heard that story that you told.

<u>Somebody else told me that, heenees-oo3itee-n, yeah</u>.
Somebody else told me that, what you told, yeah.

'oh houuneenoo-' nooxeihi' nih-'ii3-oot you know.
"And it's very serious and powerful maybe," he said about him,
you know.

Don: yeah.
yeah.

Tom: Yeah, ne'-niistii-t:
That's what he made:

Hini'iit, [hini'iit bei'ci3ei'i hini' woxu'u-no. [[gesture: money]]
[[gesture: grass]]
That, that money, out of that grass.

Don: [Yeah, [[gesture: gathering grass]]
Yeah.

Tom: Niiyou bei'ci3ei'i. Noote, nootookohei'i, nih'iit.
"Here is money. Fetch it, fetch some more drinks," Beaver
Dodge said.

Don: [[gestures as Tom speaks the preceding line, rubbing hands
together as if making something]]
Yeah, het-ce'iini, wohei het-ce'-nootookohei. [[gesture: giving
someone money]] [[gesture: pointing at bar over there]]
Yeah, "you must, well, you must fetch us some more drinks."

Tom: Yeah.
Yeah.

Ne'-neih-oot, howoh? [[gesture: claps hands together once]]
Then he scared John, right?

Don: Ne'-neih-oot howoh?
Then he scared him, right?

Nih-'iis-ce'i-no'uxotii-t, noh benei-'i, bene-' two or three times, ne'-tokohu-t. [[gesture: drinking]] [[gesture: over that way]]

After John brought back the drinks, and they drank, John drank two or three times, and then he took off real quick.

Tom: [[gesture: over that way]]

[[1.5 sec.]]

Tom: <u>Yeah hinee, neenei3P neeni'hoo3itouhu-3i' howoo.</u>

Yeah, that story, how you, I've heard it told about that, too.

Don: Yeah.

Yeah.

Tom: Nihii-n, yeah, I heard that name, heeneesi-nihii-n.

What you said, yeah, I have heard that name, what you said, yeah.

Don: Yeah.

Yeah.

Tom: <u>Nih-'oo3itoon-einoo he'iiteihi3i [that story.</u>

Someone else told me that story too.

Don: [Yeah.

                                                  Yeah.

Follow-Up: More on Medicine Power

[[1 sec.]]

Tom: Nih-'ii-betee-3i' <u>nuhu',</u> <u>teecxo',</u> [nuh'uuno 3owo3neniteeno' nuh'uuno. Yeah.

They used to be holy long ago, these Indians, these ones. Yeah.

Don: [Yeah, teecxo', yeah.

                                                  Yeah, long ago, yeah.

[[4 sec.]]

Tom: Woow hini'iit neyooxet ceikoohu-3i,
   Now that whirlwind, when it would be coming toward you,

   Hees-ii-tousi-nihiitoon heesoo-', hoowuuhu' or uhh they used to say something.
   How do you say, how it was, 'hoowuuhu' or, uh, they used to say something.

   Uhm, they had a word for it, like uhh tih-ceikoohu-t hini' neyooxet.
   Uhm, they had a word for it, like, uh, when that whirlwind was coming.

Don: Neyooxet.
   Whirlwind.

Tom: Yeah, they used to say something.

Don: Yeah.

Tom: Honobii, something like that.[31]

Don: Yeah.

   [[4 sec.]]
Tom: Nih-'ii-ceibihcehi-t nuhu' neyooxet. [[gesture: something going off to the side]]
   Then the whirlwind would swerve off to the side.

((ELAR 22b, 16:25))

((The speaker next notes that there are many whirlwinds and tornadoes in the Rawlins, Wyoming, area. This leads to a discussion of the Arapaho name for Rawlins, and of various other Arapaho place-names and the people who know those names well.))

These two stories are quite different from the Strong Bear stories in several ways. First, they are presented as absolutely true (especially the first one). They emerge out of a context of serious discussion of more-than-human power and are followed by a brief continuation of that theme. In contrast, Strong Bear's powers are described as purely physical, not sacred.[32] Whereas Strong Bear is 'strong' (*tei'eihi-*), Beaver Dodge is 'holy' (*betee-*). While Strong Bear stories are often told for fun, so to speak, the first Beaver Dodge story would never be told in that way. The second Beaver Dodge story is interesting in that it is transitional in genre between the account of more-than-human power and the folk hero stories of the Strong Bear type. Nothing much is at stake in the second story other than a few more drinks. The central feature of the story is really the humorous depiction of John Plume, appearing somewhat hapless—and certainly too eager (*si'ih'ebi-t*, 'craving a drink, drinking too much') for those additional drinks. Notice that, unlike the first story, the second one makes use of the *he'ih-* evidential/narrative past tense prefix, indicating less of a claim to truthfulness than in the first story. Notice also that the speakers explicitly claim that the first story is true.

Most interesting is that other Arapaho people comment that one normally should not use sacred powers for purposes such as the one described in the second story. This cautionary note is a central theme of traditional trickster stories, and a theme emphasized repeatedly by Paul Moss in his stories (Cowell and Moss 2005). The two speakers here made the same point themselves in another conversation recorded later the same week, again after work, and were in fact making it when they began telling these two stories. In the later conversation, they talked about special medicine powers and how a person had used the powers on his horse to win horse races he was betting on. They said that the powers should not be used in this way, and that this person's medicine power eventually went away because it was misused. And, of course, Strong Bear himself makes the same point in the story about him potentially challenging the boxer.

The acceptability of this story about turning grass into money lies partially in the fact that there is indeed so little at stake. Beaver Dodge gains nothing of any real value from this use of his power, while he also helps a friend, if only slightly, and thus does not truly abuse the power, especially not for personal gain. More importantly, the only person victimized is the (almost certainly white) saloonkeeper. Beaver Dodge scores a point for the Arapahos against the whites, in a situation that is economically dominated by whites and helps out a fellow Arapaho, while also demonstrating that traditional Arapaho more-than-human power not only exists but can trump white economic power. The first story is very involved with sacred medicine power, but it occurs in the purely Arapaho context of the Sun Dance. The second story actually makes a stronger claim about this power—that it can be taken into the Euro-American world as well.

In this sense, the story is a complement to the Strong Bear stories, though the latter focus on the ways that Arapaho *physical* power can be used successfully in Euro-American contexts.

These two Beaver Dodge stories also allow both speakers to affiliate with each other, as well as with traditional Arapaho values. And John Plume in this story stands in for all the modern Arapaho doubters of traditional more-than-human powers—another topic that the same two speakers had been discussing earlier.

The Beaver Dodge stories are similar to the "legendary Tom LaPorte" stories from Maliseet tradition in several ways. Tom Laporte is labeled a "shaman" in the Maliseet stories and has more-than-human powers. Those powers sometimes scare both the people who witness them and those who hear about them (LeSourd 2004, 553). While shamanistic power is part of a "traditional Maliseet world view" (548), the stories are set in a context of the fur trade, relations with French traders, Catholicism, gambling with cards, drinking liquor, buying supplies from stores, and especially concerns with money. Of the seven Tom Laporte stories, four turn at least in part on the need for money or concern with trade goods such as guns or whiskey that are expensive and hard to obtain. Thus, the Tom Laporte stories, like the second Beaver Dodge story, show how the "powerful one" could become a liminal figure in an oral narrative tradition in the context of colonialism. Colonialism is crucially about differing degrees of power, but also different ontologies of power. The "powerful one" is an exponent of the traditionalist ontology of power in many indigenous communities. He or she is thus the perfect person to juxtapose against the exigencies imposed on indigenous people by colonial ontologies of power—most crucially, the monetization and marketization of subsistence and human relations. Both Beaver Dodge and Tom Laporte exercise their power and confront the colonizer in the context of the need for liquor or trade goods—the classic initial meeting space between colonizer and potential colonial subject. I would argue that their power to magically convert natural products (grass, wood chips) into money is an ironic echo of the virtually magical power of markets to convert seemingly all natural products and items of daily use into monetized commodities in a market system, held in relation to each other by the mediating force of money.[33]

The Strong Bear stories and chain operate in a fully desacralized domain, in contrast to the Beaver Dodge stories. None of the threats to the tribe in them are more-than-human in nature, and none of the solutions to the threats are more-than-human either. The Strong Bear legends within the Arapaho tribe represent an externally oriented anticolonial type of indigenous response to oppression. In contrast, many traditional genres,

Paul Moss's historical narratives, and some of the Beaver Dodge stories are tribe-internal-focused narratives about access to more-than-human power. The Strong Bear stories are in this sense are truly folk hero narratives and seemingly new to Arapaho culture. Certainly, no similar texts can be found among earlier Arapaho oral literature.

The Chain

With these observations in mind, we can now return to the initial chain of Strong Bear stories and consider its dynamics more closely. Evidently the topic has come up in conversation, and Paul responds by telling a Strong Bear story. He concludes with a strong signal that his turn is complete: "Well, that's how it was."

The following speaker then jumps in with a mild challenge addressed to a third speaker—"Do you know anything about Strong Bear?"—then himself produces a simple account of an exploit of strength. This is followed by a second similar account (closely resembling Richard Moss's story of Strong Bear and the wagon). Both include the comic line, "Gee, whiz, you guys should be able to do that!" The stories are good-humored, good-natured, and relatively anodyne.

The narrator then moves to a much more complicated story of encounter with whites—the story of Arapahos being thrown out of a gambling tent—which resembles the later "Strong Bear Shakes Hands" story in that Strong Bear does to a white man what he has been doing to the Indians. Note the evocation of combined racial and gender issues in the whites' objection to Arapaho men attempting to engage white prostitutes. Like the "Strong Bear Shakes Hands" story, it evokes issues of multiple languages and crosslinguistic encounter. In Paul Moss's story, the Swede is unable to understand Strong Bear's Arapaho. This turns out to be an advantage for the Arapaho, as the Swede misses the warning contained in the ambiguous use of "play," which can mean both 'play, gamble' and also 'play with, treat harshly.' Bilingualism is an advantage for the Arapahos, and the native language is not a handicap or obstacle. In the shaking hands story, the narrator evokes pidgin English ("me go now"), but Strong Bear uses it to mock the Swede's stereotype of the poor, uneducated Indian. The narrator also evokes the common white use of "chief" to address all Indians and responds to it with a very funny code mix: *heet-chief-hiihe3en* 'I will chief you.'

The next story then logically follows from this one as a continuation of the same episode. Now the physical domination of the Arapahos that occurred in the gambling tent, which is symbolic of colonial domination more generally, shifts to a potentially fatal level of violence. The central dramatic moment occurs when Strong Bear seizes the Swede's rifle and bends it in two, then again switches languages, hands back the rifle, and tells him now he can "shoot."

The narrator then de-escalates the series of stories, telling about how Strong Bear shakes hands. As Richard Moss did in his version, he includes the white man saying "chief," the code-switch on *heet-chief-hiih-e3en*, and the ambiguous use of "play." The story is highly parallel to the one about throwing whites out of the gambling tent. He then completes the cycle with two briefer and fairly anodyne accounts of feats of strength, before the session breaks into a looser discussion of Strong Bear's identity and characteristics. The overall structure is thus as follows:

> Brief feat of strength
> More extended feat of strength (pulling the horse out of quicksand)
> Encounter with whites in gambling tent
> Subsequent, potentially fatal encounter with whites after the gambling tent incident
> Encounter with whites in saloon
> Brief feat of strength (freeing wagon from mud)
> Brief feat of strength (carrying horse)
> Brief feat of strength

There is an overall arc to the chain of stories, which is carefully managed by the narrators.

The Shaking Hands Story (Richard Moss version)

The story about shaking hands evokes an issue that still resonates strongly in Indian Country today—comparative handshake styles. Native Americans on the Great Plains normally shake hands with a very gentle grip—more a touching of the palms, in fact, than a true grip and shake. In contrast, male Anglo-Americans often use a very firm grip and pronounced shake of the hand. This difference is widely known to Native Americans and has important cross-cultural saliency: when Native American and Anglo-American males meet, Native Americans are quite attuned to the degree of strength used in the handshake. Use of a light, touching handshake by Anglo-Americans indicates a cultural knowledge and sensitivity that Native Americans appreciate. In "Strong Bear Shakes Hands," the two contrasting styles of shaking hands are taken to their extremes, and at the same time, the styles are assigned ideological implications.[34] The white man in the saloon is both literally and metaphorically attempting to crush the Indians he meets. The story takes white-style handshaking and elevates it to the level of parody, yet the parody underlines what many Native Americans see as the truth of the encounter.

The setting of the saloon further heightens the tension between the two cultures: because of the volatility that alcohol adds to any situation, the saloon is one of the places where cross-cultural disputes and misunderstandings are most likely to erupt within the life of the average Native American. In general, visiting a bar is a potentially volatile occasion for Native Americans within the context of white racism and oppression in the rural West. Again, the literal crushing of hands evokes the metaphorical crushing and oppression that whites often express so strongly in this particular setting. (The town of Shoshoni further heightens the drama because it was a white-dominated railroad camp and frontier settlement of the rawest type.)

Note, finally, that the story states of the white man "the ones who go in there, right away he goes to them" and crushes their hands. The white man represents an aggressive domination and oppression, which seeks out Indians even when they might seek to avoid confrontation. When the encounter occurs, it again evokes all the stereotypes of white behavior that still are described on the reservation today. The white man not only approaches aggressively, but speaks loudly, quickly, and with much (comical) repetition, essentially dominating the interlocutor verbally (and metaphorically as well): "It's good you've come, it's good you've come. I'm going to shake your hand, it's good to see you . . . it's good to see you, I'm going to shake your hand." The scene is strikingly close to the ways that Western Apache people represent and parody white social interaction, in terms of aggressiveness, volubility, and intrusion on personal space (see Basso 1979, 48–55).

At this point, however, Strong Bear interrupts the white man, literally and symbolically, with a single, concise, understated remark, "I'm going to shake your hand, too." The narrator then continues with the equally understated "then that's when he closed his hand," before describing in great (one might even say sadistic) detail the crunching of bones, agonized cries, desperate contortions, and bloody pulp left after Strong Bear is finished. Strong Bear then concludes with the devastatingly ironic pidgin Indian English phrase "me glad to see you." The phrase, which so often evokes the oppression visited on the Indian, and the linguistic behavior required of Indians as part of the oppression is reappropriated and used from a position of power.

The Story about the Boxer

I wonder if this story might have been indirectly inspired by the case of Jack Johnson, the famous African American heavyweight champion from 1908 to 1915. Johnson was notable as being a Black man who not only defeated the best of the white champions, but also refused to compromise with or accommodate to white expectations in the way he lived his life. Thereby, he inspired other racial minorities by his example (see Runstedtler 2012). In the Arapaho story, however, Arapaho values are emphasized, rather than individual accomplishment. Strong Bear is urged by his Arapaho relatives to fight the champion (clearly assumed to be white), because they see this as a way of again defeating the whites and maintaining the legitimacy of the Arapaho as capable people. Strong Bear refuses, saying that if he were to fight, he might kill the champion. To Euro-American ears, this may seem to be bravado, but it reads quite differently in an Arapaho context. One of the central values emphasized by traditionalist elders is that one does not "do something for no reason" or simply to show off. Indeed, one of the great failures of the trickster/ *Nih'oo3oo* is precisely that he cannot resist the temptation to show off or experiment with his powers for no particular reason. Thus, Strong Bear's refusal is quite consonant with traditional Arapaho oral literature and morality. At the same time, however, the story could be read from a more anticolonialist, indigenous perspective. By boxing with the white man, Strong Bear would be engaging with the whites on their own terms, so to speak, betraying his own deep cultural values in order to score points against the whites by showing off his strength. Moreover, in this case, the white antagonist has taken no explicit action against the Arapaho people or Strong Bear or his relatives. Thus, Strong Bear's challenge would be unprovoked. His refusal to take on the white champion could therefore be read as a general model of the appropriate forms of resistance to white society.

Strong Bear, then, can be understood as a de-sacralized version of Beaver Dodge. Like Beaver Dodge, he performs fantastic feats that amaze those who see and hear about them. Those feats again occur in the context of encounters with the colonizer—with bars and liquor again making an appearance, along with the supply wagon and the gambling house. Yet, the different ontologies of power are replaced in his case by a single ontology focused on physical strength—though Arapaho cultural values concerning the deployment of that physical strength are strongly emphasized. In this context of pure power, Strong Bear succeeds as the stronger man. But he does not simply enter into the dynamics of Euro-American power structures, assimilating to a world of "might makes right." His strength is always exercised in solidarity with the Arapaho tribe, so that he engages with whites on their terms with regards to physical strength, but does not become white himself. His ethics of strength remain Arapaho.

3

Believe-It-or-Not Stories
and the Tall Tale

In chapter 2, we saw that narratives of more-than-human power are a common type of Arapaho traditional narrative, and that one key element of such narratives is the spectacular accomplishment of the power bearer. Folk hero stories are one modern development of narratives of spectacular power or accomplishment, but they lack the more-than-human power component. Another type of spectacular accomplishment story is the "believe-it-or-not" story (*hi3oowotoo wo'ei3 ciibeh'i3oowotoo* 'believe it or don't believe it'), which can be compared to the general category of tall tales. These Arapaho stories, like the folk hero stories, lack any focus on sacred acquisition of power or any requirements of ceremonial protocol related to their deployment. In this sense, they form a striking contrast to traditional Arapaho stories of the acquisition and use of more-than-human power (as in the stories in Cowell and Moss 2005).

In contrast to Arapaho folk hero stories, which recount more or less believable human-powered exploits, believe-it-or-not stories focus for the most part on utterly impossible accomplishments and typically are highly humorous. They could, in fact, be considered an example of the genre of tall tale in the global tradition of such stories, with their desacralized component being a central part of what links them to this broader folkloristic genre (and which separates that genre, as well as the Arapaho stories, from traditions such as the miracle story or saint's legend). The believe-it-or-not stories also now very often focus on Euro-American technologies and ironic Arapaho twists (sometimes literally) on those technologies. Thus, as in the previous chapter, I intend to argue that the context of cultural encounter and colonialism has produced a new genre of Arapaho oral narrative, which draws on traditional antecedents of form, content, and genre, but which operates in ways that are sometimes quite different ontologically from the antecedents. In particular, the new genre again converges with a genre of Euro-American folklore to some extent, while still maintaining an Arapaho and Native specificity. This concept of cultural contact and the changes in folklore that can result at such boundaries has been widely studied (see Georges and Jones 1995, 193–204, 211–24; and Barnouw 1977, 181–225 for an extensive single-group survey on the Wisconsin Chippewa), but I have found little on the topic relative to Plains Indian groups.

Ethnohistorian Loretta Fowler (1986) has argued that "compartmentalization" was a key strategy whereby twentieth-century Northern Arapahos managed to both engage with the Euro-American world and assimilate into their own culture many of its technological or conceptual benefits, while also maintaining internal cultural coherence in their society, by controlling and managing the technologies and benefits in an Arapaho way. One variety of this compartmentalization, in my view, has been the increasing limitation of sacred practices—and the narratives associated with them—to "traditional" mechanisms of cultural continuity and unity, while deploying non-sacred forms of practice—and the narratives that accompany them—to both engaging with and resisting Euro-American colonial domination. Put another way, the Northern Arapaho use sacred ceremonies such as the Sun Dance not as a way to directly resist colonialism, but rather as an internally oriented ceremony to strengthen Arapaho tribal unity. There was a conscious effort to protect the sacred from controversy and conflict, in order to enhance its healing power, and the same could be said of sacred narratives. On the other hand, legal and political strategies and resistance—and non-sacred genres of oral narrative such as folk hero and believe-it-or-not stories—are used to directly engage, analyze, critique, and confront Euro-American society and colonization (though as we saw in the previous chapter and will see again here, there is always some "leakage" between the compartments, the genres, and the sacred versus non-sacred).

The believe-it-or-not story is a traditional narrative genre in Arapaho, or at least a genre that has existed since the nineteenth century. I have not been able to find many exact equivalents in other Native traditions, but generally humorous stories about encounters with Euro-American technology are widespread, and there are also seemingly similar tall tales. Leman (1979, 198) reproduces a Northern Cheyenne story, "The Geese," which is apparently a believe-it-or-not tale: a man shoots a goose, which is falling to the ground. The rest of the flock flies down, catches it, and flies back up with it. Once they've helped it, it starts flying again as well, and the flock all flies off together. Cunningham (1992, 131) provides several Navajo examples.

Two facts support the claim that believe-it-or-not is a traditional Arapaho genre. First, the content of at least some of these tales is completely traditional in the sense that the subject matter in no way reflects Euro-

American civilization or its material components. Second, the genre is recorded from as early 1899, in one story documented by Alfred Kroeber (1983), and another from 1914, told by a man who was in his sixties or seventies at the time, and documented by Oliver Toll (2003 [1962]). Both these stories have entirely traditional content. Yet, the genre seems to have truly come into its own in the twentieth century. In particular, the technological subject matter of later narratives is often explicitly Euro-American, and the tales often are told to or about Euro-Americans. Of note is the fact that the earliest story does not have the "believe-it-or-not" Arapaho tagline. In fact, we could speculate about connections between this expression and the English expression "believe it or not," especially known in connection with the "Ripley's Believe-It-or-Not" franchise, but I have been unable to substantiate any connection.

The standard plot of a believe-it-or-not story is as follows: some unidentified (presumably Arapaho) person is involved in an activity requiring use of a Euro-American technology (hunting with a gun, using a telescope, flying in a plane). That person encounters a problem and uses the technology to solve the problem, but in a way that exceeds the actual, real-world capacity of the technology. Conversely, the person may encounter a problem with the functionality of the technology itself, which is then resolved based on some surprising (and oversimplified) understanding of the technology. Following are examples of these stories, from various contexts.

Story 1: The Bent Gun

((Alfred Kroeber, who recorded this story, provides no context for it. Note that the story is told using formal traditional narrative style (with the key markers underlined here).[1]))

Arapaho Version

HHinen he'ih-'iinoo'ei.
He'ih-noohob-ee siisiiko'uu koh'owuu'.
He'ih-cohoutee koh'owu'.
He'ne'-too'usee-t.
He'ih-kokoh'u3ecoo, hotn-ii-bohoxoh'-oet.
He'ne'-noohob-ee hohoot-no [he'ih]-niisookuu-nino.
He'ne'-cecei[b]nonousen-o' hi-kokuy.
He'ne'-cob-oot.
Noh he'ne'i-bohoxoh'-oet.

English Version

A man went out hunting.
He saw some ducks in the creek.
The creek was crooked/twisting.
Then he stopped there.
He thought about the situation, how he was going to shoot them all.
Then he saw two trees standing together.
Then he bent/twisted his gun on the trees.
Then he shot the ducks.
And then he shot them all.

Story 2: The Broken-Back Bear

((This story was recorded as part of a 1914 pack trip to the area of what is now Rocky Mountain National Park, in which members of the Colorado Mountain Club (CMC) joined three Arapaho men to document Native place-names in the area (Toll 2003 [1962], 41). The hope was to use the "exotic" Arapaho names to make the park proposal more appealing to Congress (see Cowell 2004). In his write-up of the trip, Oliver Toll of the CMC noted that the Indians enjoyed telling stories in the evening (which were translated by a bilingual interpreter):

> Another tale told us by the Indians was as follows: "This is the way that Old Man Gun [the narrator's father] used to hunt bears sometimes. Now you may not believe it, but it is so. He used to daub himself all over with mud and lie down in the bear trail. A bear would come along and not know what to make of him, turn him over with his paw, feel of his heart and his mouth. All at once Gun would spring up and give a terrible yell. The bear would jump back so quickly that he would break his back.[2]

Story 3: Jumping the Canyon

((Told by Ralph Hopper (real name); note that he uses the same formal narrative style as found in Story 1 (Salzmann elicited the story circa 1950 but provides no context; Salzmann 1956).))

Arapaho Version

Hi3oowotoo wo'ei3 ciibeh-'i3oowot-oo.
He'ih-'iitoni-co'ouut hohe'.

Honoh'oe he'ih-'ii-beet-ooxuu-ceno'oot.
He'ih-ciixootee.
Kookonoo' he'ne'-ceno'oo-t.
3oo3ooniihi' he'ne'-nih-'ei'o'oo-t.
He'ne'-ce'iinee-ceno'oo-t.

English Version

Believe it or not.
There was a high mountain on both sides of a gorge.
A man wanted to jump across the gorge.
It was a long way across.
But, anyway, then he went ahead and jumped.
The middle was as far as he made it.
Then he turned around and jumped back.

Story 4: The Telescope

((In October 2003, Richard Moss (real name) told a series of stories to Hartwell Francis, then a graduate student working with Andrew Cowell at the University of Colorado.[3] Francis asked Moss to provide some Arapaho stories, with no further specification. Francis audio-recorded the stories, while Richard's daughter washed dishes in the background, occasionally laughing uproariously at the funny parts. Moss began with an adaptation of the biblical story of Jacob and Esau, retold as the story of the White Man and the Indian, which he then translated into English. After a pause of a few seconds, he launched into a trickster story, which he then translated. He followed with a second trickster story, which he did not translate. After a pause of around five seconds, he followed the two trickster stories with three consecutive believe-it-or-not stories, which he introduced as follows.))

Heenee'iihi' nih-'oon-oxoo3oo3itee-3i' nuhu' hinono'ei-no'.
From time to time the Arapahos would tell laughable stories.

Howoo heentou-'u hi3oowot-oo wo'ei3 ceebeh-'i3oowot-oo.
There is also the genre of believe-it-or-not.

Neen-entou-'u.
Those stories exist.

((He proceeded to tell a version of the "Jumping the Canyon" story, of which other versions can be found earlier and later in this chapter, concluding with the Arapaho words *hi3oowotoo wo'ei3 ciibeh'i3oowotoo*. He then translated the story into English, concluding with "believe it or not." After some laughter, he continued with the following story. As with the Kroeber and Ralph Hopper stories, Moss here uses quite formal traditional style, with narrative past marker *he'ih-* (but not narrative sequential marker *he'ne'-*), and with a closing formula. He adds much more detail, and includes direct quotation as well. I have seen Richard Moss tell this story multiple times, and certain key hand gestures always occur. Therefore, I have added them in the transcription, even though I was not present for this specific telling. The English translation is mine.))

Arapaho Version

There's another one. This guy went hunting . . .
He'ih'ini, ni'-ii-too3noohoo3ootiini-', ni'iiP ni-'ii-noohoot-o'.
Hini'iit, noh heetn-i'-ii-too3no'eni-'i heeyouhuu.
Nih'iiP nehe' hinen he'ih-nii3in;
He'ih-'iinoo'ei.
Ciisiniihi' he'ih-noohob-ee bih'io.
He'ih-noohob-ee nuhu' he'iitnei'i.
[Beet]neh'ei-t nuhu','oh he'ihP
Hoowu-ni-'iiP, hoowu-ni-'iiP,
[he'ih]coo-co'oxetiin, hoowuuni.
Ho3es 3ii'ookuu-t.
BeneeP beneetoh-noh'-oot hinee.
Wohei ne'P noonoko' heetniini . . .
Wohoe'-ne-ih-cih-neyei3ih-oo.
'oh hiihoowuh-ciixoku-t.
Ne-ebeh-ko3oo3-oo.
Wohei hini'iit ni'-ii-too3noohoo[3oo]tiini-', he'ih'ini . . . ;
Ne'-woo-wo'ben-o'. [[gesture: twisting a telescope back and forth to
    focus it]]
Heihii he'ih-'e3ebkooP too3iini.
He'ih-cih-'ii3itoniini honoot hee3P hee3e'eekuu-t. [[gesture: focusing
    the telescope]]
'oh ne'P ne'P [he'ih]-cih-wo'ow-too3-no'en-ee. [[gesture: focusing the
    telescope]]
Ne'-beeP bee-besteh'ein-oot, nuhu' hit-iicoon[in]o. [[gesture: touching,
    feeling something]]

He'ih'ini, he'ih-koxcei'in. [[gesture: feeling something again]]
Ni'iiP ni'iiP, woow too-to3ihi-n.
He'ih-3i'ookuu-n;
Ne'ini, ne'-cob-oot.
Noh nenee'.
Hi3oowotoo wo'ei3 ciibeh-'i3oowotoo.

English Version

There's another one. This guy went hunting . . .
There was, people use a telescope sometimes, to see something.
A thing will be brought closer up to you with that telescope.
This man had one;
He was out hunting.
Far off somewhere he saw a deer.
He saw it somewhere.
He wanted to kill it, but it was. . . .
He could not, he was not able to use,
There was no brush around to use for cover.
The deer is standing out in the open.
He wants to kill it.
Well then, "I might as well . . ."
"Maybe I could give it a try."
But it is sitting too far away.
"I might miss it."
Well that telescope, he . . . ;
Then he focused it. [[Gesture: twisting a telescope back and forth to
    focus it]]
Soon the deer was closer over there.
It was made closer and larger until it was standing in front of him.
    [[gesture: focusing the telescope]]
And then he made it even closer to him. [[gesture: focusing the
    telescope]]
Then he felt around its belly, its ribs. [[gesture: touching, feeling
    something]]
It was fat. [[gesture: feeling something again]]
It had been brought very close to him [by the telescope].
It was standing right there;
Then he shot it.
And that's it.
Believe it or don't believe it.

Story 5: The Two Bullets

((After concluding his English translation of "The Telescope" with "believe
it or not," Richard Moss gave another laugh, then he started up again. Note
that in the following story Moss continues with the formal style he has used
previously.[4] This story actually marks subsections via the use of *wohei*. This
particle can serve for topic initiation in Arapaho, but in longer narratives it
can also serve to mark individual segments of action, as seen here. Thus,
this story shows a greater degree of elaboration and internal segmentation
than any of the previous ones in this chapter. The translation is mine.))

Arapaho Version

Another story, nuhu'.
Toot he'=hinen he'ih-'iinoo'ei.
Coo-co'oxeti-'i hiit totoonee.
Coo-co'oxeti-'i.
He'ih-cebisee,
Ne'-noohowuskuu3-oot bih'ih-ii.
He'ih-niisi-nino: ceese' he'ih-3i'ookuu, ceese' he'ih-3i'ok.
Wohei hiihoowuh-beex-ciixoku-3i'.
Hecexoo'oe' he'ih-niiwoh'un; heniis-ciitohuni-'.
Wohei ne'e-eten-o' ceese' kokuyono3;
Hiit nuhu' hini-icito ne'P he'ne'-toun-o'. [[gesture: putting something in
    one's mouth]]
Wohei nee'eeneetP, neh'ini cebisee-t nuhu' heet-coo-co'oxeti-'i.
Hee3neeniini, nooxow-too3-no'oxuuheti-t;
Noh heihii he'ih-tootoku-nino.
Wohei heetn-ii3itoniini neyei-tootisee-noo.
Heet-ne'-wo'oweenei'oku-3i'.
Heet-ni'P ni'-cob-ou'u.
Wohei nee'eh-noo-nonouukoohu-t.
'oh hinit he'iitnei'i he'ih-ceto'owoo.
Nuhu' toh-ceto'owoo-t, 'oh ne'-nihi'kuutii-t nuhu' kokiy.
Wohei hini'iit 3ii'ookuu-ni3 he'ih-bes-ii.
Wohei nuhu' toh-'e3ebiini heeti'eisi-', 'oh nuhu' kokuyono3, nuhu' hini-
    icito he'ihP he'ih-toun, nuhu' hei'P, hitoxko' 'oh hei'-to'usetii-t, 'oh
    ne'ini ko'oeteese-' hini'iit kokiy.
'oh hu'un 3ii'oku-t woow he'ih-koheisihcehin;
Ne'iini, wo'eii3ow ci'=ne'-bes-oot.

Nenee-nini' hini'iit.
Hi3oowotoo wo'ei3 ciibeh-'i3oowotoo.

English Version

Another story, this one.
I guess somewhere a man was out hunting.
There were clumps of vegetation here, everywhere.
There were clumps of vegetation.
He was walking along;
Then he caught a glimpse of some deer.
There were two of them: one was standing, one was sitting.
Well, they are sitting a little too far away.
He was carrying a small gun; it was already loaded.
Well, then he took out one more bullet from his pouch;
Here this, in his teeth, then he held it. [[gesture: putting something in
    one's mouth]]
Well that was where . . . he walked through there where all the clumps
    of brush were.
He was really, he is managing to work his way up real close now.
And pretty soon the deer were sitting very close.
"Well, I will try to walk even closer."
"That's how they will end up even closer to me."
"Then I will be able to shoot them."
Well, then he set off running all bent over.
But right there somewhere he tripped.
And when he tripped, then he accidentally fired this gun.
Well that one that was standing, he hit it.
Well then, because he hit his head there [on a rock], this bullet, the one
    he was holding in his teeth, then when, when his chin hit [the rock],
    then that bullet went off.
And that one that is sitting, now it has jumped up suddenly;
Then, just right at that moment, he hit it as well.
That's the story of what happened.
Believe it or don't believe it.

((Moss then translated this story into English, once again concluding:
"Believe it or not. That's what they say. Nih'ini [*it was . . .*]. This story
comes from South Dakota, you know. Yeah. Yeah. Yeah, there's a lot of
those believe-it-or-not stories, you know. Yeah."

After a four-second pause, Moss launched into a completely different type of story, an account of how the Arapahos lived nomadically in the old days and survived through harsh winters.))

Story 6 : The Two Snakes

((This story was told by Joe Goggles (real name) in 2002 as part of a documentation and elicitation session focused on stories, recorded by Hartwell Francis.[5] Goggles chose to tell a sequence of believe-it-or-not stories, including the story of the bent gun (Story 1) and the broken-backed bear (Story 2). Note that here Goggles embeds the story into a semi-scientific, or at least naturalistic, observation framework, as if the story represents serious wisdom handed down over the ages. This embedding serves to further increase the tension between the framework of elder authority and the unbelievable nature of the narrative. This type of embedding is used by other narrators as well with "comicals." For example, one story begins by describing traditional Arapaho fall hunting practices, seeking elk in the Colorado Rockies, but the hunters eventually find an alien spaceship, whose occupant is taken back to camp and teaches the Arapahos how to do the "fancy dance" style of powwow dancing!

Structurally, this story is equally as formal as the preceding one by Richard Moss, in terms of its use of narrative markers and segmentation devices. Note the especially elaborate closing formulas.))

Arapaho Version

Wohei nihii heh-he'=nee'eeneesoo-' hiine'etiit:
Nih-'een-entoo-3i' nenitee-no'.
Nih'iini koo-kokoh'ou3einiiini heen-e'iyeiniiini hit-iine'etiitoon-inoo.
He'ih-'eeneixoneihi-no' wohei nih-'eeneisiini.
Wohei nehe' nenitee he'ih-'ii-heeneinisee.
Noo-notii3ei'i-t nihii,
He'ih-noo-notnoo'ein heenei'isiihi'.
Nih'ii-beetiini nosouniiini cee-ceneeyohwuuni heen-e'iyei-3i'.
3oo-3ooxuuyei'i-t hi'in nih-'iis-ce'esiini.
Nih'ii-nii-niitowoot-o' hoo3itoo-no wo'ei3 heenei'isiihi'.
Wohei nee'ei'ini heeneinisee-t.
Kookon he'ih-niitobee hiit hihcebeehe';
He'ih-koo-kohtobeinoon.
'oh hini'iit siisiiyei-no' nii-nohceineeyei-3i', he'ih-neeni-no'.
Noh xonou he'ih-nehtowoot.

Noh he'ne'iini noo-nonoo'eini-t.

Ne-ebeh'ini too3-no'usee.

Neestoonooteihi-3i' nuhu' nii-nohceiyooni-3i' siisiiyei-no'.

Wohei noh nee'eesiini noo-noo'oeniini noo-notii3ei'i-t heetoteinooni-'.

Ne'-niitowoot-o';

Ne'i-yihoo-t;

He'ih-nee[he]yeisee;

'oh he'ih-cii-noohoo3ei.

He'ne'-wo'wusee-t.

'oh he'ihP hiitouuk he'ne'i-noohow-oot niisi-ni3i nuhu'
    hiinohceineeyoonii-siisiiyei-no.

He'ih-boo-boo3eti-no'.

[He'ih]-'eeneinci3eti-no'.

He'ih-noo-no'oteinoon nuhu' hi'iiniini cee'eiyoo-no, hi-cee'eiyoon-inoo.

He'ih-neeni-no' ni'iit-ou'u, hiinohceineeyooni-3i' ni'ii3eihi-3i'.

Hoonii, hoonii he'ih-'eeneinci3eti-ni[no] kou3iihi'.

He'ne'i-ceenoku-t.

He'ih-'esooku'oo.

He'ih-ciiP, hoow-cih-3ooxuunon-e'.

Hiitowuuni heen-esiniheti-ni3i.

Nee'eesiini.

Wohei ne'iini, sii=he'ne'ini heeneitobeti-ni3i hini'iit niitiini
    [hi]ce'eineeyoon-inoo.

Wohei ne'-cesisiini bii-biineti-ni3i.

Noh he'iicisiihi', 'oh he'iitox 'oh sii=he'ih-'iiP, heecise-esoohow-oot 'oh
    he'ih-cii-noohoo3ei.

[He'ih]-hoowooh-noohob-ee nuhu' siisiiyei-no.

Bonoo3eti-ni3i,

Nih'ii-hoon-otoobeti-ni3i.

Nee'eh-cii-noohow-oot.

He'ih-'otoobeti-no' nuhu' siisiiyei-no.

He'ih-ciiP, he'ih-'iiyohou'unoo'oo-no'.

Wohei nenee'.

Ne'=nih-'ii3oo3itee-t nehe' nenitee.

Noh huuwoonhehe' niiP ne'=niisiini, nii-nosouniini 3oo-3ookut-ou'u
    nuhu'.

Nii-niitowoot-ou'u nuhu' siisiiyei-no'.

Noh nehe' nenitee, nih-nee'eesiini, nih-nee'eenee3obee-t.

'oh hu'un nenee' nee'eesiini, too'eihi-' nuh'uuno nihiit.

Nuhu' hoo3itoo, ne'=nih-'iisiini,

Nee'eesiini.

English Version

Okay, well, I guess life was like this in the past:

There were people all about.

They found out things about life by examining and studying the natural
    world.

They were useful to each other, since they shared whatever they
    discovered.

Okay, this person was wandering around.

He was looking for things such as, uh,

He was looking around for various things.

They wanted to keep right on finding out about things, persistently.

A person noticed things that were different.

He would hear stories and so forth.

Okay, so then he was wandering all around.

Then he heard something or other nearby here;

There was a funny sound.

And those snakes that have rattles, it was them making the noise.

And right away he recognized the sound.

And then he looked all around.

"I might have gotten too close to them" he thought.

"They are dangerous, these rattlesnakes."

Well, then like this, he looked all around for where the noise was
    coming from.

Then he heard it clearly.

then he went over there;

He walked up close;

But he didn't see anything.

Then he went farther.

And, sure enough, he saw these two rattlesnakes.

They were fighting each other.

They were wrapped around/grappling with each other.

There was a lot of noise from their rattles.

That's what they call them: "they have rattles," they are called.

After a long time, they were wrapped around each other, grappling for a
    long time.

Then he sat down.

He watched them.

They didn't, they haven't noticed him.

They were too busy getting each other riled up.

That's how it was.

Well, then, then they each got a hold of the other one's rattle in their
  mouths.
Well, then they began to eat each other.
And after a while, after some time, well darned if, while he was
  watching them, then he didn't see anything anymore.
He didn't see these snakes anymore.
They're fighting,
They were swallowing each other up.
He didn't see them anymore after that.
They swallowed each other up, these snakes.
They didn't . . . , they just suddenly disappeared.
Well, that's it.
That's how this man told the story.
And today that's how, they still tell it this way.
They hear it, the sound of these snakes, and then tell the story.
And this man, it was like that, that's what he saw, this man.
That's it, that how this short little story goes.
This story, that's how it was,
That's how it is.

Story 7: Jumping the Canyon

((This is Richard Moss's version of "Jumping the Canyon." It was one of
the first stories Moss told me upon my arrival on the reservation to study
the Arapaho language. The story was told in response to a general request
to record "some stories."[6]))

Arapaho Version

Hinen he'ih-'iinoo'ei beebei'on no'o'.
He'ih-no'usee heet-bii3oonoo-'.
He'ih-co'ouu3oo tokooxuuniihi'.
He'ih-co'ouu3oo hini'iit heetoh-'oxtoono'uuni-'.
Tokooxuuniihi' he'ih-cih-'iinootii hiwoxuu;
Noh beneetP, beneet-neh'ehei-t nehe' hinen.
Noh hiihoowuh-ciixoku-ni3 beete'.
Wohei nuhu' wooxe, hetne-ihoow-no'P no'unoo'oo.
Wohei ne'-noxuute'eini-t beebei'on huu3e', hi'in heeteh-beex-ceeniini,
   heetn-iit-ni'-oowusee-t.
Wohei hiit hoowu-niihiihi' heet-cihP, 'ee, beebei'on he'ne'{t}-ehP
beex-eh-ceeniini;

3eb-wootooyei-no'usee-hek, 'oh 3eb-ce'-no'usee-hek, 'oh hetne-
   ihoowe-entoo nehe' hiwoxuu.
Not-noohoot toon-heetn-iisiini;
'oh wootii hoowu-ciisP hoowu-ciisiini nuhu' wohoe'-niicii.
"Wohoe'=henei=cii-tokooxuu'oot-owoo," heeh-ehk.
"'oh noonoko' heet-neyei3itoo-noo."[7]
Ne'o-oseitisee-t.
Teeceeneet-o' heetn-ii3ei'nee-nihi'koohu-t.
Heetn-eh-'e3eb-ceno'oo-t tokooxuuniihi'.
'oh coo'ouute-'.
Wohei, ne'o-oseitisee-t.
Teeceeneet-o' heetn-ii3ei'nee-nihi'koohu-t;
Heetn-ii3ei'ne-esiikoohu-t.
Heet-ne'-eh-ceno'oo-t.
Wohei ne'-too'usee-t.
Ne'-cesisihcehi-t.
Hee3eb-yiis-cesisihcehi-t.
Hee3eb-eh-no'koohu-t heet-ses3ooni-'.
Ne'-ceno'oo-t.
Wohei ne'-3ebiihi', hee3ebi-ihco'oo-t.
Wohei nuhu' neehii3ei' hei'-no'o'oo-t, ne'-nei'oohoot-o';
He'ne'-niihoowuh-ciixootee-'.
He'ne'P ne'e-e'in-o' tih'et-ciistii-t.
Ne'-bi'-ce'iinihcehi-t.
Ne'-eh-ce'iino'oxuuheti-t cesis-ceno'oo-t.[8]
Noh ne'=nih-'iistoo-hok nehe' hinen.
He'in-o' tih-'etn-eh-ciistii-t,
Bi'-ce'iinihcehi-t;
Ne'-ce'-ceno'oo-t.
Noh nee'eesoo-' nuhu' hoo3itoo.
Hi3oowot-oo wo'ei3 ciibeh-'i3oowot-oo.
Ne'=ni'iit-ou'u.
Nohuusoho'.

English Version

A man was hunting way out in the mountains.
He got to a canyon/ravine.
It was really deep from where he was to the other side.
It was really deep since there were cliffs on both sides.
There was an elk grazing on the other side;

And this man wants to kill it.

It was sitting too far away to reach with a bow and arrow.

Well, this arrow won't reach it.[9]

Well, then he looked way over there upriver, to a spot where the slope
  went down more gradually, where he would be able to get down to the
  river.

Well, here downstream as well, way down there, the slope went down
  more gradually too.

But even if he made it over there sooner than he expected to the shallow
  slope, and got back there to the other side, well, the elk would be gone
  by then.

He was trying to see how he could solve the problem.

And I guess it wasn't too far across this stream or creek or whatever
  it was.

"I might not be able to reach the other side," he said.

"But, heck, I might as well give it a try."

Then he walked backwards.

He is calculating how fast he will have to run.

He will jump across from here to there.

But it is high.

Well, then he walked backwards.

He is calculating how fast he will have to run;

how quickly he will need to run.

He will jump from here.

Well, then he stopped walking back.

Then he took off running.

He took off running over in that direction toward the gorge.

He ran right up to the edge.

Then he jumped.

Well, then he was soaring upwards in that direction.

Well, when he reached the middle, then he looked at the situation;

Then it was too far.

Then he knew that he wasn't going to make it.

So, then he just turned back around real quick.

And he managed to get himself back around to where he had started
  his jump.

And that's what this man apparently did.

He knew he wasn't going to make it,

so then he just turned back around real quick in the air;

then he jumped back.

That's how the story goes.

Believe it or don't believe it.
That's what they call this type of story.
That's it.

Additional Believe-It-or-Not Stories

Plot Summaries

Story 8: Variants of Story 1, recorded by Kroeber, are numerous: there are two ducks on either side of a river, so the man takes a double-barreled shotgun, bends the two barrels to point in different directions, fires, and hits both ducks. In some cases, the hunting involves deer rather than ducks. In others, the animal is on the other side of a hill, so the barrel is bent up and then down. The man then fires over the top of the hill, with the bullet traveling down to hit the game.[10]

Story 9: A man is flying in a plane. The pilot announces that the plane is running low on gas. So the plane stops, a ladder is lowered, and the man climbs down to the ground to get some gas. He fills a can with gas, climbs back up the ladder, refuels the plane, and they fly on to their destination.

Story 10: A man tries to wire some money from the reservation to Casper or Cheyenne or some other big city using Western Union. The money does not arrive. The man is told that the wires must be broken. So he goes out and follows the telegraph line until he finds the spot where it is broken. Sure enough, at the end of the wire, lying on the ground, is a big pile of money.

Story 11: A man is out hunting. His people are all starving, since the whites are not providing the rations they have promised, and they have killed off most of the game. Finally, he sees an antelope. He shoots it. When he reaches it, he cuts it open. Instead of internal organs, he finds coffee, sugar, flour, bacon, and so on—reservation-era provisions (see also chapter 6).

Story 12: A man is out hunting. He sees a duck. He takes aim, but as he looks through the scope, he sees the duck waving at him to stop. He puts down his rifle and goes over to the duck, which is waving for him to come over. The duck shakes his hand and says, "Please don't shoot us, we're really diminishing in numbers these days" (see also chapter 6).

Story 13: Wox Betebi is lying in bed in his camp, with a loaded gun placed in a rack above him. He is idly fingering the gun when he accidentally pulls the trigger. The bullet shoots down one of the two Washakie Needles rock formations in the Absaroka Mountains. His wife goes to get the chunk of rock that he shot down. It is still hot, and she cooks his breakfast on it (see also chapter 6)

Story Meanings: Internal Content

These stories are often not localized in terms of time or place, nor are specific individuals often associated with them.[11] Some specification sometimes occurs, but the story itself is in no way dependent on this. It is not uncommon for "a man" to be replaced with some (typically well-known but now deceased) identifiable Arapaho individual, especially when the tales are told for an Arapaho audience. One sometimes hears "my uncle/dad/cousin" or the like used in place of "a man" as well (but never a woman, so far as I have heard). The story of the broken-back bear occurs in at least two quite different and highly specified versions. In the version recorded in 1914 (Story 2), it is the father of the narrator who used to hunt bears according to the method described, in Colorado. Another version, told to me in 2005, locates the story on the Wind River Reservation, specifically near an area known as Seventeen-Mile Crossing (where the cross-reservation road crosses the Little Wind River). In this version, a particular individual was fleeing a bear and turned to the methods described in the tale as a last resort to save himself from the bear.

Also noteworthy is that beyond the potential for specification, the tales can be told in highly elaborate as well as very brief forms. The version of "Jumping the Canyon" recorded by Salzmann around 1950 (Story 3) consists of only five brief sentences (Salzmann 1956). The same story told by Richard Moss (a relative of the original 1950 narrator, by the way) in 1998 goes on for forty-two sentences, several of which contain one or more subordinate clauses, so that the effective length is around ten times as long (Moss and Cowell 2006). Thus, like many oral narratives, there is very wide latitude for expansion, contraction, and specification depending on the particular circumstances in which the story is told.

Some of the stories invoke a (false) analogy between older and newer forms of technology: Story 10 suggests that wiring money is putting it in a pipe or tube that carries liquids. Story 9 suggests that a plane which travels in the air is like a car which travels on the ground. "The Two Bullets" (Story 5) suggests that the striking together of teeth is like the striking of a trigger on a gun. Other stories (falsely) extend a traditional mode of knowledge and experience to a new technological context: Story 4 suggests that just as bigger means closer when looking with the naked eye, so bigger must mean closer when looking through a telescope as well. Other stories (falsely) extend the power of a single technology through analogy: Story 1 suggests that if a straight gun barrel fires a bullet in a straight line, then a curved gun barrel must fire a bullet in a curved line.

The stories with non-Euro-American content are actually quite similar: if one snake eats another snake, the second snake disappears, so by extension, if they both eat each other, wouldn't they both disappear (Story 6)? If one can jump up and down on land, why can't one do the same in the air? The basic mode of thinking in the genre—an exploration of false analogies, false logical extensions of knowledge, or false reasoning—is present in both fairly traditional and more modern versions. I imagine that there may well have been an earlier version of Story 1, for example, in which an arrow was bent crooked so as to follow a crooked trajectory, though I have no concrete documentation of such a story. All of these stories, then, could be understood in general terms as explorations of traditional Arapaho modes of knowledge and experience and traditional understandings of technology and the way the world works, whose "logical" extension, in a certain sense, seems perfectly reasonable. But with an increasing rate of encounters with new technologies in the nineteenth and especially twentieth centuries, such stories and the issues they raise must have gained increasing saliency within Arapaho culture, leading to the creation or adoption of a number of new stories specifically focused on Euro-American technologies.

The types of logical extensions dramatized in the stories often appear reasonable. Moreover, failures of such logical or metaphorical extensions as modes of understanding are hardly unique to the Arapahos. Euro-American audiences are reported to have shrieked in fear when early movies showed trains roaring toward them, or leapt upon the stage to shoot a villain threatening a poor damsel in a film—also examples of (false) extensions of traditional modes of knowledge and experience to an encounter with a new technology. The Arapaho must certainly have experienced similar feelings when they encountered various novel Euro-American technologies throughout the eighteenth, nineteenth, and twentieth centuries, and the newer type of believe-it-or-not stories serve to illustrate the discontinuities in ways of understanding the world and processing external information that the new technologies introduced. The stories could thus be read in part as means of making fun of the (earlier) Arapaho collective ignorance about the workings and effects of these technologies, or as making fun of certain out-of-touch Arapaho individuals who still might naively think according to these false analogies.

But it is important to recognize that it is, in fact, the Arapahos in the stories who come out ahead, so to speak. The hunter gets his game, the passengers get to their destination, the jumper doesn't end up like Wile E. Coyote at the bottom of the canyon.[12] And to the extent that there are failures, they are failures of Euro-American technology, such as the telegraph wire—the Arapaho man, at least, gets his money back. Moving from a reading that is internal to the story and focuses on the characters within the plot, to a reading that looks at the stories themselves as performances, we must recognize these narratives as celebrations of a certain kind of wit and inventiveness—after all, in the stories, the fantastic metaphorical extensions are in fact successful, despite the impossibilities we all recognize. Indeed, the Arapaho narrators take fantastic new technologies and make them even *more* fantastic, while somehow also reducing them to absurdity at the same time. Notably, the fantastic extension of the new technology is based on an analogy with an older, *simpler* technology. Planes do even more wondrous things than fly around—they stop to refuel and go on, just like cars do. Telegraph wires do even more wondrous things than carry messages via electricity—they carry cash, just like a tube or pipe can do. Thus, the metaphorical extension of the power of the new technology involves a reduction of the technology to merely a "fancier" version of the same old thing to which it is being compared.

To summarize, the stories work on two different levels. They dramatize the literal failure of certain metaphorical or logical extensions as a mode of understanding new technologies in the real world. But performatively they apply the same metaphorical or logical extensions successfully in order to produce magical new results for the technologies in question. Simultaneously, the successful extension, while increasing the quantitative power of the new technology, reduces its qualitative uniqueness: planes are just cars that go faster and travel through air rather than on land; otherwise, the same parameters apply to both. Wires are just tubes or pipes that send their contents more quickly; otherwise. the same rules of understanding and functionality apply to both of these as well. The paradoxical dual processes of inflation of power and reduction of newness and uniqueness, each occurring simultaneously, are perhaps captured in a *mise-en-abyme* fashion in the story of the snakes eating each other. That story dramatizes the paradox of aggrandizement and disappearance simultaneously, of two processes feeding off each other until a *reductio ad absurdum* is produced.

It is important to recognize as well that metaphorical extension has a deep significance within Arapaho culture. As Alfred Kroeber documents, much of Arapaho thought about magical power and healing (which are intimately related) have traditionally relied on the notion of metaphor. Thus, for example, smooth stones were given to a woman who was having difficulty with labor, in the hopes that "by analogy" her birth passage would be smooth as well. The plant *Lygodesmia juncea* (skeletonweed), which has thick, white, milky sap, was given to mothers whose breast milk was inadequate. Individuals wore amulets of pronghorn antelope so that they would be able to run fast, like the antelope (see Kroeber 1983 [1907], 410–54, for these and many other examples). In the traditional Arapaho belief system, analogies of color, form, texture, and other sensory qualities were considered to be useful guides for understanding the deep, powerful relationships that existed between and among the many objects within the world, and for gaining access to that power. Thus, speculative thought in the form of metaphorical or logical extensions based on sensory experience was a key component of Arapaho ideology and cosmology. Within the context of traditional healing, vision quests, and religious ceremonies such as the so-called Sun Dance (all still practiced today), this mode of thought continues to be operative.

On the other hand, another key intertext of these stories are Arapaho *Nih'oo3oo* 'trickster' stories. These also often involve fantastic powers, which the trickster typically tries to use without fully understanding them. They often involve false visual analogies as well, which the trickster fails to grasp (for example, seeing plums at the bottom of a stream, he dives in to get them, not realizing that he is seeing a reflection in the water and that the plums are actually overhead). A key theme of the entire trickster genre is the idea that one must be careful in drawing analogies and extending metaphors, especially in unfamiliar situations. Similarly, one deep implication of the believe-it-or-not stories is an exploration of the limits of the analogical mode of thought and, perhaps, a growing disquiet with regard to the changes in the increasingly technologized world of twentieth-century Arapaho people, which introduces increasing unfamiliarity and increasing disruptions to traditional modes of thought.

Story Meanings: Performance Context

To more fully understand these narratives, we need to consider the performance contexts. While the specific versions recorded here were told specifically to researchers, two more traditional contexts can be identified. The first is with children, and the second is with Euro-Americans. These two audiences combine one particular feature: a certain otherness or "lack of initiation" compared to the typical teller, who is always an older or elder Arapaho person.

Alonzo Moss Sr. (real name) says that these narratives were often told to children, in Arapaho and more recently sometimes in English. Because they are short and lend themselves well to gesture as an adjunct to the narration, they are good stories to tell beginning Arapaho students. Moss states that when he taught school, he told these stories to students "straight," as if they were true. Because narrative performance traditions at Wind River are less widely practiced now, the children were largely unfamiliar with the genre. There are, however, still important components of age-grade respect relationships operative at Wind River, especially in the case of an Arapaho language and culture class (which Moss taught). According to Moss's descriptions of the students' reactions, it is clear that they were doubtful or dubious with regard to the stories based on their own knowledge and experience. Yet, some of them were either hesitant to outright deny the stories, or uncertain whether or not to believe them, given that a respected elder was telling the story, and in a school setting, which was supposed to be about education. This was exactly the reaction that Moss hoped to evoke. In talking to me about the tellings, Moss clearly relished the dilemma he had set up for the students, seeing it as both a very serious aspect of Arapaho culture and part of his personal relationship to the students, as well as an amusing situation which he enjoyed producing and recounting to me. He added that he told the children to go home and ask their parents whether the stories were true or not. This further complicated the dynamics of authority, as few parents would be willing to tell their children that a fluent Arapaho elder at the school was "lying" or to challenge Moss directly. Moss was thus able to project a spreading dilemma of belief and authority across a wide segment of the community. A number of years later, I was able to talk with a student who had been in Moss's class, and she clearly remembered the telling of these stories. From her perspective, the situation had been intimidating. She recalled him telling the students in the class, "If you don't believe me, raise your hand," and asking, "Why don't you believe me?" She also recalled him saying to the students, "I want to hear you call me a liar *in Arapaho.*" I worked closely with Moss over many years, and he reported making many similar statements to his students. The last statement pointed to the inadequacy of the students' Arapaho language skills, which Moss often lamented. However, it also indirectly indicated that his statements could be challenged and might indeed not be strictly true—but that this type of negotiation of belief and authority needed to happen through the Arapaho language. Moss often insisted that if a person could defend their claim, position, or interpretation of something *in Arapaho*, then this was satisfactory to him.

This account suggests one obvious circumstance for these tales, which appears to have been common in earlier times at Wind River as well. As the dynamics of Moss's account make clear, the stories place young children in a difficult position. On one hand, the events in the stories range from the clearly impossible to the at least highly improbable (from a child's perspective). On the other, they are told by a respected elder to a young person, so the younger person has little or no latitude to openly doubt or question the narrative according to Arapaho expectations. (Of course, this would vary according to the exact makeup of the tellers and listeners, with intimate family settings obviously creating a different dynamic than a school classroom.) Moreover, traditionally, serious Arapaho narratives of superhuman powers and events were common—and indeed remain so today—in the context of discussion of traditional healing, ceremonies, and the like. Thus, the line between "unbelievable" and "believable" within Arapaho culture is drawn across different territory than is the case in Euro-American culture, which renders the believe-it-or-not story relatively more problematic for the young Arapaho listener. Moreover, the explicit content of the stories could be read as making fun of those who believe that certain things *can't* happen—after all, in the stories, amazing things *do* happen, to the benefit of Arapaho protagonists.

The issue is further complicated by the fact that there are in fact deep truths in these stories—fundamental truths about life, values, wisdom, and the capacity for judgment. Cherokee elder and storyteller Hastings Shade, talking about similar types of stories that are "phenomenologically unverifiable" says, "There's nothing false about 'em. They're all true. The thing is, you've got to prove it. It's left up to you to prove it if they're true or not. That's what I always tell my students: 'Don't believe me. Come try it, then you'll believe it yourself.' That's what happens with these stories. They're all true." (Teuton 2011, 137).

The meaning of "true" here is, of course, specific to Cherokee values and rhetorical traditions, but what Shade said seems to be broadly what Alonzo Moss was saying as well: a person must learn to find the correct "truth" in a story, within the context of an Arapaho-specific rhetorical system, and not try to apply Euro-American standards of narrative and rhetoric to the stories. Moss and Hastings could both be seen as proponents of what Christopher Teuton describes as "Indigenous Textual Studies," whose job is to "situate analyses of Indigenous communication within appropriate contexts . . . and to understand how these forms of communication express Indigenous epistemologies" (Teuton 2011, 135).

In 2018, I was talking to a different Arapaho speaker, asking some clarification questions about a different believe-it-or-not story that he had happened to tell during a conversation which I filmed. While we were working, he spontaneously added that he had told the story of Wox Betebi and the Washakie Needles (Story 13) "straight" (that is, as if true) at one point in the recent past to a younger Arapaho deliveryman, who was delivering meals for the elderly and stopped by his house with a meal. He said that the deliveryman's response was a hesitant, "I don't know about that," and then the deliveryman did not come back the next time he was supposed to. Clearly, this speaker challenged the delivery-man in the same way Moss did with his students. And, clearly, the deliv-eryman was perturbed by the encounter, not knowing how to deal with this type of narrative from an elder, or more generally with the conflict between respect for and belief in elders on the one hand and personal knowledge and evaluation on the other. This storyteller said to me that kids don't believe things today—for them it is "hard to believe." But he also characterized the believe-it-or-not stories as like the comic books of white people. They are "our [Arapaho] comic books" (precisely echoing William C'Hair's comment quoted in chapter 1).[13] It does not seem that this storyteller truly wanted or expected the deliveryman to "believe" his story, despite his remark about kids not believing today—otherwise he would not have used the comic book characterization. Rather, I believe he was indexing the more general problems of loss of respect for the knowl-edge and ways of the elders, and lack of belief in this older version of Arapaho culture more generally. The real failure of the deliveryman was indicated by his remark that "I'm not sure about that," because it sug-gested he was evaluating the story on a simplistic truth basis and did not understand the differing contexts of Arapaho culture and the appropriate belief systems and ontologies related to each of those contexts.

This failure of interpretation—and, more broadly, of ontological under-standing—recalls an incident recounted by Barry Toelken about a Navajo storyteller telling an etiological narrative explaining why it snowed in his local home canyon (Toelken and Scott 1997, 88–134). After he finished, a younger member of the audience noted that it snowed in other canyons too, so why was that (94–95)? The Navajo man said it was a shame that the child did not know how to listen to Navajo stories in the right way (due to white schooling, he suggested) and recognize that the story was not to be taken purely literally, though it did contain important moral lessons (95). Toelken notes in a different work that there are always "two kinds of audiences (insiders and outsiders)" involved in tall tales (Toelken 1996, 144). It would seem that this insider-outsider division is a key com-ponent of their social function.

The Arapaho storyteller just discussed displayed exactly the same atti-tude. He had told several believe-it-or-not stories during the conversation I filmed. One of those involved a duck hunter (Story 12). He was about to shoot a duck, when he saw it waving at him to come over. He went over, and the duck said, "Please don't shoot me. We ducks are really dwindling in number." When the hunter said okay, the two of them shook hands. The punch line of the story was that the duck *nihtootoyoow3ee3eit* 'he had cold hands!' Upon completing the linguistic checking, the teller spontaneously added moral thoughts for me. He noted that animals sacrifice themselves to hunters, just as the buffalo did in the old days. In addition, he said the story had a moral lesson for Arapaho people: don't hurt each other; don't kill each other. He concluded our discussion by saying he did finally see the deliveryman again later and asked, "What happened to you?" The younger man made some vague excuses for why he had not been back by. The storyteller then said to me again, discussing the incident, "They don't believe." Again, his emphasis was on belief in—and understanding of—Arapaho culture and values, not in the particular story itself. The events in the story may not be strictly true, but the story itself is "real," in that it is a traditional story with an accompanying interpretive tradition, and thus is a highly salient part of Arapaho tradition for the narrator.[14] As he said, "These stories are important to me." For those who lack access to the Arapaho language or the narrative and interpretive traditions that produce and encapsulate the stories, however, they are *not* "real" anymore.

These believe-it-or-not stories thus raise issues of belief and authority, creating liminal moments for children or young adults; the stories challenge them to find a place in their own process of learning and receptivity toward Arapaho culture that will allow them to negotiate among respect for authority, belief, recognition of appropriate cultural frames and narrative genres (which are, of course, differently coded in terms of expectations of belief and truthfulness), and individual judgment. Cross-culturally, all children have to learn what counts as a "lie" and what doesn't, and how to recognize different speech frames and their expectations. The stories (and tellers' commentaries) also suggest that the proper way of engaging in this learning and negotiation is through acquisition and use of the Arapaho language and deeper engagement with Arapaho culture, which provide the necessary negotiating tools. In a sense, just as the stories themselves present different contexts internally, which must be carefully negotiated (air versus land, pipes versus electricity), the stories offer a larger performative framework for negotiating cultural contexts and relationships.

The other very different context in which the stories are often told (in English) is between Arapaho tellers and white audiences, which creates a very different insider-outsider dynamic. When a group of Arapaho elders came to Boulder, Colorado, in 2001 to plan a powwow in conjunction with a group of local citizens, I witnessed a male elder tell a believe-it-or-not story in English to one of the local white participants. That telling was itself another liminal moment that raised many of the same issues as the tellings involving Arapaho children and youth. Obviously, the intercultural and interracial setting of the telling was highly salient. In this case, the powwow was a highly charged cultural event in which the Arapaho were hoping to reestablish ties to Boulder, which they considered their traditional homeland, and more generally, to stake a spiritual and physical presence in the area. The powwow was in fact officially named a celebration of *ce'no'eeckoohuut* 'coming home again' by the elders. Arapaho individuals are often interested in testing the boundaries of belief between themselves and whites, and telling stories that probe those boundaries is a common way of doing so.

The story told in Boulder was the "Broken-Back Bear" (Story 2). It is especially suited to this purpose, as it is not utterly fantastic in the same way as jumping back from halfway across a canyon is. To the extent that the Euro-American audience picks up on the humor, these can be important moments of bonding. On the other hand, polite acceptance of the story, with a failure to comment or question, is typically seen as patronizing and distancing—as a kind of infantilizing judgment on the part of the listener, who refuses to grant that Arapahos are as rational and sensory-based as the listener. Even worse, the listener may simply appear foolish to an Arapaho for believing such a story. Thus believe-it-or-not stories place non-Arapaho listeners in a similar position as Arapaho children, in that they are forced to negotiate between issues of deference, respect, cultural difference, and competing attitudes toward belief and possibility, friendship, and bonding. Appropriate responses can be very tricky to judge, especially as Arapaho individuals themselves have different attitudes toward traditional Arapaho beliefs and ceremonialism, as well as different expectations with regard to Euro-Americans.

The same story (Story 2) was told in 1914, not too far from Boulder, to Oliver Toll. A member of the Colorado Mountain Club, he was accompanying two elders and an interpreter on a trip through the future Rocky Mountain National Park, in an effort to learn about Arapaho place-names that could be applied to the area in order to make it more "exotic" and appealing as a national park site. During the two weeks of traveling by mule train, the two elders told many stories. Toll reported the story as recorded earlier in the chapter. He makes no comment on his own belief—he states that he generally tried to simply write down what he was told, without evaluation (Toll 2003, 3). We can imagine the Arapaho elders experiencing a great deal of amusement at this, tinged by disappointment that Toll did not try to "ontologically engage" with them. On the other hand, when the story was told again in Boulder in 2001, the reaction of the Euro-American listener was polite laughter which, I thought, concealed a tinge of uncertainty. The Arapaho teller laughed confidently and knowingly, as did several other older Arapaho men who were listening, but none of them ever revealed to the listeners their explicit attitude toward the story.

I should note that Wayne C'Hair (real name) offered a quite different take on these stories in May 2018. Reacting to stories such as shooting at deer on the other side of a mountain by bending a gun, he noted that such stories were common and were told "just to make us laugh." But then, as our conversation continued, he added that in modern times, there are now weapons that can shoot over the horizon, such as guided missiles. He added that the believe-it-or-not stories showed that "Arapahos already knew about it—[they] knew better about it than the whites." Wayne and others say the same thing about trickster and other types of stories as well: when the trickster throws his eyes up in the air to see (Cowell, C'Hair, and Moss 2014, 162–65), this presages satellites, which finally came into being in 1958. When a person is trampled then revived using a single drop of blood on a blade of grass (382–86), this foretells DNA and cloning. Thus believe-it-or-not stories can be used not just to test white people, but to trump them as well!

Conclusion

As the preceding paragraph shows, Arapaho uses and interpretations of these stories are diverse. But a dominant theme is clearly a confrontation with the hard-to-believe. As much as these stories tend to open up gaps in listeners' comfort levels, in their relationships with the teller, in their view of the world, or in their understanding of their place in the community, they also force the listeners to bridge a gap and engage in a form of collaborative co-creation of meaning with the teller. If we reflect for a moment, we will recognize that the humor of these narratives depends on this collaboration.

In the first place, if one truly believes the narrative, it is not funny—it is remarkable perhaps, but not amusing. On the other hand, if one doesn't understand the nature of the metaphorical extension of reasoning that leads to the punch line, the narrative is not funny either, just mystifying. One can imagine a young child simply asking, "But how could he turn around in the air?" or an especially uncooperative listener simply saying, "But a bullet can't go in a curve." In order to appreciate the humor of the narrative, the listener must successfully recognize the metaphorical extension (from tube to wire, from straight gun barrel to crooked gun barrel) which is operative in the narrative, and furthermore, recognize that the extension indeed has a certain logic to it. Only then, I argue, does one really laugh *at* the story *with* the teller.

In other words, it is not just the telling of the story that can open up gaps in relationships for reconsideration and renegotiation. The actual content of the story also inscribes at its core a gap of reasoning. This gap of reasoning has a specific ontological quality to it, and when this quality is not fully recognized and the gap is not successfully negotiated, the telling results in a social gap in the world. But when the gap is success-fully bridged in understanding, the social gap also closes down, laughter results, and a bond is created in the world. The bond rests on a mutual acceptance of the reasonableness of the metaphorical extensions implic-itly suggested (but never explicitly stated) in the story, as well as a shared knowledge that this reasonableness is finally betrayed in the "real" world.

Having talked about bridging gaps of logic and relationships, I will conclude with some examples that bridge between genres. While some speakers simply talk about believe-it-or-not stories, others call this genre Wox Betebi 'Old Lady Bear' stories. Wox Betebi (real name) was in fact a man, despite the personal name. He reportedly often told these stories, and in fact, often told them in the first person, as if they were his accom-plishments. This sub-strand of the genre links the stories loosely back to the medicine man/shaman tradition of more-than-human power and great accomplishments, though here those accomplishments are desacralized.

Another group of speakers talk of these stories as Wox Nihooneih 'Yel-low Bear' stories, again ascribing them to an actual deceased individual, who likewise claimed to have accomplished some of the feats. In some cases, people tell believe-it-or-not stories and insert Wox Nihooneih's name as the protagonist in the story. In other cases, however, the events ascribed to Wox Nihooneih do not seem to occur in the broader believe-it-or-not tradition and tellings, which suggests a partial linkage to the folk hero genre. Some of the stories ascribed to Wox Nihooneih seem rather "Strong Bear like," while others are more truly unbelievable: on a more realistic level, he is described as having been so strong that when he hit someone with boxing gloves, feathers flew out. Less realistically, he is described as throwing a shot put so far that it goes into orbit, where it can still be seen circling the earth. Thus, Yellow Bear shares with Strong Bear the qualities of being Arapaho and amazingly strong, but otherwise he does not really engage directly with whites or overtly espouse Arap-aho cultural values—in other words, he lacks an explicitly anticolonialist indigenous component to his identity.

Following are two brief English renditions of Yellow Bear/believe-it-or-not stories (from the 1988–89 *Woxu Niibei/Bear Singer* Wyoming Indian High School annual). My editorial additions are in double parentheses.

"On the Money"

One time Wox Nihooneih went for a visit to Oklahoma. He stayed there for quite some time. Soon he was out of money. He had no funds to return home to Ethete. Wox Nihooneih called home and told Hoh'onookee 3i'ookuu (('Standing Rock')) to send him some money. So Hoh'onookee 3i'ookuu wired Wox Nihooneih a lot of money.

Wox Nihooneih waited and waited for the money, but it never arrived.

So Wox Nihooneih put a tracer on the money. The money was found somewhere in Kansas, where the wire broke. Hoh'onookee 3i'ookuu had sent too much money and it got too heavy and broke the wire.

That is why all of the money fell out in Kansas.

"About Yellow Bear"

Wox Nihooneih went fishing down along the river one time. When he got through fishing and was on his way home, he noticed something moving around by a big log off to the side of the path. When he went over to investigate, he saw two snakes fighting.

One was a bullsnake, the other a rattlesnake—both snakes really had it on. They had a battle, the only way that snakes fight, I guess.

Wox Nihooneih said the snakes were coiling around each other and trying to squeeze the life out of one another, but only to get away from the other snake's grip.

The fight went on like that for a while.

Soon the bullsnake started to eat the rattler. Wox Nihooneih was watching, and he said that the rattler got the idea and started to eat the bullsnake. He said that when they got through eating each other up, there was nothing left of the snakes—so Wox Nihooneih went on home thinking about it. ((Specifically, each snake eats the other one from the tail end.))

And that is exactly what these stories are about—people are supposed to go home thinking about them! Perhaps the most interesting component of these stories is the way they often imbricate into their plots and narratives the metanarrative, performative, and relational frameworks that typically surround their tellings, either implicitly and symbolically or, in this case, quite explicitly in the final line.

4

Old Folks Stories

As we saw in chapter 3, ostensibly comical Arapaho believe-it-or-not stories can actually raise quite serious questions surrounding elder authority and traditional belief systems. The issues are especially challenging because Arapaho society has traditionally been described as "age-graded" (Eggan 1955). In such a system respect automatically accrues to older individuals in favor of younger ones, regardless of other mitigating criteria. Age is certainly not the only basis of respect among Arapaho people, and no matter how old one is, one may gain or lose respect for various reasons. But age-gradedness is institutionalized in traditional Arapaho social practice in ways not normally found in Euro-American society. For example, older Arapahos say that if their older brother or sister is saying something in public with which they disagree, they cannot contradict the person nor can they leave the room. Even if what is being said is critical of them personally, they must simply accept the comments with equanimity, neither arguing nor departing. This is an idealized description of what *should* happen, of course, not what always does happen, but the idealization reveals strong sociocultural beliefs and links to common social practices. More generally, talking reverently about the "old men" and "old ladies" is a pervasive aspect of social discourse in traditional Arapaho society. Noting who is older than whom, and who is the oldest person present, are common practices at meetings and gatherings. Requests for prayers and invocations are often based on age-specific criteria, for both men and women. The oldest people are often given the opportunity to speak first (in response to cultural or historical questions, for example), and there are often-complex ways of mediating between older and younger speakers in formal settings (see Cowell 2018, 18–22).

Given all this seriousness and respect, it may appear surprising that there is a genre of Arapaho reservation-era narratives that could be called the "old couple" story, which seems to undermine many of the values and practices just described. In this type of story, old people are presented as clearly physically aged—old and wrinkled, hard of hearing or sight. They are often presented as out of touch with modern technologies or practices (see the John Plume stories on visiting the doctor in chapters 5 and 7 for a similar presentation). The elderly folk are typically presented as somewhat hapless, or even befuddled, and become the object of physical as well as social humor. They may also be represented as still sexually active, at least in thought if not in deed, in a way that directly contradicts expectations regarding ceremonial elders.[1] Yet as Richard Bauman notes about such joking stories, they allow "a kind of scepticism and relativism that takes pleasure in refusing to take ideal, normative moral expectations too seriously" (Bauman 1986, 75). But perhaps more importantly, they can serve as a way of channeling the very real challenges and occasional embarrassments of old age into opportunities for narrative performance and humor that reestablish the social competence and even mastery of the teller.

I have not found many published examples of this type of story from other Native American communities, but based on both personal experience in some other communities and second-hand reports, I believe this type of story to be quite common. Some good examples come from Brightman (2007, 161–64) regarding the Rock Cree. Notably, the narrator explicitly begins, "This is the story of an old man and his wife and a moose." Navajo examples can be found in Cunningham (1992, 145, 147). Following are some Arapaho examples of such stories.

The Old Couple and the Old Car

Told by Carl in 2010, this story arose during a visit between two good friends. They decided to tell me some stories and said it was fine if I recorded them. I do not discuss the entire chain of stories in this anthology, only this particular story. The two men (the other was Roger) were taking turns telling stories, in a formalized "first you then me" way, as illustrated by the first line of the transcription. This type of very explicit recognition of turn-taking is characteristic of conversational Arapaho storytelling. At this point in the sequence, one of the men's daughters arrived home. Not aware of the exact nature of the situation at first, she simply saw me present with a camera as the two men were visiting and apparently assumed I was doing some kind of "official" cultural documentation. She interrupted the other man (her Indian-style uncle), who was telling a story, and urged her father to talk about what his Arapaho name was and how he got it. He told her that he had shared that information earlier, but he mentioned his name again, as well as that of his friend, then this led to the two good friends teasing each other about their names. The uncle, who had been interrupted, was named Red Shirt, and his friend teased him that "he's got no pants, no diaper," leading to loud laughter from all present. At this point, the uncle never had completed his story, but given the long interruption, he decided to explicitly cede the floor to the father, using both the topic-initiation device *wohei* and an explicit *biiti'* 'you next.' The father took a few seconds to gather his thoughts, then launched into the following story. Note his use of *wohei* to stake his explicit claim to be telling a story; his use of *hi3oowo'* 'you know/remember' as a signal of forthcoming interesting information and an appeal to maintain his turn; and his use of a definite marker (*nuhu'*) to introduce the key characters of the story—a common practice in Arapaho to signal new referents that will be of subsequent interest. He thus presents a quite marked and formal story initiation, despite having been explicitly ceded the floor.

((ELAR video 69c, 4:54))

      [[3.5 sec.]]

Roger: Wohei biiti'. [[uncle points at woman's father]]

       Okay, your turn to tell a story.

      [[2 sec.]]

Arapaho Version

Wohei hoon-oo3itoon-ou'u nuhu' hinen, hisei;

Hi3oowo' hentoo-3i' nuhu' howoh'oowu-u', Lander. [[points toward Lander]]

Heet-ce'eeckoohu-ni', nih-'ii-3i'.

Ce3koohu-3i'.

Hi3oowo' hentou-' hill.

'oh co'ouuteni'. [[looks upward as if at a high hill; gestures as if going down a steep hill]]

KoxuuP too-to'oxo' hu'un brakes. [[gesture: stepping on brakes repeatedly]]

Hoowuuni brake! [[taps on floor with foot as if hitting brakes]]

'eiyo', 'eiyo', he-et-toustoo-n? [[taps on floor with foot as if hitting brakes]]

He-et-toustoo-n?

Nuhu' heesiini . . .

'iiheihoo neyei-too-too'uhcehi! nih-'ii3-oot.

Konoo',[2] nih-'ii3-oot, hoowuuni. [[taps foot on floor as if hitting brakes]]

Nii-coon-too-too'uhcehi-noo! nih-'ii3-oot. [[taps foot on floor as if hitting brakes]]

No brakes.

[[chuckles]]

Konoo'=hoowu-ceno'oo! nih-'ii3-oot. [[turns as if talking to wife next to him in the car]]

[[chuckles]]

Nih-koo-kokoh'u3ecoo-t nehe'.³

Neihoow-beetP wootii, neihoow-beet-eenesisin! nih-'ii3-oot.

Konoo'=hoowu-ceno'oo! nih-'ii3-oot.

Konoo'=hisei hoow-ceno'oo-t. [[gesture: pointing to woman jumping out of car]]

Tee-tee-teco'oo-t. [[gesture: woman rolling over and over]]

[[laughter]]

Tee-tee-teco'oo-t, weeds, tumbleweeds, that gravel, dirt. [[gesture: woman rolling over and over]]

Ne'-se'isi-'. [[PSL gesture: someone falls down and hits the ground]]

Honoot hill heentou'u-' hini', too'uhcehi-3i'. [[gesture: going up hill; gesture: stopping]]

[[chuckles]]

Nehe' hinen hoowu-ceno'oo-t.

'oh nehe', in the mean time hisei, got up, brushed that dust off. [[gesture: standing upright; gesture: brushing oneself off]]

Nih-'esiikoohu-t.

You all right? Keesis? nih-'ii3-oot.

Hiiko, neihoowP; he got her mad.

Ne'-to'ow-oot. [[hits his open hand with his fist]]

[[laughter]]

I'm all right, nih-'ii3-oot.

[[laughter]]

You made me jump off a car for nothing! nih-'ii3-oot.

[[laughter]]

English Version

Well, I am going to tell the story of this man and woman;

You know, they were in Lander, Lander. [[points toward Lander]]

"We will return home," they said.

They set off driving.

Remember, there's a hill there.⁴

And it is high. [[looks upward as if at a high hill; gestures as if going down a steep hill]]

Coming down the other side, the man was kicking those brakes over and
over. [[gesture: stepping on brakes repeatedly]]
"There is no brake!" [[taps on floor with foot as if hitting brakes]]
"Oh-oh, oh-oh, what are we going to do?" [[taps on floor with foot as if
hitting brakes]]
"What are we going to do? "
"With things like this now . . ."
"Golly gee whiz, try to stop!" the woman said to him.
"Anyway," he said to her, "it's no good." [[taps foot on floor as if hitting
brakes]]
"I can't stop!" he said to her. [[taps foot on floor as if hitting brakes]]
No brakes.
[[chuckles]]
"Anyway, just jump down/off!" he said to her. [[turns as if talking to
wife next to him in the car]]
[[chuckles]]
This woman thought about it.
"I don't want to, I don't want to get hurt falling off!" she said to him.
"Just jump off anyway!" he said to her.
So anyway the woman jumped off. [[gesture: pointing to woman
jumping out of car]]
She went rolling along head over heels. [[gesture: woman rolling over
and over]]
[[laughter]]
She went rolling along, through the weeds, tumbleweeds, gravel, dirt.
[[gesture: woman rolling over and over]]
Then she was lying there. [[PSL gesture: someone falls down and hits
the ground]]
Until there was that hill farther down the road, and the man and the
car came to a stop going uphill. [[gesture: going up hill; gesture:
stopping]]
[[chuckles]]
This man jumped out of the car.
And this, in the meantime the woman, she got up, brushed that dust off.
[[gesture: standing upright; gesture: brushing oneself off]]
Her husband ran real fast.
"Are you all right? Did you get hurt?" he said to her.
"No, I'm not . . ."; he mad, got her mad.
Then she hit him. [[hits his open hand with his fist]]
[[laughter]]

"I'm all right," she said to him.
[[laughter]]
"You made me jump off a car for nothing!" she said to him.
[[laughter]]

((After concluding the story, the narrator adds:))

There was no brakes, but he coasted in.
She jumped out, she didn't get hurt too bad, but she was all right.
Turned around and hit her husband.
[[chuckles]]
[[7 sec.]]

The father's switch to a brief concluding English translation was directed at the researcher, just to make sure he had understood the story. The climax of the story is the sequence of three rounds of laughter immediately preceding this. Following the English remarks, only chuckles occur, suggesting that the speakers see these remarks as not part of the story narrowly conceived. A fairly long, seven-second pause ensues, then the uncle begins a story about a time when he and his older brother had car trouble and lost their brakes, so he had to jump out of the car and throw a piece of wood in front of it, to stop it rolling. He follows this up with yet another story about car trouble. There is in fact a genre of Arapaho stories that could be called the "rez car story," about cars in poor condition and the funny things that happen when driving them. One could say that the uncle reacts to the father's "old couple" story as more of a "rez car" story in his choice of subsequent narrative, but he nevertheless shows that he knows stories appropriate to follow up on the first story, in theme if not exactly in genre.

The Good Garden

A variant of the "old couple" story is the "old lady" story or "old man" story, which both focus on the comical doings of elderly people. I often asked Robert if he could "tell me some stories." This was all the invitation he needed to share multiple stories, one after the other. I never suggested what stories he should tell, so the genre, number, and sequencing were always up to him. On one visit, when I entered the house, the following conversation occurred, which led to the emergence of this story. The story is about a woman who is hard of hearing but still comically romantically active, at least in thought. But the story is clearly also a humorous reflection on the narrator himself, who talks about his own poor hearing—and jokes about his own potential romantic thoughts—prior to telling the story. I responded *wohei* to show that I understood all of this and am ready for the session to continue. Robert responded by also using *wohei*, to initiate his story. I begin the transcription with the opening conversation leading to the emergence of the story.[5]

Conversational Prelude

Cowell: Koo-he-neeteih? Koo-he-neeteih?
Are you tired? Are you tired?

Koo-he-neeteih? Tired?
Are you tired? Tired?

Robert: Heeyou?
What?

Cowell: Neneeni-n, koo-he-neeteih?
You, are you tired?

Tired? Neneeteihi-n.
Tired? You are tired.

Robert: Nei-hoowuu-ni'ehton-e3.
I can't recognize what you're saying.

Cowell: Okay.
Okay.

I, I just asked if you were tired.
I, I just asked if you were tired.

Robert: Oh! koo-he-neeteih?
Oh, are you tired?

Cowell: Hee.
Yes.

Robert: Uhm, yeah. I thought you meant koo-he-no'oteih?
          I thought you meant, are you tough/strong?

Cowell: Yeah hei-hoow-neesetee. Right.
          Yeah, you don't hear well. Right.

Robert: Ne-ih-'oowuuP nei-hoowu-ni'-niitobee.
          I couldn't, I can't hear things well.

Cowell: Yeah.
          Yeah.

Robert: Nuhu' bi'-beenhehe'.
          Just a little bit in this ear.

Cowell: Yeah.
          Yeah.

Robert: 'oh nuhu' beneexu-ni'iini.
          But this one is kind of okay.

Cowell: Okay.
          Okay.

Robert: 'oh neniitowootobee-nooni nihiit-ono, nei-hoowuuPnei-
          hoowuu-xouuwooP xouuwoote'in heeneesi-nihiitooni-'.
          *Whenever I hear words, I can't really figure out what people
          are saying.*

Cowell: Okay.
          Okay.

Robert: I just, 'oh niiP, kookon, tohuuP, like non3einooni-', cenihP
          nih-'eeneisiini.
          *I just, well I just, it just makes no sense, whenever, it's like
          nonsense sounds, what all the person said.*

          Niini'P nii-ni'-niitobee-noo, 'oh nuhu' hi'eenetiit, 'oh
          ne'-ii'P nei-hoowuuP, Nei-hoowuu-beh-xouuwoo[t]e'in
          nih-'eeneisi-nihii-n.

*I can hear sounds, that someone is talking, but what he is
talking about, I can't, I can't really properly understand
everything that you said.*

Cowell: Ahh.
Ahh.

Robert: He-ih-tousP . . . , coo'ouu3i-', ni'ehtP nehtobee-noo.
*What did you . . . ; if a person talks loud, I'm able to
recognize it.*

Beebeet nohootineihi-n he'ii3ou'u.
You just ??? something.

Cowell: Oh, okay.
Oh, okay.

Robert: Nii-beet-neyei-yihoon-o' nii-notonotii-3i' nuhu', nuhu'. . . .
*I want to try and go see one of those doctors who doctor
these ears. . . .*

Wohei howoo nuhu' nii-3ei'in-ou'u, hini'iit ni'ii-ni'ehtowootiini-'.
*And, also, they put these hearing aids in there, those
hearing aids.*

Wo'ei3 heetP heetn-iini hi3-heetniini, 'oh heet-ne'ini
bebiis-nehtobee-noo.
Or I will, later I will . . . and then I will hear things properly.

Wohei nuhu' nesiisei'i ci', heetnii-neyeih'ini bei'ci3eiyookuu.
And my eyes too, I will try out some glasses.

Cowell: Ahh, bei'ci3eiyookuu.
Ahh, glasses.

Robert: Beexuni noohoo3ei-noo nuhu' hihiiteeniihi', 'oh nuhu',
hoowuuni huni', hoowuu-noohoo3ei.
*I see a little from this side, but this other one, I don't see
anything from that one.*

Hiisiiten-owunoohok bei'ci3eiyookuu nuhu', beenhehe'
heet-ne'-xook-noohoo3ei-noo nih'oo3eeyoub-e'.

*If I get a hold of some glasses, then I will be able to see
through these curtains a little bit.*

Heetniini'-xook-noohoo3ei-noo heeyouhuu,
nih'oo3eeyoub-e'.

I will be able to see things through the curtains.

Wohei heetn-iini heen-esoohow-ou'u nuhu' hisei-no'
nii-cebsee-3i'.

Well, I will watch those women who walk by outside.

Hini'iit nih'oo3eeyou heetnii-xook-noohoot-owoo hunee.

I will be able to see through those curtains.

Cowell: <u>Wohei.</u>
          Okay.

Arapaho Version

((Recording mp3-17, 2:54, Center for the Study of Indigenous Languages,
University of Colorado, Boulder))

Yeah. <u>Wohei</u>, heetn-<u>oo3itoon</u>-e3en.
<u>Wohei</u> heetn-<u>oo3itoon</u>-e3en <u>ceesey</u> hi'in noowuuhu'.
[<u>He'ih</u>]-3ii-3i'oku-no' ceee3i'.
Ceee3i' [<u>he'ih</u>]-3ii-3i'oku-no'.
Hesitee': bebene niihoonkoo' nii'ouu3i'.
Hee3neene-esitee-' noowuuhu'; nee'ee3eenei'P.
Kookuyon nihii toukoyeiniihi', [<u>he'ih</u>]-3ii-3i'oku-no'.
Woow nih-beexu-u3ou'oo-'.
'oh nuhu' kookon [<u>he'ih</u>]-noonoo3itoohu-no';
Nuhu' [<u>he'ih</u>]-noon-oo3itoohu-no'.
Wohei ne'-cih-no'koohu-t;
Nooxeihi' teebe nih-ciin-niisi3ei'i-t.
Hotoohe' hiit niisi3ei'i-3i', heen-ei'tobee-noo.[6]
NihP hinee niit-niisi3ei'i-noo niitowoot-owoo nuhu' hoo3itoo.
Niitowoot-owoo;
Heetn-oo3itoon-e3enee.

Hinit woteeniihi' niit-3ii-3i'okuutooni-', nihii 3i'okuutooo-no neen-
  einootei-'i he'iitnei'i.
He'ih-neh'i-no' hisei-no'.
Woow beexei'esei-3i' heh-niisi-3i'.
'oh nuhu' neneesi'owoo-t, he'ih-betebihehiin.
Hoow-ee3nee-betebihehiin;
'oh woow, woow niitootosoo' cebe'einiihi', ne'=nih-'iitoxcecnibee-t.
'oh nuhu' hoo3oo'o', bebene yeiyoo' yoo3oniini',
  ne'=nih-'iitoxcecnibee-3i'.
Wohei nehe' hisei, ceese' hisei he'ih-'ei'towuun-ee hi'in ceexoon.
'oh nehe' betebihehi' neehii3ei' nee'eet-3i'oku-t;
Nee'eet-3i'oku-t.
Hoowu'u-ni'etobee.
Hoowu'u-ni'etobee.
Niisi-cowo'oo-t, 'oh nuhu' tohuu-bee-bee3soh'oe-3i',
  [he'ih]-nei'oohob-ee.
Ne'=nih-'iis-beexe-e'ino' neeneisi-nihiitooni-'.
'oh hoowu'u-ni'etobee;
Hoowuuni.
Wohei he'ih-'ei'towuun-ee hi'in ceexoon.
Nehe' hisei, hinee nei-tooto'on-eiitooninoo, nih'oo3oo nih-'iiniine'etii-t,
  nee3neen-oonoxoni-i3eti-ni'i hi-ciineyoo-no.[7]
Howoo hiiwoonhehe' nuhu' cec, hee3nee-ni'oonoxoni-i3eti-ni'i hi-
  beskootee-no; no'o3iici3oo-ni'i.[8] [[makes gesture to indicate a long
  corn cob]]
Yeinou'u heneebe3-ce'eihi-ni3i, he'ih-'ii3-ee hi'in ceexoon. [[makes
  gesture with both hands to indicate big, round, heavy tomatoes]]
'oonei, hei-tousi-nihii? he'ih-'ii nehe' betebihehi'.
Hei-tousi-nihii?
Noh nei'towuun-o' nebi hinen, neehebehe';
Nuhu', nei'towuun-o', hinee nih'oo3oo nei-tooto'on-eiitooninoo;
  hee3neen-oonoxoni-i3eti-ni'.
Hi-ihoowu'u-ni'etobee nehe' betebihehi'.
[He'ih]-noxootoohob-ee.
Bee-bee3soh'oe-ni3; nii-ni'-hei'towuun-o':
Hinee nei-tooto'on-eiitooninoo nih'oo3oo, nee3nee-tesi-i3eti-ni'i hi-
  ciineyoo-no hiiwoonhehe', nuhu' cec;
Hee3neen-oonoxoni-i3eti-ni'i, hee3nee-no'o3iici3oo-ni'i hi-
  beskootee-no. [[long corn cobs gesture again]]
Yeinou'u too-tou3ei3e-nino. [[large tomatoes gesture again]]
'ii tousihi'? nih-'ii-t.

[[narrator laughs for several seconds]]
Nee'ei'ise-' nuhu' hoo3itoo.

English Version

Yeah. Okay, I will tell you a story.

Okay, I will tell you a story about one time down in Oklahoma.

They were sitting around outside.

Outside they were sitting around.

It was hot, around September.

It was very hot down south; that's how much heat there was.

People were just sitting around in the shade, doing nothing in particular.

It was already a little toward evening.

And they were just telling stories to each other to pass the time;

These ones were telling each other stories.

Wohei, then someone else showed up;

Maybe she just now finished working.

"??? here where they are working, at my job I was told about it.

"That place where I work, I heard this story.

"I heard it;

I will tell you a story about it."

Right there in town where people would sit around, well, some chairs
were set out somewhere.

I guess there were three women.

Already they are older women, two of them.

But this third one, I guess she was an old woman.

She was not extremely old;

But already, already beyond sixty, that, that's how old she was.

But these others, around forty-five, that's how old they were.

Wohei, this one woman, I guess she told this other one about something.

And this old woman—in the middle is where she is sitting;

That is where she is sitting.

She did not hear too/very well.

She did not hear very well.

How she got along, well, when they would make gestures or use sign
language, she watched them.

That's how she knew a little bit what people were saying.

But she couldn't hear very well;

She couldn't.

Wohei, I guess the newly arrived younger woman told that other younger
woman about it.

This woman at work said, "This white man who lives real close to us, his vegetable garden is tremendous.

"Also, now this year, they are really tremendous, his corn cobs; they are super long. [[makes gesture to indicate a long corn cob]]

The tomatoes are very big and round," she was saying to that other woman. [[makes gesture with both hands to indicate big, round, heavy tomatoes]]

"Gee, what did you say?" said the old lady.

"What did you say?"

And "I am telling her about my older sister at work, there is a white man, my sister at work was telling about him";

I am telling her that this woman at work said, "That white man who lives real close to us, his vegetables are extremely good."

She didn't hear too well, this old lady.

She was just staring at them.

The younger one showed her with gestures; "I am telling her about it:"

"That one white man who lives real close to us, his vegetables are tremendously good now this year;"

"They are really tremendously good, his corn cobs are super nice and long." [[long corn cob gesture again]]

"And you should see how big and heavy his tomatoes are!" [[large tomatoes gesture again]]

"Oh my, what's his name!?" [the old lady] asked.

[[narrator laughs for several seconds]]

That's how the story ends.

((In case anyone has missed the point, the old lady has interpreted the gestures describing the corn and tomatoes as a description of the genitalia of the man next door, and now is interested in finding out more about him! From a linguistic perspective, this story shows a semiformal style: initiation with *wohei* as well as with an explicit invocation of storytelling, plus use of *ceesey* 'one time'; occasional use of narrative past tense *he'ih-*; and a formal closing formula. In contrast, the story told by Carl lacked many of these features and was completely informal.))

The Old Couple and the Ghost

The following story occurred in the same session as the "Good Garden." Following the garden story, we talked about believe-it-or-not stories for several minutes, specifically at my suggestion. Robert commented, "Yeah, there's a lot of those believe-it-or-nots, you know. Yeah, you hear them.

Once they get started on those kind you hear all kinds." After discussing a couple more believe-it-or-not plots and stories, Robert then explicitly changed genres, back to the theme of old people that had been evoked in the "Good Garden."

((Recording mp3-17, 14:57, Center for the Study of Indigenous Languages, University of Colorado, Boulder))

Robert: Yeah, they uh . . . they have pretty good ones.

  This story, this story I heard, it's not a believe-it-or-not, it's sort of like a ghost story, you know.

Cowell: Okay.

Robert: There was an old man and his wife, you know they, at the house.

Cowell: Why don't you tell it in Arapaho? Hinono'eitiit [Arapaho].

Robert: Yeah

Cowell: It's always better, you always tell it better in hinono'eitiit [Arapaho].

Robert: Yeah.

Cowell: Heetniitone3en.

  I will understand you.

Robert: Yeah, well, it was told to me in English.

Cowell: Oh. . . .

Robert: I don't know just how well I can put it in Arapaho.

Cowell: Oh, I see. Okay, well, go ahead and tell that one in English.

Arapaho Version

Yeah, <u>wohei</u> hi'in <u>nihii</u> beh'eihehi' <u>wohei</u> hi-betebihow
   [he'ih]-niisnenii-no'.[9]
<u>He'ih</u>-bih'iyoo.[10]
Woow <u>he'ih</u>-'iis-eeneisibi-no', niis-eeneisibi-3i'.
Nih-'eyeih-noo-nokohuutooni-'.
He3ebii <u>he'ih</u>-'iiP <u>he'ih</u>-beebee-no';
[<u>He'ih</u>]-he3eb-yih'oow-oono'.
Nih-'ii-ce'-tokohu-3i'.
No'uuhu' tecenoon-e' woo-woteisibeti-3i'.

Koox=ne'-eh-ce'-yih'oow-oo3i'.
Ne'iini yehei noh ne'-cih-ce'-tokohu-3i' hi'in woo-woteisibeti-3i'
    tecenoon-e';
'oh nehe' betebihehi' "3iwoo neyei-he'inon-inee toon-he'iiteihi-3i.
Wohoe'=cih'e-entoo ceee3i'.
Hiineniini-n, nih-'ii-t, beh'ee.[11]
He'ne'-kohei'i-t.
3eb-no'oehi-t.
Nuhu' tece' he'ih-3ebii-noo-notnoo'ein.
[He'ih]-3eb-wo'wusee.
'oh hoowo-e'in toh-cih-to3ih-eit hi-betebihow.
Nih'ii-cee-ceeniini [he'ih]-noo-notnoo'ein.
He'ih-cii-noohoo3ei.
'oh nuhu' he3ebii heetn-ii-beebee-3i', ne'=nii'-ce'-tokohu-3i'.
He'ih-cii-noohoot tooniiP;
Woow heetn-iineesee-t;
'oh ne'-cih-tii'en-eit hi-koob-e'.
Keih-cii-noohoo3ei?
Yohoohohoe![12]
[He'ih]-honinoo'oo.
Neneih-eit;
Neneih-eit.
Hoowo-e'in toh-neeni-ni3 hi-betebihow.
Toon=hei'-ce'-beex-heen-e'inoo'oo-t,[13] noh hini'iit koo-koonooku-t,
    [he'ih]-cih-noxow-no'oe'eini-n hi-betebihow.
Behixooke'eiP, konou'u'ei-t.
Hei'-noohow-oot "yeheiiiiii!"[14]
Ce'-neeti-neih-eit.
Nee'eesi-neih-eit hi-betebihow.
[[narrator laughs for several seconds]]

English Version

Yeah, okay, that uh, old man, *wohei*, he and his wife, I guess they lived
    alone.
I guess it was nighttime.
They had already gone to bed how they normally did.
They were almost asleep.
The dogs were barking outside;
I guess they were chasing something over that way.
And then would run back again.

They ran right up to the door and into it, chasing something.
Then yet again they chased it away.
Then, gee whiz! then they came running back and ran right into the
    door again;
And this old lady said, "Well, why don't you go try to find out who that is."
It might still be here outside.
"You're a man," she said, "old man, you go do it."
Then he got up.
He went outside there.
He looked around, out there in the night.
I guess he walked farther along.
But he didn't know that she was following right behind him, his old lady.
He was looking all around, far and near.
He didn't see anything.
But these dogs would bark, then they would run off again.
He didn't see anything whatsoever;
Now, he's ready to turn back around;
And then his wife touched him on his back.
"Do you see anything?"
"Yikes!" he cried out.
I guess he fell over.
She has frightened him;
She has frightened him.
He didn't know that it was his old lady.
Whenever he again came to a little, then he opened his eyes and her face
    was right close to him, his old lady.
Her whole face, her face was all wrinkled like a ghost.
When he saw her, "yikes!" he cried out again.
She made him faint again.
That's how his old lady scared him.
[[narrator laughs for several seconds]]

The Old Ladies and the Anthropologist

Told by Carl in 2010, a final example in this genre, again focusing on old
ladies, comes from the same chain of stories between Carl and Roger
described earlier. At a certain point in the discussion, Roger shifted away
from relatively comical or fun stories and topics, and began to complain
about differences between the past and the present, especially the fact
that people today don't understand things about Arapaho language and
culture. He concluded these remarks as follows (English translation only

given here). He then very explicitly transferred the speaking turn to Carl, as before. And as before, Carl took a moment to gather his thoughts, then launched into a story. Note that rather than explicitly talking about story-telling in his opening, he used *hei'towuun-* 'tell someone something' or 'share news.' He once again used *hi3oowo'* as well as definite markers to indicate new referents of interest.

((ELAR video 69d, 11:05))

Roger:	But a long time ago, the old men they helped each other. They would help each other.
Carl:	"Come here (and help)," that's what they would say. But they really don't know about that today.
Roger:	And when people help each other, they get something for themselves in return. People feel good inside.
Carl:	Yes. [[glances up at Roger]]
Roger:	All over.
	[[7 sec.]]
	And it's good that way.
Carl:	Uhm.
Roger:	That's what my grandfather said.
	[[2 sec.]]
	Okay your turn. [[points at Carl.]]
Carl:	Uhm.
	[[1.5 sec.]]

Arapaho Version

Heet-bi'-hei'P heet-bi'-ei'towuun-e3en, be.
Nuhu' hisei-no' nih-'eenentoo-3i' hi'in by the river, heeP heenentoo-3i'.
  [[gesture: points toward the river]]
'oh nehe' nih'oo3ou'u, nuhu' heetP, wootii heetP, [[gesture: uses finger
  to represent a white man]] [[gesture: pointing to various locations]]
nuhu' uhh wo3onohoe, heetP, nehe', [[gesture: writing]]
write it down, kee'in, hinono'einiihi'. [[gesture: writing]]
Hi3oowo' nih-no'usee-t nuhu' hinen. [[points at river over there]]
Hei'P hei'towuun-oot nuhu' husei-no, [[gesture: addressing multiple
  people]]

3iwoo, heet-wo3onP, heet-wo3oninoo'oohP, I'm gonna take your
   picture, nih-'ii3-oot. [[gesture: addressing someone, as in lecturing
   with finger]]
Nooxeihi' gonna have you, have a full costume, full buckskin dress.
   [[gesture: indicates full body]]
These old ladies, "noh heet-ni'iini, heet-ni'iini heetP."
Heet-ne'P nii-nee-niiteheiw-oono' nehe' hinen, nih-'ii-3i'.
heeneisi3ecoo-3i', that's what they thought.
we're gonna help him out. [[gesture: "that man"]]
he's gonna take our picture." [[gesture: indicates self]]
Wohei, nooxeihi' heet-won-neyoo'uu-no', nih-'ii3-oot.
We're gonna dress up. Put our buckskin dress on. [[gesture: "that man"]]
Ne'P hi'in nih'oo3ou'u, hinee he'=niisih'iinou-'u, camera, [[gesture: "that
   man"]] [[gesture: hands make a camera]]
Well while you're, uh, getting ready, getting ready, I'm gonna focus this
   camera, [[gesture: "you over there"]] [gesture: focusing a camera]]
nih-'ii3-oot nehe' hisei. [[gesture: "that woman"]]
Nehe' hisei, koo'eini-t, [[gesture: turns head quickly to the side to look
   at someone else]]
Hey, keih-cii-niiton-oo hu'un nih'oo3ou'u? [[gesture: points at person
   over there]]
Heeyounii, keih-niiton-oo?
He's gonna focus us, nih-'ii3-oot. [[leans forward, as if letting others in
   on a secret]]
[[laughter for 2.5 sec.]]
Nih-cii3-tokohu-t, locked the door. [[gesture: closing and locking a door]]

English Version

I'm going to just tell you about something, friend.
These women were over there by the river, they were around there.
   [[gesture: points toward the river]]
And this white guy, he is going to, like . . . [[gesture: uses finger to
   represent a white man]] [[gesture: pointing to various locations]]
in this book, he will, this guy, [[gesture: writing]]
Will write it down, you know, about the Arapaho culture. [[gesture:
   writing]]
So, you know, this white man arrived. [[points at river over there]]
He told these women, [[gesture: addressing multiple people]]
"Let's see, I will, I will, I'm gonna take your picture," he said to them.
   [[gesture: addressing someone, as in lecturing with finger]]

"Maybe I'm gonna have you in full costume, a full buckskin dress."
  [[gesture: indicates full body]]
These old ladies said, "It will be good, it will be good."
"We are going to help out this man," they said.
That's what they thought, that's what they thought.
"We're gonna help him out." [[gesture: "that man"]]
He's gonna take our picture." [[gesture: indicates self]]
"Okay, maybe we will go dress up," one of the women said to him.
"We're gonna dress up. Put our buckskin dress on." [[gesture: "that man"]]
Then that white man, that what-you-call-it, camera, [[gesture: "that
  man"]] [[gesture: hands make a camera]]
"Well, while you're uh getting ready, getting ready, I'm gonna focus this
  camera," [[gesture: "you over there"]] [gesture: focusing a camera]]
he said to this woman. [[gesture: "that woman"]]
This woman turned around to look at her friend, [[gesture: turns head
  quickly to the side to look at someone else]]
"Hey, did you hear that white man?" she said to her friend. [[gesture:
  points at person over there]]
"What is it, did you hear him?" said her friend.
"He's gonna focus us," she said to her friend. [[leans forward, as if
  letting others in on a secret]]
[[laughter for 2.5 sec.]]
She fled inside, and locked the door. [[gesture: closing and locking a door]]
((The joke here is that the woman misunderstands "focus" as "fuck us")).

Thematically, these stories have a number of elements in common. First,
they tend to focus on limits of sight, hearing, or environmental awareness,
which of course, is common in old age. A related theme is crosslinguistic
misunderstanding and older people's failure to adequately master English.
Second, they often involve older people having difficulty with, or at least
lacking awareness of, newer technologies. Third, they typically avoid ceremonial themes—there do not seem to be any humorous stories about old
men making mistakes in the Sun Dance due to their age, for example. Note
also that chiefs, councilpersons, or leaders are rarely depicted in these stories, so anything that might question authority or the capacity of older
leaders to exercise authority is avoided. Indeed, no specific individual is
ever named in the stories. Fourth, they present images of older people as
incongruously sexual. And finally, to the extent that whites are involved in
the stories, these outsiders are never "in on" the joke.

The stories can be understood in a somewhat more serious way, however, and partially in parallel to the believe-it-or-not stories. As discussed,

the latter raise issues of authority and ontology, subtly suggesting that elder authority and truthfulness are not universals of Arapaho society, but rather are context-dependent, and elders need not be granted universal authority or belief. The old couple or old folk stories likewise illustrate that age-gradedness and elder respect, despite being universally acknowledged as central to Arapaho society, are also not absolutes or universals. The stories present the non-ceremonial side of elderhood and the limits of the need for automatic respect or reverence toward older generations.

It is exactly this contrast that seems to be operative in Carl's deployment of the "focus" story in the chain of stories with Roger. It is difficult to grasp the dynamics fully without seeing the video, but Carl largely gives perfunctory assent to Roger's comments about the "good old days." His gaze is unfocused and distant, and he seems somewhat bored with Roger's encomium of the older generation and their wisdom, despite his verbal assent to the claims. As a means of shifting away from this topic, the moment he is given a chance to take the floor, he introduces a bawdy "old lady" story, which is quite funny in the incongruous contrast it establishes between these old ladies and Roger's near-reverential descriptions of elders. Roger himself was sensitive to this, because he complained to me afterwards as we went through the video together that he was trying to keep the stories "clean" and proper, but that Carl kept trying to take things in the other direction, introducing "dirty" elements.

The deployment of the "Good Garden" and "Old Car" stories can be interpreted quite differently. In both those cases, the tellers first engage in good-natured teasing, either of each other or of themselves. This can be seen as similar to what Basso describes for Apache jointly enacted stories or scenarios, where participants embarrass each other or themselves in order to demonstrate their own solidarity or self-confidence through their ability to publicly put up with such embarrassing comments or situations (Basso 1979, 37–44, 67–76). The ensuing stories, in both cases, then depict individuals who are clearly inadequate to the moment and embarrass themselves. It is as if the tellers want to tell the story to further underline that they, too, have just engaged in or been through similar moments of potential embarrassment. Yet, by following up not with anger or silence, but rather with very pointed awareness of their own situation, they illustrate their mastery of self, of the close relationship they have with the other interlocutor, or both. They turn potential inadequacy into narrative performance of a high order, which demonstrates they possess a narrative repertoire adequate to respond appropriately to any situation. The physical limitations of old age are replaced by the wisdom, cultural knowledge, and high performative competence of old age.

5

Story Sequence A

Estes Park, Colorado (2005)

The following story chain occurred at a hotel in Estes Park, Colorado, just outside Rocky Mountain National Park. A group of Arapaho elders had come down to the park to work with me on a language and cultural documentation project funded by a National Park Service grant. Once the day was over, part of the group retired to a hotel room, simply to chat and tell stories. Participants included Art, Earl, Ron, myself, a grad student research assistant working for me, and a young Navajo National Park Service ranger intern. The evening began with general conversation, then Art and Earl exchanged trickster stories. Perhaps inspired by the bawdy trickster, one of the participants then recounted some anecdotes where people made mistakes in Arapaho while speaking in public and accidentally said something off-color or obscene. Such accounts are themselves a genre of Arapaho oral tradition. Both stories described World War II veterans who returned home and were honored for their service at public gatherings. On such occasions, the honorees are asked to tell their war stories. One individual, describing fighting the Japanese on a Pacific Island, told about firing over and over into a dark hole (cave) surrounded by thick brush. Due to the description and certain Arapaho-specific double meanings in some of the words, this story ended up sounding like a description of sexual intercourse. Another individual described how he permanently injured his arm in a battle, but accidentally concluded by saying, "That's how I ended up with a bad vulva" rather than "a bad arm" due to the similarity of the two words in Arapaho.[1] Art spoke in Arapaho as he recounted these stories (which are well known and told by others as well), then I translated into English for those present who could not understand Arapaho. After I finished translating the "accidental obscenities" stories, Art added in English, "There's a lot of stories like that." A pause of more than nine seconds then ensued, after which Art launched into the following story.

Old Couple Story: The New Car

ELAR 19a, 59:42.

Art: <u>Nihii</u>, <u>ceesey</u> <u>nihii</u>, beh'eihehi' noh betebihehi'
<u>he'ih</u>-woonotiibee-no'.[2]

*Well, one time, uh, an old man and an old lady, I guess they got
a new car.*

<u>Neisonoo</u> nih-'oo3itoon-ei'eet, tih-'okeciihihi-noo.

My dad told us this story when I was a little kid.

<u>Nihii</u> <u>he'ih</u>-woonotiibee-no'.

Well, I guess they got a new car.

<u>He'ih</u>-'ee3nee-ceesiikoo: fifteen mph.

I guess it was not really very fast: top speed was fifteen mph.

WoteenP, nuhu' hooxono'o, nuhu'.

They got it in town, in Riverton, this car.

Earl: Yeah.

Yeah.

Art: Huu3e' nihii, Seventeen-Mile Crossing, ne'=nih-'iit-iine'etii-3i'
nuhu'.

*Over there, uh, at Seventeen-Mile Crossing,[3] that was where
these old folks lived.*

Earl: Uhh.

Uhh.

Art: Nuhu' toh-no'oeckoohu-3i',

When they got home,

'Oh he'iiP he'=iis-tou'kuuhu-3i nuhu', nih-'ii-t.

"Well, I wonder how you stop this car," the old man said.

<u>Hit-o'oowu-u'</u> nenee', <u>he'ih</u>-bi'-cih-noo'oekoo.

*At their house what happened, I guess he just drove around it in
circles.*

Noonoko' heetP koohinP
"You might as well . . . could you . . . ?"

3ebiini. . . . hiis-noo'oekoohu-noohok, heet-ne'-oowu-
ceno'oo-n, nih-'ii3-oot hi-betebihow.
*"There. . . . once I have driven around, then you will jump down
out of the car," he said to his old lady.*

Earl: Yeah.
Yeah.

Art: Ahh, ne'P hiis-noo'oekoohu-3i', hi-betebihow
ne'-oowu-ceno'oo-ni3.
*And then, after they had driven around, then his old lady
jumped down out of the car.*

Nih-teeteco'oo-t.
She went rolling over and over.

[[laughter]]
Noh hiiteto'oo-t.
Now it's his turn.

Noo'oekoohu-t.
He was still driving around the house.

Wohoe'-etn-iisiini nuhu'.
"I wonder how to manage this," he thought.

Nuhu' uhh haystack he'ih-[noohoot, woxu'.
This uh haystack, I guess he saw it, hay.

Earl: [Yeah.
                                          Yeah.

Art: Noonoko', heet-bi'-yihkoohu-t.
"I might as well . . ." he will just drive over there.

Sii=heete3eiP cih-niiyou [[gesture of smacking fist into hand]], he'ih-bi'-eete3ein nuhu'.

He just collided [[gesture of smacking fist into hand]], I guess he just ran into this haystack.

[[laughter]]

That's how he stopped his car.

[[laughter]]

((Brief explanation of the story in English))

The first time he, he just told his wife, "jump off!" and she went rolling like that.
[[laughter]]
When you told 'em in, uh, Arapaho, you know, you got much more meaning. When you change it to English, not . . . you lose about half of the story, the moral or the, how comical it is, and stuff like that.

((I retell the full story in English, for those present who don't speak Arapaho, concluding with:))

Cowell: He can't figure out how to stop the car, so he drives it into the haystack.

Art: Uhm-hmm.
          [[laughter]]
          Yeah.
          [[.3 sec.]]

The Old Couple and the Guts

Ron: [NihcenP
          She jumped . . .

Art: [That. . . .
          That . . .

Art: ci' ceese' hoo3itoo nihii . . .
          And another story uh. . . .

[[2 sec.]]

Betebihehi' noh <u>nehe'</u> beh'eihehi':

There was an old lady and this old man:

He'P he'=iisiini, nihP niihencebkoohut, <u>teecxo'</u>
he'ih-'itotiibi-no'.

*And somehow or other, a car, a long time ago I guess they
had a car.*

<u>He'ih</u>-noo'eiyei-no'.

I guess they were driving.

He'iitneeni-ni'i, teexootee-ni'i.

Somewhere or other, intestines were in the car.

Noh he'=iisiini he'iitnei'i [he'ih]-ceiboowuhcehi-no' hi'in
booo, booo.

And somehow somewhere, they swerved down off that road.

[he'ih]-hi3ecinoo'oo-no'.

They overturned.

'oh hoowe-esiinii-no'.

But they weren't injured.

'oh beebeet nuhu' nihii noo'oeyoo-no <u>he'ih</u>-noh'eise-nino.

But these intestines, I guess they were just scattered all over.

Nihii nehe' nih'oo3oo <u>he'ih</u>-ceikooh.

So, then I guess this white man drove up.

Cih-'oowuuni.

He came down here.

<u>He'ih</u>-noohoot nuh'uuno noo'oeyoo-no.

I guess he saw the guts.

Noh sii=ne'-necinoo'oo-t.

And then he fainted dead away.

Noo'oeyoo-no.
He saw the intestines.

Necinoo'oo-t.
Then he fainted.

He fainted.
[[laughter]]
He thought they, he thought they had a big, bad accident, and all the guts and everything were scattered all over.

[[laughter]]
Actually, they had just got it from the, from the . . . you know where they . . . the cattle yards and stuff like that.[4]

Cowell:　Okay, so it's the car that rolled off the road, yeah.

Art:　Uhm-hmm, and then scattered the insides, noo'oeyoo-no *[guts, innards]*.
They thought these people lost their, lost their guts.
[[laughter.]]
He fainted.

Cowell:　necinoo'oo-t.
He fainted.

Art:　Uhm-hmm, necinoo'oo-t.
Uhm-hmm, he fainted.

He, he fainted.
There's a lot of little stories like those there.[5]
[[2 sec.]]

Strong Bear Shakes Hands

Art:　howoo Tei'ox.
Also there was Strong Bear.

Nooxeihi' hee'inon-ot Tei'ox.
Maybe you know about him.

Earl: Tei'ox, yeah.
        Strong Bear, yeah.

Art: Uhm-hmm.
        Uhm-hmm.

Cowell: Hee.
        Yes.

Art: Nuhu' Sosoni' . . .
        At Shoshoni . . . [6]

Earl: Yeah.
        Yeah.

Art: Nih'eebe3iini nih'oo3oo tih-'entoo-hok.
        When whites were around, they would hang around there.

        Nuhu' hinono'ei-no', tih-'e3ebi-yihoo-3i',
        These Arapahos, when they went over there,

        He'ih-'ii-neniniixoo3-ei'i.
        I guess this guy was shaking their hands.

        He'ih'ini . . .
        I guess he was . . .

Earl: Yeah.
        Yeah.

Art: 3oo-3o'ohoen-ei'i.
        He was crushing their hands.

Earl: Yeah.
        Yeah.

Art: Nih-3oo-3o'ohoen-ei3i' hi'in.
        That guy was crushing their hands.

"Hello, chief."
"Hello, chief," he would say to them.

Ne-ihoowu-'unP.
"We can't do anything about it," the Arapahos said to Strong Bear.

He'ihP he'ih-bii-biih-ei'i.
I guess he was making them cry.

Heni'-bi'-cih-neesP nee'eesi-nihii-3i'.
That's just what they were saying about it as they returned home.

Nehe' Tei'ox ne'-cih-'e3ebP.
Then Strong Bear was coming there . . .

Nih-'e3ebP
He was going that way . . .

Wo'ooto' he3ebisee-t.
Just at that very moment he was going that direction.

No'usee-t.
He walked over there.

Wo'ei3 he'ih-no'uukoh-e'.
Or I guess maybe he rode there.

Earl: Uhm.
         Uhm.

Art: wohoe'-etP too-tousiini?
         "I wonder . . . what's going on?" he asked.

         Huu3e' nih'oo3oo nii-3oo-3o'ohoen-ei'eet.
         "Over there a white man is crushing our hands."

Nii-bii-biih-ei'eet.
"He's making us all cry."

Wohei chief, xoxu'un(?) nuhu'.
" 'Hello. chief,' this guy says to us."

Ne'-yihP yihxoh-oo3i'.
Then they took Strong Bear over there.

NiiP heebe3iihi' nih'oo3oo.
Here was this big white man.

<u>Wohei</u> hi'in nonoohow-oot Tei'ox.
Well, that guy sees Strong Bear.

Hello there, chief, hello there, chief, how are you?
"Hello there, chief, hello there, chief, how are you?"

I'll chief you, <u>he'ih</u>-'ii3-ee.
"I'll chief you," I guess Strong Bear said to him.

I'll chief you.
"I'll chief you."

Heet-neniiP neniniixoo3-eit.
The man is going to shake Strong Bear's hand.

Earl: Yeah.
          Yeah.

Art: <u>He'</u>=nehe' nih'oo3oo xonou ne'-hoonoxoniini nihii neyeisee-
          seyoun-o' hinee [hiicet-in.
          *I guess this white man, right away then, as hard as he could,
          he was trying to crush his hand.*

Earl: [yeah.
                                        yeah.

Art: 'oh <u>he'ih</u>-noxohoe-niisiwoo'oo, nih-'ii3-oot.

But I guess pretty quickly he was going down on his knees from the effort, Strong Bear said about him later.

Nih-<u>coon</u>iini.

He couldn't do it.

Wohei niixoo heet-seP niixoo heetniini seyoukuutii-noo heecet.

"Well now me too, I'm going to squeeze your hand too."

Bi'-nee'eestoo-t ceesey. [[gesture of rapidly closing one's hand]]

He just did like this one time.

Ne'-koxuuten, ne'-biih-oot hu'un nih'oo3ou'u.

Then suddenly, then he made that white man cry.

'oh "hoowooh-'uni,"nih-'ii-t, "ne-etne-ihoow-ooh-kohtowuP."

And "no more," the white man said, "I won't bother anyone anymore."

They said his hand looked like a little old geese or something, hanging.

They said his hand looked like a little old goose or something, hanging.

[[laughter.]]

<u>That's the story of Strong Bear.</u>

That's the story of Strong Bear.

Cowell: Yeah, Tei'ox.

Yeah, Strong Bear.

Art: Yeah, Tei'ox.

Yeah, Strong Bear.

There was a lot of 'em [stories] on him. Some pretty comical too. But he was real. When he died, it took twelve men to carry his coffin. And he was a real person. Those, my dad told a lot of short stories like that, about him, about the. . . . There's a lot of little short stories. Of course there's, nuhu' [*these ones*], true stories, like here [in Estes Park]. Gonna take a long time to tell. You know, like nii'ehiiho' ["*The Eagles*"], woxkoneehiiho' ["*The Bad Dreamers*"], nehe' honoh'oe ["*The Boy*"], uh. . . .

Cowell: Hinono'ei Honoh'oe *["The Arapaho Boy"]*

Art: Yeah, "The Arapaho Boy." You know, he went clear down to the caves [near Walsenburg, Colorado]. Those take a long time [to tell]. Uh, "The Apache Captive" that they [Utes] got from [the] Casper [band]. He was captured from here [in Estes Park area], but they moved from there [Casper].

Cowell: Yeah.

Art: From here they moved to Casper.

((ELAR 19a, 1:06:28))
((At this point Art continues mentioning other historical narratives told by his father and briefly evoking the plots of these (see Cowell and Moss 2005). Since I was interested in getting the conversation back to stories in Arapaho, I turned to the other two Arapaho speakers to ask if they could follow up on the story that Art had told about Strong Bear:))
((ELAR 19a, 1:08:17))

Cowell: Koo-he-e'in-eebe hoo3itoo-no hi'iihi' hinee Tei'ox?
           Do you guys know stories about that Strong Bear?

           [[1 sec.]]
Earl: Tei'ox beenhehe'.
           Strong Bear just a little bit.

           Beebeet nenee'.
           Just this one we heard.

           Ne-ihoow-no'ote'in, 'oh huut . . .
           I don't know a lot of them, but here. . . .

Believe it or Not: The Broken-Back Bear

Earl: Ceese' hinono'ei he'ih-'entoo.[7]
There was this one Arapaho.

'oh wot=he'ih-'oowuu3ei, hi'in.
And I guess he wasn't afraid of anything, that guy.

Hi'in heeyoohuu-ho he'ih-'ii-beet-neyei3itoo.
That one wanted to try just everything.

Nooxeihi' hoowuuP
Maybe he didn't. . . .

Hii-tousi-nihiitoon nuhu' tohuuP tohuu-cii3ootiini-',
How do you say it, when they don't fear anything?

Art: Hiihoho'neihi-t, howoh?
He is brave, right?

Earl: Hiihoho'nP [yeah,
Brave, yeah,

Art: [yeah.
yeah.

Earl: he'ih-'iihoho'neih.
He was fearless.

Heeyouhuu he'ih-bi'-neyei3itii nuhu'.
This one just tried anything.

Howoo hoh'eni' he'ih-'entoono' he'iitoxnenii-no'.
And one time there were a number of them up in the mountains.

Nooxeihi' hihcebe', teesi' he'ihP he'ih-noohob-eeno' woxuu.
Maybe up there, on top of a mountain, they saw a bear.

He'ih-cih-niihisee-n nuhu' booon-e', cih-'oowuuni.
It was going along a trail coming this direction, downhill this way.

Noonowun, wohei heet-ne'-oowusee-noo.
In the meantime, "Well then, I will go down there," the fearless one said.

Heet-cou'uh-o' nuhu' wox, he'ih-'ii.
"I will mess with this bear," he said.

Nehe' ne'iini . . . woxec ci' nooxeihi', he'ih-'ini woxec.
Then this guy. . . . a marsh maybe too, there was a marsh there.

[He'ih]-bis-nehee3ei.
He took off all his clothes.

He'ih-bisiini woxesii nuhu' wo'teenoxes.
He painted himself all over with this black mud.

Ne'iini hiisibi-t nuhu' booon-e'.
Then he lay down in the trail.

Hini'iit wox he'ih-cih-no'usee.
That bear walked down here where he was.

Noh he'ih-3i'ookuu nuhu'.
And this bear stood there.

[He'ih]-noo'oexoot-owun.
The bear walked around the place where he was.

Heihii hii'oxon-oot.
Eventually, it got closer to where he was.

[He'ih]-no'oxuuhet nehe' wox.
The bear worked his way up to the spot.

Nooxeihi' <u>he'ih</u>-nee-nehyonih-e'.
Maybe it was checking him out.

[<u>He'ih</u>]-heenei3ecen-e'.
It rolled him over several times.

Noh <u>he'ih</u>-neciibee.
And the man played dead.

Heihii <u>he'ih</u>-no'oxuuhet hi'in hihe'(?) nowoo3iihi'.
Eventually, the bear worked his way over to the man's left side.

[[chuckles]]
Heihii <u>he'ih</u>-3i'ookuu.
Eventually, the man was stood up by the bear.

[[chuckles]]
<u>He'ih</u>-3owoto'oo.
He was being pushed upright by the bear.[8]

[[laughter]]
Beexoo3iihi' "'oh hei-toustoo?" <u>he'ih</u>-'ii.
A little later, "What are you doing?" the man said.

[[chuckles]]
Nih-i'-tooyeit-o' wox.
The bear screamed involuntarily due to this.

Ne'-einei3e'ee-towotoooyo-' nuh'uuno.
Then it twisted around so suddenly it broke its back and fell down dead.[9]

[[laughter]]
<u>He'ih</u>-'ii-benoot nuhu'.
It was sniffing this guy.

Art: Yeah.
         Yeah.

Earl: Nowoo3.
         On the left side.[10]

         [[2 sec.]]
Art: Hoh'onookee NooP Hoh'onookee Nookeih
         nih-'oonoo3itoon-einoo.
         White Rock told me that one too.

         [[1.5 sec.]]
Cowell: Hee'inon-o',
         I know that story about that one,

Art: Yeah.
         Yeah.

Cowell: Hinee, hinee wox.
         That, that bear.

Earl: Wox, yeah.
         Bear, yeah.

         [[laughter]]
         [[1.5 sec.]]
Art: Ci'=nih-'oo3itoon-einoo hini'iit nihii, nehe' nihii hinen: he'ih-
         'iisiiten-e' nehe' wox.
         *He also told me that one, uh, about this, uh, man: this bear
         grabbed him.*

         He'ih-coonP coon-cesiikoh-oe.
         He couldn't get away from her.

         Konoo'=nih-'iis-cih-koxo'-ceenoho'oe-t.*[11]
         *So he just decided to slowly lower his hand down here
         under her.*

Nuh'uuno nooxeihi' nihii hoxehesei neneeni-ni3.
This bear maybe, uh, it was a female bear.

<u>He'ih</u>-cooP coocoo'uh-oe.
He was molesting her.

Heihii <u>he'ih</u>-ni'eeneet-owun.
Pretty soon she was liking it.

Hee3nee-ni'ouuwutP ni'ouuwutii-ni3.
She was really feeling good there.

<u>He'ih</u>-'eh-ciinen-e'.
She loosened her grip on him.

<u>He'ne'</u>-oosei3o'oo-t hi'in honoh'oe.
The young man fell backwards away from her.

Ne'=nih-'iis-tokohow-oot.
That's how he ran away from her.

<u>He'ih</u>-ce'e'ein.
He turned and looked back.

he'=iis-ce'eeti3-e'.
She was calling him back.

[[laughter]] [[3 sec.]]

((Audiotape 19a, 1:11:12))
((Art then repeats the story in English, concluding with this line:))
((Audiotape 19a, 1:11:43.5))

Art: And he looked back, and the bear was calling him back.
       [[laughter]] [[4 sec.]]
       <u>That's a Nih'oo3oo [trickster] story.</u> Uhm-hmm.
       [[3 sec.]][12]

At this point, no one followed up with a story, and the conversation moved back to talking about different genres and types of Arapaho stories, including discussion of historical stories about the Estes Park area. Then the conversation moved on to discussing who still knew these stories, as well as criticizing those who take on ceremonial roles without the proper knowledge, without really knowing about the ceremony. From there, the conversation moved to a long discussion of proper respect, proper modes of storytelling, the imperative not to cut stories short or leave out parts (with the same being true for ceremonies), and similar ideas. By then Earl had apparently had enough of this mode of talk, because he reoriented the conversation, leading to a second story sequence. Here the transcription begins with the concluding parts of Art's comments, followed by Earl's intervention.

((ELAR 19b, 19:00))

Art: Ahm, you can, you can tell from my dad's [true, historical] stories, how it's translated, how it kind of changes, you know. I had to translate it . . . they don't translate, translate literally. And then XXX, they said, "leave it alone. Don't translate it. You might maybe be gettin' away from the real point of the story." I had to streamline "The Eagles." But, you know, I might be getting off. . . .

Earl: nih'ini, nih-'oonoxoobeti-3i'.
They said things to make each other laugh.

Nuhu' beh'eihoho', tih-'ii-notonihei-3i', nuhu' heesowobeihi-ni3, 'oh nih-neyeiP heeneecohoxuuh-oo3i'.
These old men, when they were doctoring, this one, the one who is sick, well they tried to work him back to strength.

Nih-'oonoxoohowooP.
They made him laugh.

Art: Uhm-hmm.
Uhm-hmm.

Earl: Ne'=nih-'iisiini tonoun-ou'u nuhu' heeteetoo-no.
That's how they used those old-time stories.

Art: Yeah.
        Yeah.

Earl: neyei-hoowooP hoowu-kokoh'oeneet nuhu' hesowohiit; wootii
        he3ebiini,
        *The patient tries not to think about this disease; and I guess as
        time goes on,*

Art: Yeah.
        Yeah.

Earl: 3ebiini, heihii ne'e-e3eb-nonih'i-t nuhu' hee3ouubeihi-t.
        Later, pretty soon, then he forgets about how he feels.

Art: Uhm-hmm.
        Uhm-hmm.

Earl: Ne'=nih-'iis-een-eeceheteebeti-3i'. . . .[13]
        *That was how they eventually talked each other back to
        strength. . . .*

Art: Uhm-hmm.
        Uhm-hmm.

Earl: Nuhu'.
        These old men.

Art: Yeah.
        Yeah.

        [[1 sec.]]

John Plume: Story 1

Art: Howoo nihii, nehe' nihii, John Plume [14]
        That reminds me of this John Plume,

Earl: Yeah.
        Yeah.

Art: Nehe' koyih'o, nih-notonih-oot.
This R. was doctoring him.

Ahh, henee3neen-esowobeihi-noo ne3e'ee, nih-'ii-t.
"Ahh, I am really sick, nephew," John P. said.

heetP heet-cihP heet-cih-won-noteiitih-e3en, noh heet-notonih-in.
*"I will come seek you out to help me," John P. said, "and you
will doctor me."*

Earl: Hee.
Yes.

Art: Wohei, nih-'ii-t, nehe' R.
"Okay," R. said.

Nihii, wohei, heet-notonih-e3en.
Uh, "okay, I will doctor you."

Toot-he-esowowutii?
"Where is it hurting?"

Wohei nuhu' ne-3eesino', noh hinee heet-tontinee-noo.
"Well, between my testicles, and my rectum."

[[laughter]]
Ne'-ii3-eit nee'eetP 'oh hookoh nee'eesowowutii-noo, neet-cihP
heet-cihP
Heet-cih-notonih-in.
*Then he told him, "That is where, and because that is where I
am hurting, you will doctor me here, in this place," John Plume
said to R.*

[[chuckles]]
Noh hee3P heet-nee'eesiini.
And "that's what I will do," R said to him.

[[chuckles]]

So ne'P wohei, nih-'ii3-eit, het-nehee3ei-t, nehe' John Plume.

So then, "okay," R told him to take off his clothes, he told this John Plume.

Hee; nih-yii3e'eini-t.

"Okay," then he put his head down there.[15]

Ne'=nih-'ii'-be3eeyeitoo-t nuhu'. [[retching sound]]

Then he was making a retching sound to suck out the badness in the body [[retching sound]]

[[laughter]]

'oh nehe', nei-nistoot, nehe' nei3oo, ceib-toun-o', heetihP . . .

"And this thing of mine, my penis," John Plume. says; he was holding it off to the side, so that . . .

[[laughter]]

heetihP heetihP heetih-ni'iini niiniP niini'iiton-eit.

so that R could fix up the sore area for him.

[[chuckles]]

Ceibi-toun-o' nuhu'.

He was holding it off to the side.

'oh nih-'ii-be3eeyeitoo-t.

And R. was making that retching sound.

[[chuckles]]

He'iitP nuhu', he'iiP he'iiP he'ii-cisiini ne'-cesP cesiiP cesiikoh-einoo

nehe' nei3oo, nih-'ii-t.

"At some point this, at some point, then my penis got away from me," John Plume. said.

Earl: yehei!

Gee!

Art: Nih-'ee3neen-eete'eih-iit nuhu'.

He really knocked him loopy on the head with his genitals.

[[laughter]]
[[2.5 sec.]]
That's one of them crazy ones, crazy stories.

((ELAR 19b, 21:50.5))
((Art explains the story in English for some of the listeners.))
((ELAR 19b, 22:31))

Art: There's a lot of stories, funny stories like that.
[[chuckles]]
[[3 sec.]]
Uhh, R., uhh, R., uhh, Koyih'o hih-'oowoe'iyei.
R., he was woozy, unconscious.

Earl: Yeah.
Yeah.

Art: Yeah. Nih-no'o3ih-einoo, nih-'ii-t.
Yeah. "It really knocked me for a loop," he said.

[[laughter]]
[[3 sec.]]
Art: So he must have had a big . . .
So he must have had a big . . .

Earl: A big one.
A big one.

Art: A big one.
A big one.

[[laughter]]
'Cause he said when it slipped out of his hand, it hit R. over the head.
[[laughter]]
[[1.5 sec.]]

John Plume: Story 2

Earl: <u>Ceesey</u> nih-3iixowotoooyo-'ohk, <u>nuhu' wooxo'oe-t.</u>
One time he apparently strained his back, this John Plume.

Ne'-yihkoohu-t Lander.
Then he drove off to Lander.

Doctor, he-ih-toustoo? <u>he'ih-</u>'ii3-e'.
The doctor, "What did you do?" I guess the doctor said to him.

His back, nii-coon-xouuwuwoo3ii-noo.
His back, "I can't straighten it out," he told the doctor.

Art: Umm.
Umm.

Earl: Wohei, <u>he'ih-</u>'ii, neetotoohoe, ceenen-oo hon-otooho, <u>he'ih-</u>'ii3-e'.
"Okay," I guess the doctor said, "Take off your pants, pull down your pants," I guess he said to him.

Ne'-ceenen-o'.
Then he pulled them down.

[[chuckles]]
Rubber gloves, nih-ciiciito'on-oot.
He put on rubber gloves.

[[chuckles]]
Vaseline.
He put Vaseline on his anus.

[[chuckles]]
'oohoohei, too-tou3ei'oo-nino his fingers![16]
"Oh my gosh, how big the doctor's fingers are!" GQ thought to himself.

[[laughter]]
[He'ih]-heebetook.
George's eyes were big.

[[chuckles]]
Ne'-inowohoe-t huu3e'.[17]
Then the doctor stuck his finger(s) in there.

[[chuckles]]
Koseineekuu3ei-t.
John Plume's back made popping sounds.

[[chuckles]]
Ne'-xouuwukuu3-oot.
That made him stand up straight!

[[laughter]] [[1.5 sec.]]

Art: <u>That's what they do, them doctors</u>, you know, when you have a pulled back or something. They get rubber gloves, put Vaseline on there. Goose you. You have to be careful, [[chuckles]] because you always have to make sure that the two hands aren't holding you. It might be his penis that's going up your rectum.
[[laughter]] [[5 sec.]][18]
Hoonoyooh-owu', hoonoyoohoot-owu' heet-cihP hiicet-ino nuhu' notoniheihii.
Watch out for that doctor's hands!

[[laughter]] [[2 sec.]]

Earl: Yeah.
Yeah.

Art: Niisoonee-ni', niisooneeniini-'ehk, 'oh hihctii'kuu3-eit.
If there are two of them on him, then he's having anal sex with him

[[laughter]]
Said he's grabbing a freebie off you.

[[laughter]]

A lot of stories like that, when they're told in Arapaho, they're a lot [more] . . . real funny, comical.

[[3 sec.]]

So, you can make a little book out of [them], like that, out of small, short stories. And they're, they're common. But, you know, if we, let 'em go, just, we'll lose 'em forever, the small stories, short stories, these comical ones.

Because an uncle used to tease his nephew. Same thing, vice versa.

Cowell: Yeah

Art: They used to tease each other.

Cowell: Hee, tii3i3.[19]
           Hello, kidney!

Art: Yeah. And uh, that's, they used to always tell stories. Even his grandpa would tell a story about him, because R. was on crutches.

        He said, ahh, nehe' neito'ei, heet-niitookooyei-t.

        "Ahh, my relative is taking part in the fasting/ceremony," his grandfather said.

        Koyih'o, heet-wone-esoohow-o', nih-'ii-t.

        "R., I will go watch him," the grandfather said.

        Cii-niiheniini.

        "On his own he can't dance properly."

Earl: Yeah.
         Yeah.

Art: Tebkuusiini, heetn-iisiini nuhu'.

        "Only in a broken way, that's how this one will dance."

        Wone-esooku'ooP

        He went over to watch on,

heii; nih-bee-bee3too-3i'.

"Okay, come on!" the announcer called; they were finishing up the preparations.

ne'-cesisto'owu-t,

"Then when the drum starting being hit,"

ne'-ee3nee-niihen-nih'ko'usi-', nih'iit.[20]

"Then he was truly self-propelled, going off in all directions," he said.

[[laughter]]

((ELAR 19b, 25:52))

((Art provides a brief translation of the preceding story. The conversation then moves into a general discussion of teasing relationships in Arapaho, with Earl taking the lead in telling a story about a joke some kids played on one older man.))

In this chapter, I have actually presented two story sequences that occurred within the same long conversation. The sequences are not quite as seamless as those in other chapters, because the speakers felt the need to stop and translate their stories into English for some of those present, or allow someone else to do this for them, but the general features of story chains are clearly present in both cases. The first chain is initiated after a significant (nine-second) pause in the conversation. The preceding anecdotes are in general funny and, secondarily, focused on poor choices of words or mispronunciations in the context of a description. In concluding these stories, the speaker notes that there are "a lot" of stories like that, which is a clear invitation for someone else to tell something similar. When no one does, the same speaker then begins the story about the old couple and their new car. It, too, is comical and, more specifically, features a comic misunderstanding in which someone makes himself look foolish, so it is a fitting follow-on from the preceding narratives.

The story of the old couple and the new car, however, brings some entirely new themes into the conversation. Like other "old couple" or "old folk" stories (including John Plume stories), it centers on the gap between older people and new Euro-American technologies. Based on the top speed of the car, the story appears to be set in the early 1900s, perhaps even prior to World War I, though it was certainly very uncommon for any Arapaho people to own cars at that time (many Arapaho families did not get their first car until the 1950s, relying on wagons until that time). The narrator notes he heard this story when he was a little kid, from his dad. The narrator was born in 1938, his father in 1911, so he would likely have heard it in the 1940s. The story may simply be proverbial, of course. (I presented another version of the story in chapter 4, where the issue is brake failure, rather than purchase of a new car where the braking mechanism is not understood.) In both versions however, the central comic moment of the story for Arapaho listeners is the image of the old lady rolling and tumbling over and over after she jumps out of the car.

The follow-up story of the old couple and the guts refers to the common practice of searching for cattle intestines in the Wind River, downstream from Riverton, Wyoming, before and after World War II. There was formerly a meat-processing plant in Riverton, and cattle waste from the processing was simply dumped into the river. The Arapahos, most of whom were chronically short of money, would wade into the river and retrieve the intestines, which they cooked and ate, along with other cattle parts. In this story, the old couple are again not especially familiar with the technology of the car, as they run off the road and overturn (again, at a slow rate of speed, suggesting a very early model of car—though this story has an even stronger feel of being prosaic). In this case, it is the white man who is target of the most intense humor, when he comes along and sees the spilled cattle guts all over the road. He thinks that they are human internal organs and faints from shock. Note that here, as in many other stories, the conclusion is provided in a fairly deadpan and understated way, leaving the listener to recognize the full implications of the situation. The element of misunderstanding or comic haplessness is the unifying feature of the two stories, as well as the feature tying them to the preceding anecdotes. As noted in chapter 4, "old folks" stories are often told after the narrator has personally been in an embarrassing or potentially face-threatening situation. In this case, the stories follow stories of third parties (war veterans) being placed in such a situation. These stories seem to have a general mitigating function regarding moments of threat to or loss of face. They perhaps all have a generalized connotation of "it can happen to other people too," which generalizes and de-individualizes the loss of face.

We have also seen that old folks stories sometimes involve Euro-Americans, but these figures are peripheral and never seem to "get the joke" or be aware of the humor in the situation. The second story told here is an extreme extension of that tendency—the Euro-American himself becomes the butt of the joke (though he also makes one think of the old Arapaho man described in chapter 4 who faints from fear when his wife touches his back, then faints again when he regains consciousness and sees her face).

Why then follow these two stories with a Strong Bear story? It is difficult to say exactly. One very simple explanation is geographic proximity within the stories. The guts story is situated around Riverton, Wyoming. In other versions of the "Strong Bear Shakes Hands" story, a specific location is given, and it is along the Wind River just beyond Riverton as well (plus, the new car was also bought in Riverton). So the narrator follows up with another funny story involving Arapahos and white people that occurs around Riverton.

Perhaps a more important point to consider, however, is that the narrator has just told a series of anecdotes and stories that all focus on mistakes by or lack of strong agency on the part of Arapaho people, to an audience that includes both Native Americans of other tribes and Euro-Americans. In contrast to the preceding stories, Strong Bear presents the most strongly agentive view of an Arapaho person among all the genres we have examined. The story offers the narrator a chance to counter the "hapless comic Arapaho" image with a much stronger one. Moreover, the narrator picks the specific Strong Bear story in the genre where Strong Bear acts most forcefully on Euro-Americans: this is the only one where he physically debilitates someone (turning a man's hand into pulp), as opposed to simply bending his gun, assaulting his horses, throwing him out of a tent, or shaking him like rag doll. In this sense, the story parallels the second old couple story about the spilled guts, which presents the strongest effects on a Euro-American among any story in that genre. In the Strong Bear story, the white man ends up on his knees, while in the old couple story he ends up in a dead faint on the road. The sequence thus concludes with very strong Arapaho agency and very weak Euro-American agency.

There may also have been more personal reasons for the narrator to choose this story and genre. In the earlier parts of the conversation, before the trickster stories were told, the two narrators talked about their past personal experiences, and this narrator mentioned in particular how he had been tricked into playing for the St. Stephens Mission (near Riverton) basketball team, then kicked out of the school before graduating once the basketball season was over. This was a memory that he recounted to me, or to others in my presence, multiple times over the years. He usually included the detail that he vowed to go back to St. Stephens later and beat the heck out of the priest who wronged him. But when he finally got back there, the priest was so old and decrepit, he decided it wasn't worth the trouble to beat him up. It would be difficult to say with certainty whether the Strong Bear story he chose to tell at this point in the sequence projected his own desires and feelings toward that priest at St. Stephens, which he had described earlier—in particular, his feelings of lack of agency in the past and strong desire for vengeance later—but it certainly seems possible to me.

The sequence picked up again after a break when I directed a question to Earl about whether he knew any Strong Bear stories, which obviously put him on the spot. He responded that the only one he knew was the one Art had told earlier. But he then continued with a believe-it-or-not story about a bear that breaks its back from fright. Indeed, it is the same believe-it-or-not story that Oliver Toll heard in 1914, this time shared in a hotel room likely only a few miles from the 1914 campsite. I find it interesting that Earl added details at the beginning of the story about the fearlessness of the Arapaho individual who scared the bear. I have never heard those details included with other tellings, even much longer versions. It appears that Earl added these details about the courage (and implicitly, agency) of the Arapaho hero of the story in order to present it as maximally similar to the preceding narrative about Strong Bear. This contrasts with the typical believe-it-or-not story, where the main characters are usually accidentally successful, to the extent they succeed in their endeavors at all. Earl's story also picks up on the elements of surprise and misperception that occurred in the earlier old couple stories, especially the one about the guts spilled on the road. It also resonates with other old folks stories that revolve around old people being shocked by fear, though in this case it is the bear that is shocked by fear.

Art then responds with another story about a bear that gets more than she expected—and moreover another story attributed to an elder named White Rock. It is again a story in which the bear is the butt of the joke— as typically occurs in all genres of Arapaho stories. Generically, Art calls it a *Nih'oo3oo* 'trickster' story, but in fact, he describes the person as simply a human, and when I have heard this story from others, they likewise do not mention the trickster, but rather simply "a man." It seems closer to another believe-it-or-not story than anything else. The big difference between the two stories is that one bear ends up dead, the other much happier. Probably most importantly from the standpoint of social action, Art's story serves to retrospectively validate Earl's choice of the preceding story and to reinforce the direction in which Earl took the story sequence, thus building solidarity between the two narrators.

As a sequence, we can see the stories move from comic victimhood to mitigation and then agency for the Arapaho characters, which is then nuanced by more comic forms of agency as the sequence concludes. In terms of structure and genre, two anecdotes of linguistic mistakes are followed by two old couple stories, followed by a Strong Bear story with certain thematic if not generic links to the preceding, but which is primarily reactive and contrastive in relation to the preceding stories and genres. Then two believe-it-or-not stories occur, in which links to the preceding Strong Bear story are creatively engineered in the moment, in part in response to a mildly face-threatening question regarding the narrative repertoire of one of the participants. The sequence is clearly more variable and complex than the more-or-less single-narrator sequence of Strong Bear stories examined in chapter 2. By the time the sequence is over, the two narrators have collectively produced a sequence that leads to interesting resonances between bears and Euro-Americans! Both of these characters commonly seem to misperceive situations and to underestimate the resourcefulness of Arapaho people in ways that leave them at best the butt of jokes and at worst severely debilitated (or dead).

The second sequence is quite different from the first. Earl changes the direction of the discussion by explicitly evoking the idea of "making each other laugh" and telling comical stories. This is a clear invitation for someone to produce such a story. Earl provides a very specific additional context by invoking the use of such stories in traditional Arapaho medicine and healing practices. This is not at all surprising, since Earl was a noted traditional medicinal practitioner within the tribe.

Art takes up the invitation and produces a highly appropriate comical John Plume story that focuses specifically on traditional medicinal practices, thus demonstrating his large narrative repertoire and skill at deploying just the right narrative in just the right moment. In this story, as in "John Plume Visits the Proctologist" (presented in chapter 7), John is a medical patient. The story that is told here resonates strongly with the one in chapter 7, though in indirect ways. In both, John finds himself in a funny position and the doctor (though in this case an Arapaho healer) engages in a treatment that clearly has sexual resonances. The overall situation is comical, even absurd, in both. And in both we have amusing sound effects—retching in this story, popping in the other. Furthermore, this story also resonates with the plot summary given in chapter 7, where John looks down through his bifocals at his genitals and says *'oohoohei!*, suggesting great size or quantity. While the common understanding of that story is that John's new glasses are magnifying his body parts, here he apparently really does have very large genitals—enough to knock the unfortunate healer loopy when they hit him on the head! Art has thus produced a perfectly deployed narrative from a syntagmatic perspective, and that narrative is much richer if one has paradigmatic awareness of the John Plume genre more broadly.

Earl then immediately follows this story with his own version of the "Visiting the Proctologist" story, adding syntagmatic effects to the pragmatic ones of the sequence. Note, in contrast to the version of the story in chapter 7, this version has no particular reference to the overall strangeness of the experience or setting for John, and thus little potential to recapitulate a colonial encounter. Here, the point is simply to produce a parallel comical and absurd medical scenario to the first one, with parallel sexual resonance and parallel sound effects, as a way of showing the narrator's skill while also building solidarity with the other participants.

Art further emphasizes the sexual component by his remarks at the end of the story. I find these remarks interesting in that they are a way of retrospectively undoing some of the parallelism of the two stories, in a way beneficial to the Arapaho perspective. As described in chapter 7, "Visiting the Proctologist" is in large part a mockery of Euro-American medicinal practice. The two John Plume stories in the sequence here, however, suggest a potential mockery of Arapaho medicinal practice as well, in the presence of a highly prominent tribal medicinal practitioner—not to mention non-Arapahos in the audience who may not fully grasp the dynamics going on between Earl and Art. Admittedly, the face threat is low here—Earl has invited a comical story and specifically set up the traditional healing framework, then laughed heartily at the first story before offering his own. Nevertheless, by overtly describing the possible sexual activity of the Euro-American doctor in the second case (in his remarks after the story), Art presents Euro-American doctors as actively perverse, while the Arapaho doctor is just comically unlucky, so that the Euro-American agency takes on a negative component.

Yet another face threat is avoided at the same time: the Arapaho doctor being described, whose name was given in the story, was actually Art's uncle, and all the Arapahos present would know this. But rather than presenting his uncle as the object of the joke, Art's ending comments more clearly differentiate the uncle from the putative Euro-American doctor "grabbing a freebie." Incidentally, the remarks also emphasize a general Arapaho theme that occurs across many contexts—the idea that white people are both oversexed and strangely sexed. This has perhaps greater resonance in the moment if we think back to the preceding sequence, which concluded with an implied comparison between white people and bears, and specifically with a very sexual bear. Now it concludes with a very sexual white doctor.

The situation takes an ethnographic turn at this point, as Art emphasizes the value (and ubiquity) of these common, comical stories. In calling them "short" he explicitly contrasts them with traditional myths, legends, or historical accounts, which he talked about in the conversation that occurred between the two story sequences, and which he emphasized "take a long time to tell." He then concludes this sequence by telling another story about R., who was featured in the preceding John Plume story. R. is taking part in the Sun Dance, but he was permanently injured as a child by falling into a fire, and thus has to use crutches. Generically, the story has much in common with old folks stories in that the protagonist is physically debilitated and "pitiful" in the Arapaho sense of someone who is worthy of pity and sympathy. The story also illustrates the theme of in-law teasing that Art has just mentioned. The punch line is that once the drum starts beating, R. looks like he is "self-propelled." In other words, his body seems to be moving in all different directions on its own, as if there is no single, controlling will directing it. The Arapaho word thus comically describes his attempts to dance with his crutches. The story also illustrates Art's claim that the stories are much funnier in Arapaho, as the punch line has to be explained laboriously in English. The wrap-up thus returns to many of the themes Earl set up in his opening to the sequence: humor; medicinal practice and Arapaho doctors; and the use of humor for healing, good feelings, and social solidarity.

Although I have treated these as two separate sequences, they have much in common. They each subtly play with issues of either personal or tribal embarrassment or loss of face, or at least the potential for this. They also both include depictions of lack of knowledge or agency among the Arapaho people in the face of Euro-American colonialism—a theme that is a common feature of the individual genres explored earlier. Individual status, social cohesion, or both are often depicted as under threat, either implicitly or explicitly. The sequences offer interesting examples of the way that these potentials are mitigated through humor and of how humor is used agentively in performance to produce social solidarity. Arapaho society includes institutionalized teasing relationships, as well as respect/avoidance relationships. It is also a society where the serious and the comical or absurd are often at a very small remove from each other, and where people are quick to deploy humor to capture the comical or absurd elements of even the most serious occasions. Earl's opening invocation to the second sequence, evoking laughter and healing, encapsulates this close relationship, and the entirety of what follows can be seen as an exploration of humor's connection to health, danger, and even life-threatening—if nevertheless comical—situations.

From a more performative perspective, the second sequence is a very nice example of a story request, followed by two stories that respond to that request. Note that although the genres of stories may switch, there tend to be at least two stories in each genre. This is an important element of the performance, and of demonstrating one's narrative competence: knowing one appropriate story to fit into a sequence is the minimum for successful collaboration, but knowing two different stories, both of which fit into the sequence and which also sequence well with each other without being exactly alike, is a much more impressive accomplishment. Equally important is the ability to use an appropriate thematic fulcrum or stylistic maneuver to shift between genres in a way that is not awkward or abrupt: Art uses R. as the common theme to shift from the John Plume to the old folks genre in the second sequence, while Earl uses some additional opening evaluative comments to shift from the Strong Bear to the believe-it-or-not genre in the first sequence. Yet another key skill is the ability to use just the right amount of meta-narrative commentary to either set up a following story or subtly alter interpretations of a preceding one. Both sequences are very impressive collaborative sociolinguistic accomplishments, emergent in the process of performance but also the product of much prior social knowledge and practice on the part of both participants.

My analysis has focused on issues of solidarity and collaborative achievement, but we should not forget the other individuals in the room, who are in fact not a part of this collaborative achievement. They included me (a researcher who understood and spoke Arapaho, but not fluently), another older man (a native speaker of Arapaho who never participated in the story sequences, other than occasional back-channeling, nods, and laughter), a University of Colorado, Boulder, graduate student (with some familiarity with Arapaho), and a young Navajo park service ranger (unfamiliar with Arapaho). There was no effort to include these others in the collective performance, so the solidarity in many ways was limited to that constructed between Art and Earl. One might object that Arapaho language issues limited the other participants, but this was clearly not the case with the other elder. And in fact, even when the conversation switched into English, it was dominated entirely by Art and Earl. Thus, while they developed solidarity with each other as narrators of the collective performance, they also displayed cultural and narrative knowledge in a way that clearly established their preeminence over the others in the group. Earl was a widely respected healer, and Art was at the time co-chair of the tribal Language and Culture Commission, so this status was already socioculturally ratified. The two men had also played key roles during the day's consultations in Rocky Mountain National Park, so their importance was apparent to the entire group, even those who had not previously known about the details of the two men's Arapaho social positioning. This performance was therefore not necessary to establish their roles and identities in the group, but it certainly further ratified those roles and identities. The respect for these elders and the acquiescence to their lead roles shown by the rest of the group was, of course, its own form of solidarity—solidarity with values of elder respect in particular. But that solidarity was based on recognizing differential knowledge and differential rights to participation and sharing of such knowledge.

To conclude the discussion, I turn to a few remarks on the technical and linguistic aspects of the story turns. As I will also note in chapter 6, the act of explicitly mentioning telling a story or having been told a story (intransitive *hoo3itee-* transitive *hoo3itoot-* 'tell a specific story' or *hoo-3itoon-* 'tell a story to someone') often serves as a means of invoking an extended storytelling turn for oneself. Art also regularly makes use of *ci'* or *howoo* (both meaning 'and also') either to claim the right to tell a second story of his own or to follow up someone else's story with something in the same genre or on the same theme. More subtly, he also uses the hesitation particle *nihii* ('well . . . , uh . . . ') to claim the floor, since it has the secondary implication of asking the listener to wait for the speaker. He does use this particle internally to his stories at times, but he uses it every single time that he starts a story, typically more than once, which suggests that in these cases he is using the particle as a turn-extension device. Irina Wagner (2021, 92–105) has shown that repair mechanisms such as this are often used to initiate story sequences in Arapaho more generally, and that the same is true across other languages as well.

Finally, after telling the two old couple stories, Art seems to invite someone else to begin a narrative. When no one else does, he then initiates the Strong Bear story. But he goes out of his way to ask Earl if he knows about Strong Bear (to which Earl replies yes, at least a little bit). This exchange seems to be as much a request for permission to proceed with a story in this new genre (and to continue telling stories generally, since he has used up his standard two-story sequence already) as a question about Earl's knowledge. Functionally speaking, Earl's affirmative response grants Art permission to proceed. Somewhat similarly, Earl's word-search questions to Art at the start of his story about the bear are interpretable, at least in part, as a polite indicator of the type of story he is about to tell, as well as an effort to show clearly the thematic links between his story and the preceding one, since his narrative will be of a different genre.

Having now presented a chain with a single narrator and a chain dominated by two narrators, in the next chapter I look at an even more complex chain involving several narrators.

6

Story Sequence B

Arapahoe, Wyoming (2016)

The following chain of stories emerged from a longer conversation that took place in an elementary school library on the Wind River Reservation in January 2016. Several elders had gathered to work on a new language app for smartphones. I was present to help transcribe the Arapaho for them. I had my video camera along, and with their permission I turned it on as we were waiting for the work to begin, and again as we were eating lunch. I knew that these pre-meeting moments were often occasions for interesting Arapaho conversation and storytelling. I initially filmed by holding the relatively small video camera in one hand while also participating in the interactions documented here, but later put it on a tripod off to the side. I use a camera that is hand-sized and fairly inconspicuous, not because I want to hide it, but because I feel that large, bulky cameras are more intimidating and render the atmosphere less relaxed and casual. None of the participants wore individual microphones, as this also greatly alters the interactional dynamic. I am interested in documenting naturally ongoing interaction as much as possible, and stopping conversation in order to set up large cameras on tripods and put individual microphones on people is counterproductive to this goal.

The men and women chatted, mostly in Arapaho, as they waited for everyone to arrive, then continued talking mostly in Arapaho as they ate lunch prior to the working session. The conversation was extremely wide-ranging, including talking about new words that had recently been created, talking about additional new words that were needed, extending general greetings, getting food and drinks properly served, discussing past times and differences between then and the present, and other topics. Meanwhile, the dynamics shifted from two or three subconversations among the half-dozen or so elders to a single general conversation. In the portions of the conversation immediately preceding what is documented here, a side conversation was going on between two speakers, while the other four speakers (documented in the transcription) had been discussing older people who had passed away, and where exactly they used to live on the east side of the reservation (in the area where the school is). In conjunction with each person mentioned, participants also shared memories of that person. One speaker brought up a particular person who had been a noted storyteller:

Historical Anecdote: "Chief Black Coal Planted Those Trees"

((Told originally by Ce'in; ELAR 133d, 0:21))

> Ron: <u>Keih-niitoni-be</u> betebi, uhh Betty Harper hiinoon? [[gesture: trying to remember a name]]
> *Did you hear of that old lady, uh, Betty Harper's [real name] mother?*

> Bill: Ooohh . . .
> *Ooohh . . .*

> Ron: <u>Remember</u>, she used to stay there? [[gesture: a little house]]
> *Remember, she used to stay/live there?*

> Bill: Yeah.
> *Yeah.*

> Ron: Andy['s place], yeah.
> *Andy's place, yeah.*

> Bill: Yeah.
> *Yeah.*

> Ron: Nih-<u>'oo3itoon</u>-ei'eet nih-'iitP nehe' big tree over there. [[gesture: pointing "over there"]]
> *She used to tell us stories about that big tree over there.*

> Bill: Yeah, yeah.
> *Yeah, yeah.*

> Ron: Black Coal nih-3i'ookuuh-ei3i'. [[gesture: sticking something into the ground]]

"Chief Black Coal put up those trees," [she told us].[1]

His lance, nih-3oo'oekuusetii-t. [[gesture: sticking a lance into the ground]]
"His lance, he stuck it firmly in the ground."

Nenee', neneeni-t, nuhu' tree. [[gesture: pointing at lance in ground; pointing at tree "over there"]]
"That [lance], this one is it, this tree."

Bill: Uhm-hmm.
        Uhm-hmm.

Ron: That, that was a long time ago. Me and XXX, Flora.
        That, that was a long time ago. Me and XXX, Flora.

Tom: Nih-3oo'oekuusetii-t, [good word nuhu', means stuck in the ground, nih-3oo'oekuusetii-t. [[Addressed as a side comment to the researcher]]
        He stuck it firmly in the ground; that's a good word, means 'stuck in the ground,' he stuck it firmly in the ground.

Ron: [Nih-'ei'towuun-ei'eet.
                        She told us about that.

Bill: There's a lot of . . . <u>koo-Ce'in</u>? ne'=nih-'iisih'i-t, yeah?
        There's a lot of . . . was it Ce'in? that was her name, yeah?

Ron: Yeah.
Bill: Ce'in, [that was her Indian name.
Ron: [Uhm-hmm, Yeah.
Len: I heard that name before, Ce'in. I heard [that name before, yeah.
Bill: [yeah, yeah, that was her Indian name, Ce'in.
        [[2.8 sec.]]
Bill: <u>Hinee Shakespeare</u>, nee'eetoot, Tom Shakespeare [real name]?
        That Shakespeare, that's where he stayed, Tom Shakespeare?

Ahm . . .
Ahm. . . .
[[1 sec.]]

Reference to a Historical Anecdote or Tall Tale: A Tree from a Willow Switch

((Originally told by Wox Betebi/George Antelope (real name).))

Bill: Ahm, hees-ii-tousihi' that guy, umm . . . ?
         Ahm, what was that guy's name . . . ?

Ron: Uh-huh.
         Uh-huh.

         [[1 sec.]]
Bill: Uhm. . . .
         Uhm . . .

         [[2 sec.]]
Bill: Nii-coon-e'inobeenoon-o' hi-niisih'iit.
         Uhm, I can't think of his name.

         Anyway, he's telling people, hinee, cei3iikoh-einoo, nih-'ii-t.
         [[gesture: "that guy"]]
         *Anyway, he was telling people, "That tree, I rode [it] to here,"
         he said. [i.e., on the tree, like a witch on a broomstick in Euro-
         American fairy tales, for example].*

         Nuhu' niskohoe, nih'iit, you know, the ones they used to use.
         [[gesture: imitating a horse whip]]
         This willow stick whip, he said, you know they used to use.

         [[1 sec.]]
         Ahm, them sticks, out of willows. [Red, yeah red willows.
         Ahm, them sticks, out of willows. Red, yeah red willows.

Len: [Red, red willows.
                                            Red, red willows.

Tom: [They don't have the power
anymore. ((side remark addressed to the researcher.))
                              They don't have the power
anymore.

Bill: Ne'i-iten[owoo].
        "Then I took it."

        "Ne'-3i'ookuutii-noo," nih-'ii-t. [[gesture: sticking something in
        the ground]]
        "Then I stuck it in the ground," he said.

        "'oh ne'P ne'-ihciii'oo-'," [nih-'ii-t.
        "And then it grew up into a tree," he said.

Tom: [You gotta think. ((side remark
        addressed to researcher.))
                              You *gotta think.*

Len: Huh!
        Huh!

Bill: <u>Wox Betebi.</u>
        Old Lady Bear [was his name].

Ron: Yeah.
        Yeah.

        Nih-no'oteihi-t 'innit?
        He was a tough one, right?

Bill: Yeah Wox Betebi yeah.
        Yeah, Old Lady Bear, yeah.

Ron: Nih-'ohookeeni-t 'innit?
        He was crazy, right?

        Huut nih-<u>'oonoo3P hoonoo3itoon</u>-ei'eet nehe' Richard, <u>Richard</u>
        <u>Little Shield.</u> [[gesture: sharing stories back and forth]]
        Richard Little Shield [who lived] here used to tell us stories too.

Bill: Yeah.
        Yeah.

        [[1 sec.]]
Bill: Wox Betebi, what does that mean?
        It means, uh, 'Old Lady Bear'?
Ron: Something like that.
Bill: like that, 'innit?
Ron: uhm-hmm.
Bill: Yeah, or, or Bad Old Lady?
        [[laughter]]
Ron: Wox betebihehi', yeah, 'innit?
Bill: Yeah, could be ['bad old lady,' or . . .
Ron: [Bad old lady, yeah.
Tom: Bear, bear old [lady.
Bill: [yeah, yeah, old lady bear.
Ron: [hini'iit nih-teeP <u>wooce'</u>.
                That one was always telling stories, you remember.

        <u>Wooce'</u>, nih-'<u>oo3iteeP</u> . . .
        You remember, he told stories . . .

Bill: Uhm-hmm.
        Uhm-hmm.

Tall Tale: Hunting for Ducks

((Originally told by Wox Betebi/George Antelope))

Ron: nehe' Wox Betebihehi': [[gesture: "this guy"]]
        This Old Lady Bear [told the following story]:

Tom: Yeah.
        Yeah.

Ron: [[gesture: holding a rifle]]

Heet-ne'-nee-neh'ei-ni'. [[gesture: "out there"]] [[gesture: "out there"]] [[gesture: holding a rifle]]
"I'm going to go get some game."

Won-iinoo'ei,' nih-'iis-i3i'.(?)
" 'Go hunt,' they said to me."

Nih-'eeneiniikoh-einoo, nih-'ii-t [[gesture: pointing here and there]]
"I was riding around various places," he said.

[[2 sec.]]
Ciitoh-owoo. [[gesture: loading a gun]]
"I loaded my gun."

Ne'-seh-'oowuniihisee-noo. [[PSL gesture: "stream"]]
"Then I walked off downstream that way."

Nih-'iinouwu-t, nuhu' siisiikou', nihxoo . . . [[gesture: duck moving around on the water]]
"It was swimming around, this duck. . . ."

Nih-'iinouwu-t. [[gesture: duck moving on the water]]
"It was swimming around."

Yehei, niine'ee-hek nuhu'! [[gesture: grabbing a rifle]]
"Hey, here is one!"

Sebeyooh-oe', nih'iit. [[gesture: aiming a gun]]
"I took aim at it," he said.

[[1.7 sec.]]
'oh hei'-iis-3ooxuunon-eit.
But the duck had already noticed him.

Bill: Yeah.
       Yeah.

Ron: [[gesture: aiming a gun]]

Woow ne-'ihcohee-t. [[gesture of raising arms in air, as if in surrender]]

"Now it raised its hands/arms up in the air."

Nih-too-too'esohowuun-einoo. [[gesture: waving arms in the air to say "stop"]]

"It was motioning to me to stop."

[[2 sec.]]

Yeheihoowun, nih-'ii3-o'. [[gesture: holding a gun lowered]]

" 'Oh gosh,' I said to him."

Neih-'oow-uus-bexoh-oo. [[gestures: lowering a gun; pointing at the duck]]

"I didn't shoot him."

Nih-cih-no'o'usee-t. [[gesture: duck waddling this way, out of the water]]

"He came walking out of the water."

[[2 sec.]]

[[gesture: holding one's hand out in front of one]]

No'usee-t nuhu'. [[gesture: reaching out to shake someone's hand]]

"This duck arrived there."

Nih-neniniixoo3-einoo. [[gesture: shaking someone's hand]]

"He shook my hand."

Nih'ii-tooP too-toyoow3ee3ei-t hinee. [[gesture: indicating one's hand]]

"That guy had cold hands!"

[[laughter for 5 sec.]]

Ciibeh'oohP nih'iit, neh'ei'ee. [[gesture: waving one's hands to signal "no, don't"]]

" 'Don't kill us anymore!' it said."

Woow neniiwo'ooni', [nih-'ii3-einoo. [[PSL gesture: "disappearing," "gone"]]

"We are really diminishing in numbers, now,' it said to me."[2]

[[laughter]]

Bill: [yeah.
                                   Yeah.

Ron: That's one of them, [kee'in?
       That's one of them, you know?

Bill: [Yeah, yeah.
                                   Yeah, yeah.

[[laughter]]
[[1.4 sec.]]

Believe-It-or-Not Story: The Bent Gun

Bill: Yeah, nih-i'-oo3itoot-ou'u hi3oowo' hini'iitiino siisiikou'uu: [[gesture: various places on the surface of the water]]
       Yeah, remember they told that story about those ducks:

Ahh nihP nih-'ouu3ei-'i hini'. [[gesture: ducks on the water in various places]]
Those ones were floating on the water.

XXX hee3ebiini noonotP noonoononoo'oo-' [nuhu', nuhu' niicie. [[gesture: meandering stream]]
But in that direction, this stream was very twisty and winding.

Ron: [Yeah.
                                             Yeah.

Nuhu' heetn-iis-iiniih-ou'u, nih'iit. [[gesture: pointing at someone]]
"These birds, I know how to handle them," he said.

Sii=ne'-beebeeyooneenowoo nuhu' . . . [[gesture: bending a gun into curves]]
"Then I bent this gun all into curves. . . .

[[laughter]]
. . . Kokuy," nih'iit.
. . . this gun," he said.

Ne'-coboo'oo-' nuhu'. [[gesture: quickly following the curves of the stream]]
Then this bullet went shooting along [following the curve of the stream].

Nih-'ee3nee-no'otiisisiw-ou'u. [[gesture: lots of dead ducks lying around]]
"I really shot down a whole bunch of them."

[[laughter for 3 sec.]]

Ron: Hini'iit, ni'-ii-tei'eih-ehk, 'innit?
That guy, he was really good with those kinds of stories, right?

Bill: Yeah.
Yeah.

Ron: Ni'-ii-tei'eih-ehk, hi'in.
He was really good with those, that one.

[[2 sec.]]

((**Possible Continuation of the Ducks Story**. The following lines are obscure, and consultants were unable to clarify later. There is a trickster story where the trickster kills many ducks, but when he puts them aside before cooking them, a coyote steals them. A similar scenario seems to be suggested in the next lines.))

Ron: Heet-ne'-ceniihei-noo, nih'iit.
"Then I will dress/gut them," he said.

[[laughter.]]

'oh, 'oh 'oh hei-beex-cih-'oowu-ceno'oo, nih-'ii3-o'.
"But you should jump down here," I said to him.

'oh he'ih-'entoo-no' hinono'ei-no'.
But I guess some Arapahos were present.

Cese' heet-nee-3i' nih-'iinsee3i'. [[gesture: walking down to a place]]
It's only going to be them who wandered around.

[[chuckles]]
He'ih-won-beteee-no' nuhu'. [[gesture: walking or dancing]]
I guess they went to go dance.

[[laughter]]
[[1.7 sec.]]
Neenentouhuu nuhu' hinen.
This guy really told some tall tales/big lies.[3]

Bill: Boy, that guy, after he got, if somebody had recorded all of his knowledge, it would have been . . .

Tom: They don't got that power anymore.

Ron: Francis, Francis Black was like that.

Bill: Yeah, uhm . . . Yeah, Francis was like that.
Uhm, over, me and Leo Headley went over there, you know, where they used to stay at Mill Creek there? Along that creek there, they had a house there. And then we got over there, and he was telling us, he says . . .

Tall Tale: A Modern Saint Francis

Bill: Huutiino, tih-tes-nohkuseiciini nih-no'oehi-noo, [nih-'ii-t. [[gesture: here]]
"Here, when it was very early in the morning, I went outside,"
he said.

Tom: [This is,
This is,

this is good old [man talk. ((Side remark to the researcher.))
this is good old man talk.

Bill: [Nih'iini hoon[owooyeiti-noo, nih-'ii-t,
hoonowooyeiti-noo. [[gesture: arms out to the side]]
    "I was praying," he said, "I was praying."

Tom: [This was the way it was in the past. That's the
way it was a long time ago. ((Side remark to researcher.))
    *This was the way it was in the past. That's the
way it was a long time ago.*

Bill: Nih-nee'eesohoo'oo-noo. [[gesture: arms out to the side, slowly
waving up and down]]
I was moving my arms like this.

Ne'-koo-ko'usi-'i nii'eihiiho', nih-'ii-t. [[gesture: birds landing on
each arm]] [[gesture: arms crossed in front of him]]
"Then birds started landing on my arms," he said.

Nih-koo-kou'usi-'i nii'ehiiho', nih'iit. [[gesture: standing with
arms weighed down]]
"Birds landed all over," he said.

He'ii3ou'u nih-cih-'etei'oo-', nih-'ii-t. [[gesture: looks up into the
sky]] [[gesture: points at something flying down]]
"Something came toward me, making a sound," he said.

Nih-cih-'etei'oo-', nih'iit. [[gesture: something flies down to the
speaker]]
"This thing came this way, making a noise," he said.

Ne'iini, nuhu' nei3e'eene', ne'-ko'use-', nih-'ii-t. [[gesture with
both hands: something has landed on my head]]
"Then this thing landed on my head," he said.

[[1 sec.]]

'oh nuhu', ne'-nei'ooku'oo-noo. [[gesture: points at something over there]]

"And this thing, then I looked around."

Hinit noh'eihoone', nih-noohobeti-noo, nih-'ii-t. [[gesture: standing piously with arms outspread]]

"I saw myself reflected in the window," he said.

Niine'eeno' nii'ehiiho'. [[gesture: points to multiple birds along each arm]]

"There were birds all over me."

Nih-noohowP nuhu' noh'kosoo'oo-', nih-'ii-t. [[gesture with both hands: something is on my head]]

"I saw this shiny thing on my head," he said.

[[gesture: standing with arms outstretched]]
Wootii Saint Francis neneeni-t, neneeni-t no-noohow-ooo. [[gesture: standing with arms outstretched to the side, eyes closed, looking pious]]

"I was like Saint Francis; that's what I saw."

[[laughter]]
Tom: A halo, wo'ei3. . . .

A halo, or. . . .

[[laughter]]
Bill: Had a halo.

He had a halo.

[[laughter for 6 sec.]]

Believe-It-or-Not Story: Shooting Down the Washakie Needle

Ron: <u>Nenee' ci'</u> ne'P heetniiP heetehP Tetons 'innit, with them needles? [[gesture: pointing to the north]]

There is the one also, then, about where the Tetons are, right? with those needles?

Bill: Yeah.
Yeah.

Ron: <u>Wooce'</u> nooxeihi' nih'ii-se'isi-'. [[gesture: lying in bed, hands up over his head]]
Maybe you know, Wox Betebi was lying there in bed.

Nih'ii-cou'utii-t kokiyono XXX. [[gesture: fiddling with something above one's head]]
He was messing with his guns [mounted above his bed].

<u>He'ih</u>-3eiisen, kee'in? [[gesture: still fiddling with something over his head]]
There was a bullet in there, you know?

Tii'ikuutii-t; [[gesture: touch something]]
He touched the trigger;

Ko'etee-ni'. [[gesture: points in direction of shot]]
The gun went off.

Tom: Yeah.
Yeah.

Ron: [[gesture: two rock needles; bullet hitting one of them]]
"So'onoo'ootii-noo that one," nih-'ii-t XXX. [[gesture: one rock fallen over, next to other one standing]]
"I made that one here start teetering," he said.

[[laughter]]
Ne'-ce3cenise-'. [[gesture: something falling over]]
Then it starting falling to the ground.

Nih-cihP. [[gesture: something falling and hitting the ground]]
It fell down to the ground.

[My wife], she had that casing. [[gesture: pointing to something over there]]
My wife had the casing from the bullet.

Hesitee-', nih-'ii-t. [[gesture: putting something down]]
[[gesture: an object]]

"It was hot," she said.

[[2 sec.]]
[[gesture: points at something in front of him on the ground]]
He'ne'P nuhu', nuhu' tees-bii3ibee-ni', nih-'ii-t. [[gesture:
putting something on top of something else]]

"Then we cooked breakfast on top of it," he said.

[[laughter for 4 sec.]]

Believe-It-or-Not Story: Jumping the Canyon

Bill: Nuhu', "hini', nih-beetoh-'ooxuu-ceno'oot-owoo," nih-'ii3-oot
wootii, one of them Tetons to the other.

*This guy said, "That canyon, I wanted to jump across it," he
said to them, I guess, from one Teton to the other.*

Ne'P ne'eh-ceno'oo-noo, nih-'ii-t.
"Then I jumped from there outwards," he said.

Neehii3ei' ne'e-e'in-owoo: neetne-ihoowu-n[i']huustii hii3e'.
[[gesture: being suspended in the air midway across the
canyon; points to the goal on the other side of the canyon]]

*"In the middle, then I realized, I'm not going to make it over
there to the other side."*

Ne'-iinee-ceno'oo-noo. [[gesture: turning around in midair]]
"So, then I jumped back around the other way."

[[laughter for 6.5 sec.]]
[[1 sec.]]

General Remarks on Storytelling

Ron: Yeah, boy, good ones, 'innit?
Yeah, boy, good ones, aren't they?

Bill: Yeah.
        Yeah.

Len: Hini'iit uhh hinono'ei, hinono'eiyeiP toh-'oonoo3itee-3i', ne'P
        [ne'=nih-'iiP
        Those Arapahos, when they told stories in Arapaho, they did
        that when. . . .

Ron: [Yeah.
        Yeah.

Len: [ne'=nih-'ii'-oo'eisee-3i'.
        That's when they would get together.

Tom: [ne'nih'ii'ni'iisiini.
        That's how it was.

Ron: Yeah.
        Yeah.

Tom: Nih-'oonoxoeh[etiitooni', yeah.
        They made each other laugh, yeah.

Len: [Yeah.
                        Yeah.

Bill: [Yeah.
                        Yeah.

Bill: 'oh nih'oo3ouyei[tiit], hi-ihoowuuni
        But in English you can't tell it.

        Neenen[iheihiinoo-'.
        [The humor] is lost.

Len: [‘ihee
                    Yeah, for sure!

Len: [Yeah.
            Yeah.

Ron: [Yeah.
            Yeah.

Bill: Neenen[iheihiinoo-'.
        [The humor] is lost.

Len: [Noh kookon nuhu' nih-ceh'e3tiitooni-'.
            And people would listen to just anything.

        [[chuckles]]
        He'=iisih'i-noo3i neh'eeno.
        I wonder what their names were [who did these crazy things].

        [[laughter]]
        [[1 sec.]]
Ron: 'oh hi3oowuuni, kee'in?
        That's truly how it was, you know?

        [[3.5 sec.]]

Humorous Anecdote/Pun Story: The One I Hit

Len: <u>Nuhu'</u> nih-'<u>oo3itoon</u>-einoo. [[gesture: points at Tom.]]
        This one told me this story.

        <u>He'</u>=Tom; [[gesture: points at Tom]]
        I guess Tom was the one;

        <u>Teecxo'</u> nooxeihi' nih-'iinoo'ei-3i' <u>nuhu'</u> beh'eihoho'. [[gesture: indicates multiple people]]
        A long time ago, maybe they were out hunting, these old men.

        Kokiyono nih-'eeneiten-ou'u. [[gesture: holding a gun]]
        Guns, they had gotten them.

[[1.5 sec.]]
Cee-cesisih'ohu-3i' hini'iitiino. [[gesture: birds flying away]]
Those birds all set off, flying away.

3eb-noo'oen-ihc-coocowoo'oo-3i'. [[gesture: points at sky]]
[[gesture: shooting various directions]]
They were shooting all around at them, up there in the sky.

Ceecensi-'i. [[multiple things falling and hitting the ground]]
They all came falling down.

[[laughter]]
Nih-'oono3(?)-noohow-oo3i' nuhu'. [[gesture: points at various things on the ground]]
They looked at all of them there.

"Nuhu' see'isi-', koo-neen ne-ih-besooo?" [[gesture: pointing at something on the ground]]
"This one lying here, is that the one I shot?"

[[laughter]]
Bill: "Koo-neen ne-beso'o?"
"Is that my butt?"

[[laughter]]
Len: [[gesture: points at Bill to indicate "you got the joke"]]
[[laughter for 7 sec.]]
[[3 sec.]]
Hee, nono'oteihi-3i' teecxo'.
Yeah, they were tough a long time ago.

Bill: Uhm-hmm.
Uhm-hmm.

[[2.8 sec]]

Believe-It-or-Not Story: The Antelope Larder

((This story was told to me by Alonzo Moss Sr. as well, in October 2010. In his version, an additional detail is added, that the hunter has only one bullet left.))

Bill: <u>Nuhu' Wox Betebihehi',</u>

This Old Lady Bear,

Mexican Pass, nih-'iinoo'ei-noo, nih-'ii-t. [[gesture: "over there"]] [[gesture: "here and there"]]

"I was hunting at Mexican Pass," he said.

Nih-noohow-o' nisice 3ii'ookuu-t. [[gesture: see something]] [[gesture: "standing"]]

"I saw an antelope standing there."

'oh howoo nih-bisiini nih-bee3tii-ni' ne-bii3hiin-inoo, nih-'ii-t. [[PSL gesture: "all gone"]]

"And also at that time, we had finished off all our food," he said.

Ne'iini, ne'P, neeneh'ini hotino3-o', nih-'ii-t, hinee. [[gesture: creeping?]]

"Then I was sneaking up on it over there," he said, "that antelope."

Too3iihi', 'oh ne'P, 'oh ne-ih-'oowP ne-ih-'oow-3ooxuunon-e'.

"When I got near it, then, it had not noticed me."

Sii=ne'P sii=ne'-coboo-noo. [[gesture: shot hits animal]]

"So then right away I shot at it."

Xonou honinoo'oo-t. [[gesture: animal falls over]]

"Immediately it fell over."

Hei'iini honinoo'oo-t, ne'-cih-koe'e3ein-o', nih-'ii-t. [[gesture: cutting an animal open at the belly]]

"After it went down, then I cut it open at the belly," he said.

Hei'-ko'P, hoow-3eiis. [[gesture: points to his stomach or insides with both hands]]

"When I cut it open, there were no internal organs in there."

HoowP hoowu-3eiise3ootiin, nih-'ii-t. [[gesture: indicating his own innards]]

"There was nothing inside there," he said.

[[laughter]]

Ne'-cihP ne'-ciinohei-noo wohei. . . . [[gesture: pulling something out of a place]]

"But then I got something from there, well . . ."

Niisiscoo', [[gesture: taking something out of a container]]

"Sugar . . .

[[laughter for 3 sec.]]

Woo'teenoowu' . . . [[gesture: taking something else out]]

Coffee . . .

[[laughter]]

[3o'P . . . 3o'ohoeno." [[gesture: takes something and gives it to someone else]]

Fl- . . . flour."

Ron: ['oohei!

Amazing!

[[laughter]]

Yeheihoo.

Gee whiz!

Bill: Ne'=nih-'iisP ne'=nih-'iis-nehton-bii3ihi-ni'.

"That's how we came to cheat hunger and grab a meal."

[[laughter for 3.5 sec.]]

Tall Tale: Racing the Train

((The following continues in the tall tale vein of stories. Note that this is more a mention of a story than a telling of it.))

Ron: <u>Wohei hini'iit</u> tih-cebiih-oot <u>hini'iit</u> uhh heso'oonotiib-e' <u>wooce'</u>? [[gesture: points in direction of train tracks]] [[gesture: "that one"]]

Well, remember that one about that guy who raced that, uh, train?

Bill: Uhm-hmm.

Uhm-hmm.

Ron: Hou'o'oot, backwards, [<u>wooce', he'ih</u>-cebiih-ee. [[gesture: facing backwards]]

He faced backwards against the front of it, remember [on skates], and beat it.

Bill: [yeah

                             yeah

Ron: <u>He'ih</u>-cebiih-ee, cebe'eih-oot.

He defeated it, beat it.

[[laughter]]
Nono'oteihi-t, boy.

He was tough/smart, boy.

Wintertime.

In wintertime [they would tell them].

[[1 sec.]]

Humorous Anecdote: Is That My Wife?

((This story continues the humor theme, and returns to stories originally told by Wox Betebi. Additional context, not articulated in this telling but

known by the listeners, is that Wox Betebi and his wife had been invited
to a fancy, white-man-style dinner and dancing party, as special Arapaho guests, and Wox Betebi was therefore far out of his normal cultural
context.))

Ron: <u>He had real good stories</u> about when he want to Washington,
       DC, too, one time. I don't remember how that goes, 'oh [but]
       somehow . . .

       Neeyoo'uu-noo hini'iitiino. [[gesture showing regalia and hat]]
       "I was dressed up fancy in those [white-man-style]."

       <u>You know,</u> he described the stovepipe hats. [[gesture: showing
       a stovepipe hat]]
       You know, he described the stovepipe hats.

       [[gesture: wearing a bow tie]]
       Betoootiini-'. [[gesture: pointing to a dance floor]]
       "There was a dance going on."

       Henee3nee-nii3-beteee-noo. [[gesture: dancing a white-style
       dance with a partner]]
       "I am really taking part in the dancing."

       Nih'oo3ouniihi', henee3neeP nih-nookunouhu-t, nih-'ii-t.
       [[gesture: pointing out a woman's long dress]]
       *"In white-man-style, [this woman I was dancing with] was all
       dressed in white," he said.*

       Ne'-bebiis-nei'oohow-o'. [[gesture: leaning over, looking closely
       at someone]]
       "Then I looked at her carefully."

       He'ih-neen Cetoun! nih-'ii-t.
       *"I guess it was Cetoun, [my wife]!" he said. ((i.e., he had not
       recognized his own wife, because she looked so different in the
       white-style fancy dress clothes.))*

       [[laughter for 6.5 sec]]

Ron: Nih-no'oteihi-3i', boy.
Those old guys were tough/good at telling stories, boy.

[[laughter for 6 sec.]]
Yeheihoo.
Gee whiz!

[[13.5 sec]]

((After this long pause of 13.5 seconds, one of the speakers shifts the topic entirely. He recounts how his nice new cell phone or tablet had been stolen the previous weekend. There was no apparent link between the just-completed sequence of stories and this topic.))

Bill: I'm trying to get my phone going today.
       I'm trying to get my phone going today.
       I had a big phone, heebe3iihi'.
       I had a big phone, a big one.
       Nih-'ebiitebee-noo, other week. . . .
       I had it stolen from me, the other week. . . .
       ((Conversation continues))
       ((ELAR 133d, 9:19))

The preceding is an exemplary story chain: the chain emerges naturally from a general conversation, rather than being staged as a "storytelling event"; multiple speakers tell stories, taking turns without any explicit need for cues such as, "Now it's your turn." There is commentary between some of the stories, which temporarily moves the chain back to general conversation, before someone else takes up the challenge of producing a new story. The stories chain together thematically in interesting ways, and the chain peters out naturally at the end, with a return to general conversation.

Regarding emergence, the first story in the sequence is an entirely historical account, which continues in the vein of several preceding accounts about local history and ancestors. Unlike the preceding accounts, however, the narrator here does not simply tell *about* the person in question (mimetically), but *voices* her as well (diegetically). Connected to this decision is the fact that a distinctive feature of this now-deceased elder is that she told young kids lots of stories. Moreover, in voicing the bygone narrator, the speaker Ron also voices that narrator's voicing of the even-longer-bygone Chief Black Coal (died 1893), about whom the elder woman told a story sometime in the 1940s. The speaker thus introduces a double level of meta-narrativity into the ongoing narratives, while also explicitly evoking the practice of storytelling. This conversational move opens the floor to the domain of narrative more generally, both as a topic of discussion and in the form of *voicing* the narratives of previous Arapaho elders.

The next speaker, Bill, picks up on these moves: he introduces a new person as topic (Wox Betebi), who also was a noted storyteller, and he voices a part of that person's narrative. Thus, the ground rules are established for a series of narratives that are not simply stories themselves, but explicit *voicings* of the stories of *others*, in those *others'* voices. We have already seen in previous chapters the common use of two kinds of double-voicing: the narrator speaking through the voice of a past narrator, or the narrator speaking through the voice of the putative protagonist in the story itself, who then later told the story about his or her own experiences. This double-voicing is a practice specific to the development of new reservation-era narratives and comicals.

Traditional narratives, such as those about mythological or legendary characters or trickster stories, are almost never double-voiced. The narrator simply reports the events or, when providing dialogue, includes the traditional quotative verb *heehehk* 'he/she is reported to have said' or transitive variants of it. Much more information on the style of such narratives can be found in Cowell and Moss (2005); Cowell, Moss, and C'Hair (2014), and Cowell (2002). The only attributions that occur, if any, with such stories are phrases like "so-and-so told me that story" (or more commonly, "that's how so-and-so told that particular story"). The stories are cultural property that do not belong to anyone; at most, one particular version of the story may be attributed to a specific teller.

At the other extreme, true personal anecdotes are typically told simply as "I did this, then I did that" or "s/he did this, then s/he did that." In contrast, the double-voicing found in many comicals and modern narratives is a way of distancing them from everyday anecdotal accounts that simply represent personal experience, while also distancing them from the ontology of classic narratives such as trickster or culture hero stories, which do not rely on double-voicing as a key feature of performance. Therefore, the speaker who initiates the chain presented here invites both additional narratives and narratives of a particular type.

The narrator of the second anecdote picks up thematically on the idea of trees or sticks from the first narrative. He introduces not just any Wox Betebi story, but the one most apropos to the preceding narrative, while also changing the genre of the speech event from historical anecdote to tall tale. The chain does not immediately take off, however. The first brief narratives are really more evoked, by reference to a key line of content, than actually told. Yet even in the first narrative, one person is actively *evaluating* the narrative as it is told, noting a "good word" that occurs in it, which signals that the listeners are now attuning themselves to the performative quality of the sequence. On the other hand, the speakers go on a tangent to verify an Arapaho personal name, which has the potential to return the discussion to the more historical framework. One person then tries to initiate discussion about another individual who lived in the area, Tom Shakespeare, but the others do not pick up this topic, despite the fact that Tom was a noted tribal historian. The second speaker, Bill, then cannot remember the Arapaho name of the person he is talking about, and this must be resolved. Yet another speaker tries to start discussion of a different individual, Richard Little Shield, who was apparently a noted storyteller, but this topic is also not taken up. Then the same speaker who appreciated the "good word" introduces a brief reflection on the name Wox Betebi, noting that the name could mean two different things in Arapaho, and a competing, diminutive version of the name is suggested.

The interaction up to this point shows the "controlled chaos" of a typical multi-speaker conversation. In fact, however, the speakers are working together toward a unified target, or in the language of sociocultural linguistics, negotiating and co-constructing a shared conversational task. The two brief narratives pattern strongly with each other in both form and content, and in ways quite different from the preceding discussion. Even the topics not taken up center on the theme of storytelling, indicating that all of the speakers have implicitly accepted this as the focus of the forthcoming conversation/story chain—the question is just what story or whose story to tell next. Even the one speaker who does not attempt to offer a new topic has nevertheless picked up clearly on the new metalinguistic focus, as he evaluates old words and the potential double meanings of old personal names.

In the following part of the interchange, the storytelling becomes much more clearly organized, as single tellers tell longer and more coherent stories, with back-channeling by the others, and the tellers take more orderly turns. The second speaker, Bill, is the key pivot person in the chain. He picks up on the potential provided by the double-voiced invocation of Ce'in and the references to storytelling. He then introduces one additional variable into the situation: he alludes to a tall-tale-like story and suggests that Wox Betebi, unlike Ce'in, was known for such stories. After all this conversational negotiation, Ron's third narrative is appropriately another Wox Betebi/believe-it-or-not narrative (again told in double-voiced fashion), this time about duck hunting. The central genre focus of the chain has been established.

Certain key features help the narrator of the third story "clear the floor," so to speak, and procure an extended turn for telling a true story. These are his use of *wooce'* 'you know? remember?' twice in succession, which is clearly an appeal for a right to elaborate; his explicit invocation of telling a story (*hoo3itee-*); and his use of very prominent gestures as he begins the narration—first "this guy" and then "holding a gun." The previous conversation for the most part lacked any notable iconic gestures, but once Ron. initiates his story, he uses very clear iconic gestures with virtually every line, which is a clear performance "key." And finally, he concludes with the phrase "that's one of them" (that is, one of the stories that Wox Betebi told, or perhaps one story of this genre, or one story on this topic). Whatever the exact sense of the phrase, it clearly invites "another one of them," we might say.

The fourth story then flows almost seamlessly from the preceding one. The narrator uses *hi3oowo'* 'remember,' echoing the previous narrator's use of *wooce'*, except that *hi3oowo'* is less a question than a command. Note that "do you remember" or some related form is commonly used cross-linguistically to initiate stories (Mandelbaum 2013, 496). The narrator also explicitly evokes telling stories (*hoo3itoot-*). Plus, he immediately begins iconically gesturing as well. The story he tells is another believe-it-or-not story, though this time not attributed to Wox Betebi. Again told partially in a double-voiced fashion, it is another story specifically about someone hunting ducks. Thus, the narrator shows the range of his narrative repertoire by very closely chaining the theme and events in his story to the preceding one, while also respecting the choice of genre that has been established. On the other hand, the story is rather perfunctorily told—half telling, half allusion really; it is very common and hardly needs to be told in detail. But the telling is unimportant—the narrator's goals are to show his knowledge of this story (which everyone else knows as well) *and* to show that that he has the chaining skills to deploy the story in the perfect place at the perfect time.

The story does however introduce a new thematic element—Euro-American values and technologies. I have heard many versions of this "Bent Gun" story over the years, but I have never heard a story about a bent arrow, even though there is no conceptual reason why such a story could not be told—and perhaps it once was. The fascination of most believe-it-or-not stories, as we have seen, is with Euro-American technologies and

Arapaho ways of deconstructing the technological or ideological power invoked by those technologies. As all this is happening, one person in the conversation happens to mention Francis Black.

The next teller, in telling the story of the ersatz Saint Francis, performs a dazzling feat of chaining. He happens to know a story about—and told by—Francis Black, *and* the story is another believe-it-or-not story (or at least very close to that genre), *and* it is about birds again, *and* it specifically addresses a potent Christian symbol while also providing an Arapaho perspective that renders the symbol absurd or at least highly comical.[4] The story is also again fully double-voiced. All of the participants in this discussion are from the eastern side of the Wind River Reservation, which is centered on the Catholic St. Stephens Mission (the western side has an Episcopal mission). So they all would be very familiar with the iconography invoked comically in this narrative. From talking to them, I know they have widely varying attitudes toward the Catholic faith, but the teller himself is generally critical of Christian religious traditions, and the story allows him to take a stance in this regard as well. Thus, this particular story does many different kinds of identity and performance work simultaneously for the teller, through the way it is situated in relation to the preceding chain.

Note that the same speaker who earlier evaluated old words and names now comments to me as we sit listening that this entire session is a good example of the way "the old men" used to sit around and tell stories. This is a highly interesting remark because (relatively) old men are in fact sitting around telling stories at the time. The speaker does not represent the situation as "how it is now—at least sometimes," but rather as "this is how it used to be." Thus, the entire session takes on the character of a performance or even re-enactment of the past for him. The consistent double-voicing of the stories in terms of bygone narrators probably contributed to this sense of the moment. I have suggested that the double-voicing is performing "genre work," but at least for this speaker, it is also performing a kind of "performative nostalgia" work.

The following story—about accidentally shooting down the Washakie Needle, then cooking breakfast on the hot rock is another nice addition to the chain, though not as dazzling a performative feat as the preceding story. Washakie Needles, one of the four symbolic corners of the reservation, is a 12,523-foot mountain peak in the far northwest corner of the Wind River Reservation, in the Absaroka Mountains. Part of the Washakie Needle formation did in fact collapse due to an earthquake at some point during early reservation times, and this has generated a number of local stories. The connection between this story and the preceding ones is that it is also a believe-it-or-not story, and it again touches on guns and hunting.

The next story, "Jumping the Canyon," is also very widely known and repeated—a very long and detailed version appears in chapter 3. For that reason, the story is told in a highly perfunctory manner here: its main value is that it is placed in a location near Washakie Needles, and thus has a geographic as well as generic link to the preceding story. It also again touches on the theme of hunting. Note that the chain then threatens to dissipate when an eight-second pause occurs. This is followed by general remarks on the humor of Arapaho stories, and how this humor does not translate well into English. This is a commonplace that I have heard many times from Arapaho people, but here it seems to serve more specific purposes of implicitly asking for another story while also stalling for time until such a story is produced.

The next speaker, Len, then brilliantly synthesizes almost all of these points by telling another common story, which I have heard several times over the years. The story turns on a pun on *besóoo*, which can mean either 'one's butt, rear end' or 'the person or animal that one has hit with a projectile.' The story itself can be told independently of context and still be amusing simply due to the pun. Yet, in this case, it is inserted immediately after a remark on both the humor of Arapaho stories and the untranslatability of the humor, so the pun is perfectly placed to demonstrate these points. In addition, the story involves hunting birds, and thus picks up on the hunting and guns and bird motifs of the preceding stories. Finally, the story is explicitly presented as having been told to the teller by someone else, and thus is double-voiced. This is the only time I have heard the story presented in this double-voiced way—it is usually told simply as a third-person narrative about "this guy who went hunting"—so the choice to double-voice is almost certainly a response to the context of the moment. The telling is a tour-de-force performance and contextual deployment of an otherwise common joke, with the humor and force derived almost entirely from its syntagmatic placement in the narrative chain, since paradigmatically speaking it is again fairly quickly and perfunctorily told.

The next story follows nicely as well, in that it is another story originally told by Wox Betebi, is again presented as double-voiced, is another believe-it-or-not story, again talks about hunting, and returns to the cross-cultural comparison with Euro-American culture which occurred in some of the earlier stories. The story alludes to the fact that subsistence hunting in Arapaho culture has been replaced by going to the store to buy commodities. Like the "Bent Gun" and "Modern Saint Francis" stories, this narrative nevertheless presents Arapaho people as somehow successfully being able to take advantage of the new white values and technologies, if perhaps in comic and unintended ways. More generally, it continues the classic believe-it-or-not pattern of making Euro-American practices and technologies strange.[5]

The preceding two stories are the highlights of the chain. The following story is another believe-it-or-not story, again about Euro-American technologies and Arapaho individuals integrating with and even conquering them, but it is minimally developed and neither attributed to Wox Betebi nor double-voiced. The narrative—about how a person can beat a train in a race by letting it push them along ahead of it (on roller skates, in many versions)—recalls more traditional Arapaho stories such as a race between a fox and a woodtick (where the woodtick jumps on the fox's tail at the start of the race, crawls along its back and down its nose, and falls across the finish line first when the fox stops to rest just before completing the race). This is followed by yet another double-voiced Wox Betebi story, in which he tells an amusing anecdote about himself—again in the context of an encounter with Euro-American values and practices. In this case, however, the story is more an "old couple" story—Wox Betebi fails to recognize his own wife at a fancy dance, thinking he is dancing with a pretty white woman, only to be disappointed when he recognizes his actual partner.

In moving away from the believe-it-or-not genre that has guided the development of the sequence, the speaker effectively ends the story chain. The other participants clearly recognize this, as a long 13.5-second silence follows, with no further attempts to offer either more believe-it-or-not or Wox Betebi stories, or any further meta-level commentary about storytelling or the humor in stories. One of the participants then introduces the topic of his stolen phone. While this move seems random, it is perhaps motivated by the fact that the individuals involved in this conversation are present to work on a new technology app for mobile phones, and the topic returns them squarely to that present objective and topic.

I hope readers can now appreciate the virtuosity of this storytelling performance more fully—both the individual moves by the narrators as they add to the sequence and the collective accomplishment of the entire sequence. Coherence occurs on many different levels: genre, themes and topics, use of double-voicing, and meta-level appreciations of the Arapaho-specific nature of storytelling and its social value. The sequence is far from being a meandering thread. Each addition is carefully disciplined, and speakers actively return to preceding themes on multiple occasions, resisting potential drift introduced by the many elements necessarily included in any previous story. Random centripetal forces are controlled in order to collectively complete a truly cyclic whole. In chapter 3 we saw that the believe-it-or-not genre can be used to reflect on Euro-American practices and technologies, and also as a means of testing and teaching proper relationships of trust and doubt, and proper social ontologies and evaluative skills. But in this case, while some of those elements are present in the cycle, the believe-it-or-not stories can best be seen as the raw material necessary to perform the collective social act of producing a story sequence while individual narrators simultaneously demonstrate their personal linguistic and cultural competence. The other potential themes and resources in this genre of story are not heavily exploited in this sequence. That said, the more general critical perspective on Euro-American influence is certainly reflected in this moment of quite self-conscious Arapaho-ness, involving the performance of a quintessential traditional Arapaho practice prior to beginning work on an app designed to help ensure survival and revitalization of the Arapaho language and culture. As the Arapaho elders get set to confront yet another new technology, they produce a sequence about their historical engagement with, and attempts to rhetorically and ideologically master, previous new technologies.

7

Crazy Guy Stories

The Healing Clown and
the Echo of the Trickster

From the class clown to the stand-up comic, likely every social group has one or more members who love to make people laugh, provide comic relief in moments of seriousness or tension, and generally make a comic spectacle of themselves. And likely every social group also has at least one person who likes not only to tell funny stories about their own doings but to embellish those stories. In some cases, actor and narrator turn out to be the same person, at least initially. In this chapter, I will examine two Arapaho individuals of this type and the comic narratives that surround them.

The stories belong to a general Arapaho genre or thematic grouping that could be called very loosely stories about "that goofy guy." They involve real individuals who gained a reputation in the community for being clownish or goofy in behavior. Among the Arapaho, this means the individuals often did something that made them look silly, either in a mildly socially transgressive way or simply in a humorous way as the victim of funny circumstances. In fact, it is common for many or even most Arapaho people to tell such stories about themselves, when they inadvertently do something silly or embarrassing. This is a way of building social solidarity, by presenting a good-humored and humble persona in the community, and avoiding perceptions of arrogance or excessive self-regard.

Some individuals however (Henry Snake; real name) seem to go out of their way to engage in such behaviors, actively creating moments of humor or transgression. The individuals then tell these stories about themselves, as well as being the subject of others' stories about them, such that this becomes a recognized social role in the community. Others (John Plume) simply seem to find themselves in incongruous and hilarious situations despite themselves, but nevertheless delight in sharing the details. In both these cases, the stories cannot really be separated from the actual performances of the individuals—the former serve to memorialize the latter.

When told by the individual himself or herself, they serve to complete—or more commonly, embellish—the drama or humor of the performance. In particular, this kind of storytelling about and performance of mild transgressions could lighten the mood at many gatherings. In fact, in May 2018 Bill commented that whenever Henry Snake left a place, he always left people laughing, in a good mood. These people would be laughing *at* Henry Snake, and in one sense he could be seen as risking loss of face in the community due to the actions he described in his stories—being too quick to anger, jumping to conclusions, bragging about himself, and so forth. Yet, it was apparently (almost) always understood that there was an element of overt performance and self-awareness involved in his behaviors. The actions were often as much meta-social commentaries on expected Arapaho behaviors and attitudes as they were transgressions of those behaviors and attitudes. Henry Snake told his stories about himself in the first person. John Plume also told stories about his own previous comical or goofy experiences in the first person. Others are then free to retell the stories, but in this case they are told in a double-voiced manner: "John Plume said, 'I was doing so-and-so' . . ." and the first person is still used. An example of a John Plume story follows.

John Plume Visits the Proctologist

((This story was specifically elicited by Andrew Cowell and told by Robert in June 2003, after Cowell talked about John Plume. [Center for the Study of Indigenous Languages, University of Colorado, Boulder, audio recording mp3-16, 42:54]))

Arapaho Version

I guess he had stretched or pulled his spine, you know, back here.
He could barely walk, you know, barely walk.
He'=nii'P . . . hoowo-e'in <u>toon</u>-heet-niis-woteekoohu-t.
Hoow-beet-noo'einowuun-e' nuhu' hoo3oo'o' hi-tei'yooniiw-o wo'ei3
  hini-isiihoh-o.
Hoow-beet-noo'einowuun-e'.
Hee <u>3iwoo</u> niisiini, heeh-ehk.
Wohei <u>noonoko'</u> heetn-ii-nihii neyei3itoo-noo niiheniihi'.
Ne'-nouu-teesisee-noo not-otiib-e'.
<u>Hoonii</u> heniixouuhu-noo.
<u>Hohkonee</u> heniis-teesisee-noo.
Noh, nii'iini; <u>hinit</u> ne'eh-ce3koohu-noo.

3eb-woteihcehi-noo boon-e' hee3ebii[hi'].

Wohei hee3ebP . . . heeyow=eete3einobee-nooni, heetoh-tonoti-'i
   nuhu' boon-e', 'oh nih-'ee3neene-esiini-', nooh'uhcehisine-nooni hinit.

Hohkonee seh-woteihcehi-noo, hinee heet-wo'oteeyoo-' booo.

Beexuuni ni'iini.

Hohkonee 3eb-iis-no'koohu-noo.

Noh hunit hee3e'eitee-', niitoo-t nehe' notoniheihii,
   nee'eet-too'uhcehi-noo.

'oh niiP niit-3i'ookuu-'u hi'in 3i'ookuu3oo-no, bei'ci3ei'i niit-3eiini-'i,
   toon=heetn-iicisiini hentoo-[n].

Ne'-3eiikuutii-noo bei'ci3ei'i.

Hoonii hehiix-oowusee-noo.

Hohkonee hehiix-oowuseenoo.

Ne'-cii3-nonousee-noo hini'iit tecenoon-e'.

Wohei hi'in teesciiyei'iit-ono 3eb-noh'uuhu' hee3eb-ciis-noh'oe-'.

Ne'eh-3ebouuhu-'; hoonii ne'eh-seh'ini,

Hohkonee seh-'iis-no'oxuuheti-noo;

Huut ne'eh-ciitei-noo.

Wohei heneeyeih-no'usee-n, hee3-einoo hi'in nih'oo3ousei, notoniheisei.

Wohei hunit, huut xonou, cih-ciitei, heet-noohob-ein notoniheihii.

Nooxeihi' 3eniixowotoooyoni-n.

Hee, 3iixowotoooyonihcehi-noo.

Wohei nih-noo-noh'en-owoo niiheyoti-'i,
   ne'-3iixowotoooyonihcehi-noo.

Hee, heet-notonih-ein, heetn-iiP"

Huut cih-ciitei hinit!"

Noko3iihi' niitP . . . nooxeihi' niit-teesiisibi-3i',toon=hi-nii-notonih-ooono,
   koo-kokoh'ouh-oot,

Wohei hiitoniihi' wootii touyoo-no;

Heh'ini nooxeihi' nuhu' ce'iiteyei-no' niitoh-ciineni-'i;

Howoo ne-ih-'oowo-e'in, 'oh honoot nih-'ei'towuun-i3i'.

Neetehee3ei, hee3-einoo hi'in nih'oo3ousei.

Nih-bi'-nei'oohow-o'.

Neetehee3ei!

Neneeni-noo notoniheisei.

Hoow-kohtowuuni.

Konoo'=ne'-nehee3ei-noo.

Nih-'ee3nee-3onceihinoo, hece'eekuu-noo hinit.

Wohei niiyou nuhu' heetohni-'i wootii touyoo-no.

Nuhu' he-ce'iiteyei-no' hiiton-ciinen-oo!

Cih-ce'-eh-be'e3iisibi-n.

Nee'eeneestoo-noo.
Ne'-cih-ciitei-t nehe' notoniheihii.
Nih-'eeneti3-einoo.
Hee, 3iixowotoooyonihcehi-noo.
Ne'P, wohei heet-ce'i-ni'kuu3-e3en.
Heet-i'i'ii-seh-sei'oohow-o' hi'in siikoocei3ooxo-ho cii-ciito'on-oot.
Beexeeneihi-ni3i.
Wohei hini'iit xo'eyoo ne'-eebe3-ko'un-o'.
Wohei nuhu' ne-3itin-e' cih-'eenei3en-o'.
'eiyo', heesi3ecoo-noo.
Wohei hiit hei'-iisiini ne'-cih-'inowoho'oe-t nuhu';
Oooh nih-'ee3neene-esiini-'.
Too-bih'inkuuton-einoo.
Hinit he'iitnei'i ne'-koxuuten koseineekuutii-t.
Nihi'P . . . heetn-iini . . .
Sii=ne'-beex-noxowunoo'oo-noo.
Nihii hee ne'=nii'-wootii heh-bi'-einoku-noo.
Wohei kohei'i, hee3-einoo.
Hei'-iis-eh-ce'-koxcein-een-etoho'oe-t,¹ 3i'ookuu-t.
Ho-tou3ouubeih?"
Hee, woo'wu-ni'iini.
Wohei hiit woxu'uu;
Heetn-iini biin-e3en.
Heetni-iten-ow;
Beebeet ciibeh-nohkuh'ebi ciitee[hinec] wo'ei3 nih'oo3ounec;
Heetn-iini heetn-i'-beex-neini'ei-n.
Heetn-iiP het-oonoyoohoot nuhu' hee3e'eikoohu-n.
Noh ce'i-ni'iini, noh ne'=nih-'iis-ce'-ni'ih-einoo nehe' nih'oo3oo.
Hee3eeniini ci'=hiikoot ciinoo'on-beesoo-ni'i hi-3ee3oo-[no].
Nee'eesise-' nuhu' hoo3itoo.

English Version

I guess he had stretched or pulled his spine, you know, back here.
He could barely walk, you know, barely walk.
Then when . . . he doesn't know how he will get to town.
They don't want to drive him, these others, his children or his
grandchildren.
They don't want to drive him.
"Well, let's see how it is [I can get there]," he said.
Well, might as well, I might as well try to do it myself.

Then I went out and got in my car.
After a long time I climbed into it.
Finally I managed to get on board.
And, "It is good"; then I set off away from there.
I set off for town on the road there.
Wohei, every time I hit a bump in the road, where there were potholes,
    then it was really painful whenever I was bounced there.
Finally I got onto the blacktop road that leads to town over there.
It was a little better then.
Finally I arrived over there.
And right there in front of the doctor's office, that's where I came to a stop.
And those poles that stand there, where you put in money depending on
    how long you're going to stay.
Then I put some money in there.
After a long time I managed to get down out of the car.
Finally I managed to get out of the car.
Then I went inside through the door, all bent over as I walked.
Wohei, those steps going up there, they went way up there.
They ascended way on up there; after a long time on up there from here,
Finally I managed to get myself up there;
Then I went inside there.
"*Wohei*, it's good that you've come," that white woman nurse said to me.
"*Wohei*, right there, right away, come in, the doctor will see you."
"Maybe you pulled your back."
"Yes, I have wrenched my back."
"*Wohei*, I was lifting some heavy things, and then I wrenched my back."
"Yes, the doctor fix you up, he will. . . ."
"Here, go right in there!"
And on either side of where a person lies down, whoever is being
    doctored or examined,
Well, on both sides there were these cups, stirrups;
Now maybe that's where the knees are put in place;
And I didn't know until they told me,
"Take off your clothes," that white woman said to me.
I just looked at her.
"Take off your clothes!"
"I'm a nurse."
"There's nothing strange going on."
So I just went ahead and took off my clothes.
I was naked as a jaybird, I was just standing there wondering what to
    do next.

"*Wohei,* here is this device where there are things like cups."
"Your knees are put in there on both sides."
"You bend back over that way and expose your butt."
So I went ahead and did like she said.
Then this doctor came in.
He talked to me.
"Yes, I have wrenched my back."
Then, "*Wohei,* I will make you better again real quick."
I kind of saw behind me there, from the corner of my eye, that he was
    putting on rubber gloves.
The gloves were pretty big.
Well, that ointment, then he took a gob of it.
Well, he spread this stuff on my anus.
"Uh-oh, watch out," I thought.
Well here, after he was ready, then he put his fingers in there out of sight;
Oooh, it was really painful.
He almost made the lights go out on me [made me lose consciousness].
Right there somewhere, then suddenly he caused a popping sound.
That's how he . . . he's going to . . .
Then I really got a little bit faint.
Well, y-e-e-e-s, then it was like I was just lying there like a lump.
"Okay, stand up," he said to me.
After he had pulled his hand back out of there with a funny sticky noise,
    he stood there.
"How do you feel?"
"You know, it's better."
"Okay, here's some medicine;"
"I'll give it to you."
"You'll take it;"
"Only don't drink it with beer or whiskey;"
"You'll get a little bit dizzy from it."
"You'll have to watch out where you're driving."
And better again, that's how he made me better again, this white man.
That's why [it worked], because he had pretty big fingers.
That's as far as this story goes.

The story is especially comical because Robert makes extensive use of
hohkonee 'finally' and *hoonii* 'after a long time' to indicate John Plume's
slow and painful progress at the beginning of the story, most often using
these particles line-initially for additional effect. Robert also uses many
devices to emphasize the uncertainty and lack of agency John experiences:

multiple uses of the indefinite marker *toon-* and of *nooxeihi'* 'maybe'; and use of *3iwoo* 'well, let's see now . . . ', *noonoko'* 'well, whatever; might as well,' and *konoo'* 'well, anyway, I guess I will.' Finally, he makes masterful use of deixis. In everyday Arapaho, the proximal marker *nuhu'* 'this' occurs much more commonly than the distal markers *hinee* and *hi'in* 'that,' but in this story virtually everything John Plume describes is marked as 'that' thing or 'that place there' (*hinit*) and every direction is over 'that way' (*he3eb-, 3eb-*). These devices serve to emphasize the alienated feeling he experiences in the setting.

During a follow-up discussion of this story, Robert added that the doctor in question supposedly actually existed, and was named Dr. Edwards. He continued, "There's a lot of guys, you know . . . Like, one of my uncles had a back like that, you know. One of his nephews, you know, 'I'll help you out. Dr. Edwards gave me his way!' [And the uncle said] 'Ahh, get out of here!' 'He passed that way on to me. I'll help you out,' [the nephew repeated]. 'Ahh, get out of here!'" This is a nice example of the way these comic stories can be used for teasing purposes, with the nephew-uncle relationship being a key Arapaho relationship.

John Plume Visits the Optometrist

A second John Plume story, which I have heard on multiple occasions but never managed to record in Arapaho,[2] relies on the punch line *'oohoo-hei*. This word is used in Arapaho to indicate astonishment at the size or amount of something, but it also can carry implications of someone being a simpleton, or perhaps a child, who is easily astonished or has limited knowledge of the world. In the story, John Plume's eyesight is going bad as he gets older. After some resistance, doubt, and hesitation, he finally decides to go to one of those white doctors for the first time. He heads off to the optometrist to have his eyes checked out. The doctor prescribes bifocals for him. John is quite pleased with the quality of his new long-distance eyesight. Before heading home, he goes into the restroom and steps up to the urinal. He unzips his fly, and as he prepares to urinate, he looks down through the lower lens of his new bifocals, and exclaims *'oohoohei!!*

Reflection on John Plume Stories

Other examples of John Plume and Henry Snake stories are presented in the Riverton and Estes Park story chains (chapters 8 and 5, respectively). But just from the two stories told and described here, we can see that they have much in common with old couple or old folks stories: an emphasis on physical or sensory limits; white people as ironic secondary foils who are completely unaware of the joke; incongruous sexuality or sexual implications on the part of the old people; and an emphasis on the person's lack of awareness of the Euro-American world and various Euro-American practices and technologies. The primary differences are first, that the stories are at least ostensibly about real people and events, and second, that they are told in the first person.

The John Plume story is a really wonderful example of a narrative that engages with the colonial context, which bears much further comment. First, there are numerous sexual undertones that the casual reader might miss. As one elder who was helping me translate explained on a different occasion, when John gets in his car and is driving on the bumpy road to town, the entire description has sexual undertones. The word for 'hop on a car' (in Arapaho, "on" not "in" is the preposition used) is the same as that used for a man in relation to a woman during sex, and the "bumpy ride" carries obvious connotations. John presents himself as an old man who at least imagines himself as potentially sexually active.

When John arrives at the doctor's office however, he encounters a white female nurse, who unceremoniously tells him to take off all his clothes. His comical response conveys the shock of such an incident for Arapaho men generally: attitudes toward display of the body are generally conservative in reservation-era culture, and the scene also conveys the Arapaho view of white women as often sexually aggressive, both in dress and in their approach to men. At the same time, the story makes fun of John's own particular innocence and ignorance of the entire situation he is involved in, and one could certainly imagine that John thought he was truly being sexually propositioned. On yet another level, the story captures a common Arapaho ambivalence toward cross-cultural sexual encounters, especially in the earlier days of the twentieth century: a certain sexual curiosity and desire is brought up short, so to speak, by the reality of the encounter with the stereotypically more open and aggressive white woman, leading to feelings of sexual hesitation and loss of confidence. In this sense, John is more broadly representative of older Arapaho men's positions than might be apparent from the seeming mockery of his (obviously unusual) ignorance of white medical procedures. Thus, the scene allows an Arapaho listener to laugh overtly at both John Plume *and* the white world's strange attitudes toward sex and the body, while covertly indexing a more generalized uncertainty in relation to colonial power.

The entire story could in fact be read as a recapitulation of the colonial experience. The incident of visiting the doctor is recounted as being alienating and dehumanizing, with John constantly unsure of what is going to happen next. (A student in one of my classes once commented that the story reminded her of an account of an alien abduction.) The basic joke here is that although John has a bad back, he is ignorant of western medicine and ends up at the proctologist by mistake. Even the minor detail of the parking meter brings out this feeling—the meter is described in detail as the funny metal posts that sticks up, where you put money in. This description renders it strange and bizarre—who puts money in metal posts sticking out of the ground? John is stripped of all his dignity and humanity and is subjected to invasive procedures, while being assured that it is all for his own good and that he will be the better for cooperating. Yet, the incident is recounted in terms of a sexualized experience that renders John's (passive) position hilarious to an Arapaho audience as well.

The sense of sexual uncertainty is carried to entirely new heights when John enters the exam room with the proctologist, in a scene which carries clear analogies to anal intercourse and homosexual experience. The story continues to exploit John's extreme innocence and ignorance to maximum effect, as in the description of restraints or stirrups that actually seem more like equipment one would find in a gynecologist's office. The scene evokes the humorous—and indeed, downright bizarre—nature of some Euro-American medical customs and procedures. The focus is specifically on the reduction of the individual to a pure body to be probed in a highly impersonal, "scientific" manner. Many Euro-Americans will easily sympathize with this perception, but the feeling is even more marked for Arapaho individuals, since traditional Arapaho medicine is highly holistic and ritualistic in nature, combining physical treatment with prayer, song, and ceremony. Physical treatments and medicinal plants are assumed not to work without the proper social and ritual contexts, which tend to focus heavily on the spiritual as well as physical condition of the individual under treatment.

The Euro-American medical procedure is reductively and ironically stripped of its supposed medical rationale and acceptability or normalcy, and reduced to its most strange and comic simplicity in the story. The doctor himself seems to be interested in some form of homosexual practice, and John seems to be the imminent partner in this sexual encounter. Yet, as in the preceding scene, the critique of the Euro-American environment does not preclude a good deal of laughter targeted at John as well. His special fascination with the gloved hand and big fingers of the doctor, and the sexual trepidation which they evoke, make him the target of uproarious Arapaho laughter when the story is told for a fluent audience.

At the same time, John is reduced to the passive participant in what amounts to a severe bodily and sexual assault on his dignity, as an individual and as an Arapaho, by a Euro-American who occupies one of the quintessential positions of social and scientific authority in relation to reservation residents. This seems to be a larger symbolic evocation of white-Arapaho power dynamics and of a certain de-masculinization of the Arapaho male at the hands of this power and authority. Laughter at an excessively naive Arapaho individual combines with laughter at the strangeness of Euro-American society, but both index more deep-seated—and much less humorous—sociopolitical uncertainty and ambivalence expressed in the form of sexual inversion. Whether it is the female nurse who threatens the Arapaho male's prerogative to initiate a sexual encounter or the male doctor who threatens the Arapaho male's prerogative to the active position, John's position in the story cannot be separated from the evocation of both a sexual and a sociopolitical power dynamic that underlines the more fundamental problem of the colonial subject in the (literal) hands of the colonizer.

Yet, for all the dynamics that the story sets up, in the end it avoids taking a clear stand. After the insertion of the finger and its removal (a scene that Arapaho men describe as hilarious, particularly the word used for describing the extraction of the finger), John is miraculously cured of his bad back, due to the shock of the proctology exam, as he jerks suddenly when the finger is inserted. The result certainly reduces white medical practice to a new comic low of absurdity, as the cure and the problem have no connection whatsoever, other than the physical shock John experiences in reaction to the unusualness of the procedure.

But in this shock lies an even deeper irony. The story suggests that the attempted cure itself is fundamentally misguided and could not have worked on any regular patient. It could in fact only work on someone so far removed from the white medico-scientific establishment that he would be shocked (both mentally and physically) by the very bizarreness of the procedure to the point of jerking himself into health. Thus, the person most likely *not* to pursue such a cure in the first place—or at least, the person *least* likely to go to a proctologist and have confidence in and understanding of proctological procedure—is ironically the only person who really could have been cured. Up to this point, the Arapaho audience has been laughing at the "craziness" (as they would say in English) of both Euro-American medicine and John Plume. Yet in the conjunction of the two forms of craziness, a cure is effected—the two comic targets end up as collaboratively "smarter" and "healthier" than the audience would have ever thought as the story unfolded, with this result being the product of the meeting of extreme difference. "The world is truly crazy, but sometimes things work out anyway," is the message one is left with. This is a world where nothing Euro-American makes sense, and where there is thus no rational way for an Arapaho person to respond to that world effectively. It is a world both comic and absurd.

There are other Arapaho individuals who are recalled in a similar way. William C'Hair (real name) mentioned Leo L. as a person who somewhat resembled John Plume and who used to "tell crazy stories about himself" (field notes, May–June 2018). In one story, Leo goes to a Peyote Ceremony in Lakota country. Unfortunately, the wife of the Lakota leader of the ceremony gets sick and cannot carry out her crucial duties for her husband. Leo volunteers to help out with one thing then another, and the story turns increasingly comical as the Lakota man starts treating and talking to Leo as if he is the Lakota man's wife. In another story, Leo goes to visit his cousins ("sisters" in the Arapaho kinship system), but is tipsy when he arrives. He also is wearing pants with no belt and no underwear. For some reason, one of the children present yanks on his pants and pulls them down, exposing him in front of his sisters (a disastrous situation for an Arapaho person). He leans over quickly to pull up his pants, but hits his head on a table and knocks himself over. As the situation goes from bad to worse, he ends up running out of the house with his pants in his arms. As with John Plume and Henry Snake, Leo told such stories about himself, and those who retell the stories quote him in the first person.

Henry Snake: A Clown Who Builds Social Cohesion

In the same vein as John Plume, Henry Snake, also known as Henry Gunnison (Arapaho name Hooxei Hesnee, 'Hungry Wolf') is remembered by older people as a man who always got himself into funny situations and told funny stories about himself. He passed away sometime in the late 1950s or early 1960s. As the stories in the Riverton sequence (chapter 8) show, Henry Snake presents himself as much more actively mischievous than John Plume is. He brags excessively about himself and seems to think very highly of himself, trying to do things he should not or cannot do. His excessive curiosity often gets him into trouble—he is, in fact, easily tricked, especially if one appeals to his vanity, and very gullible. In addition, he is quick to anger, he makes lame excuses for his failures, and despite being married and older, he has unfulfilled sexual desires. He refuses to acknowledge his age and the proper behaviors for someone of that age.

Based on this description, Henry Snake would not appear to have been a person whom anyone would have liked much. Indeed, he quite closely resembles the Arapaho trickster figure *Nih'oo3oo* in many ways. When I made this suggestion to William C'Hair in May 2018, he readily agreed. He "always wanted to outdo someone, talk about himself," William added. Yet Henry Snake is always talked of with fondness. The reason for this is that Henry Snake recognized his own negative personality traits (and almost certainly exaggerated them in both his actions and his narratives for comic effect), and made fun of *himself* in his stories. Even more importantly, in the end he almost always recognized the validity of Arapaho social values, regretting his actions and promising future reform. As a result, he is spoken of as someone who always made people feel good by his presence. He was effectively a socialized trickster—a kind of stand-up comic and comedian Euro-Americans might say, or in a particular Native American vein, a clown such as the Lakota *heyoka*. He could be compared to John (Fire) Lame Deer of the Lakota, for example, though whereas the Lakota figures are described as providing "comic mediation in all things worldly and spiritual" (Lincoln 1993, 62), Henry Snake's realm of action seems restricted to the worldly domain.[3] At the end of the chain of stories presented in chapter 8, the two speakers provide these comments on Henry Snake (ELAR Video 128a, 5:48):

Bill: Yeah hini'iit-iino, woow, woow hee'inobeen-o' neh'eeno he'=hi-niisih'iit, hesnP, uhh hih-tousi-nihiitP Hooxei Hesnee.
    Yeah, that guy now, now I know his name, what he was called, Hungry Wolf.

Roger: HooxeiP
    Wolf . . .

Bill: Hooxei Hesnee, [neneeni-t, neneeni-t.
    Hungry Wolf, that was him.

Roger: [Yeah.
    Yeah.

Bill: Nih-co'on-woo-wo'oo3eti-t.
    Hungry Wolf, that was him; he was always bragging on himself.

    Wootii nii'P tih-'eeneinisee-t, nih-ceeceitoonP, ceeP ceeceitee-t heenoo.

When he walked around, he always had pierced ears.

Noh beebeet, hee3e'in-owoo hini'iit-iino, nih'iiP nih-
'ii3oohow-o', beebeet nih-niiseihi-t nuhu' cee-ceitoo.
[[gesture: earrings dangling from ears]]
*The way that I remember him/see him, he was the only one
who had pierced ears among the men.*

Ceeceitoo-no, nih-'eix-o'.
He wore earrings.

'oh hoo3oo'o' hinen-no', hih-'oow-eix-owuu.
The other men didn't wear them.

'oh beebeet neneeni-t, 'oh nihP hi3oowo', hi3oowo'
nih-co'oneeyoo'uu-t.
Only him, and remember, he was always dressed fancy.

Roger: 'ihee.
           Oh yeah!/I remember that now!

Bill: Nuhu' ceeceitoo-no hee, nih-'eeneix-o'. [[gesture: earrings
           dangling]]
           These earrings, yeah, he wore them.

           Wohei hini'iit-iino, niiyou hini-i3e'ee, ci' nih-nii-niisen-o'.
           [[gesture: braids, wrapping braids]]
           And those braids, his hair, he wrapped it.

           NihP nih-niisen-o' wootii hini-i3ootee'ee-no. [[gesture: two
           braids]]
           I guess he wrapped his braids.

           Nenee-', nenee-', nenee-' . . .
           That, that, that . . .

           Ne'ini, hiiwoonhehe', 'oh bisiihi', 'oh hiiwoonhehe'
           nonoo-noohobeihi-3i'.
           Then, today, well, everyone today, they all appear that way.

'oh no'on-noohowP hinen-no' nii-ceeceitee-3i'. [[gesture:
pointing to both ears]]
And now I often see men with pierced ears.

Noh, noh beebeet nih-neeni-t, nih-neeni-t niito'
ne-ih-noohow-ooo.
But he was just the first one that I saw who did that.

Ne'P ne'P ne'P ne'P ne'-cihP. . . .
Then, then later. . . .

WonooP, woow wonoote'inon-o' nuhu' Hooxei Hesnee.
Now I remember this Hungry Wolf.

Noh nihP, heenoo nih-'ii-t, wootii nih-'oonP wootii
nih-'onowo'on-oot.
*He would, they said he always, it was like he made people
feel comfortable in his presence.*

Heenoo nih-'oonowo'on-oot wootii [nuhu' tih'ini . . .
nih-'eeneisiini wootii nih-'eeneisP nih-'eeneisoo3itee-t,
tohuu-woo-wo'oo3eti-t.
*He always made people feel comfortable since he would . . .
how he told stories, or when he bragged about himself.*

Roger: [hee.
                                          yes.

Bill: Wootii wootii nih-bisi-ni'en-o' heeyouhuu.
           It was like he could handle any situation.

           Yeah hih-'oow-oo3ontii heeyouhuu, wootii tih-'oon-oo3itee-3i'.
           *Yeah, he was never stumped by anything/never failed, when
           they were telling stories.*

Clearly Henry Snake was *different*. He was "a character . . . his own
character," William C'Hair said in May 2018. He was also very explicitly
a storyteller and a performer, and someone who contributed to social harmony and enjoyment, not despite but because of his seemingly antisocial

qualities such as braggadocio. Joseph Epes Brown said of another Lakota *heyoka*, Nicholas Black Elk, that "he was always doing funny things . . . that is why it was always good to live with him, because you never knew what to expect" (cited in Lincoln 1993, 67). This comment closely echoes the description of Henry Snake.

In concluding this chapter, I would like to return to the aforementioned genre of trickster stories and consider more carefully the intertextual relationship between that genre and comicals among the Northern Arapaho. The trickster is a notably protean character in many Native American oral traditions, and trickster stories themselves exhibit the same protean nature. Many of them are quite traditional in content, reflecting precontact culture. But many others incorporate modern content and engage specifically with the Euro-American encounter. One Northern Arapaho story recounts the trickster skating around on a frozen river on ice skates. Two young men are carrying "a nice shiny butt" across the river but are worried about the slippery ice. The trickster volunteers to carry it for them, but, of course, slips and drops it. This is why our butts all have cracks in them now. Treuer (2001, 162–63) includes a story about the Ojibwe trickster Wenabozho playing baseball. Franchot Ballinger (2004, 61–62, 142–43) reports on trickster stories that specifically involve mockery or tricking of white people and which resemble the believe-it-or-not genre of Arapaho stories, as well as trickster stories in which the trickster is specifically identified as white. Ballinger (2004, 128–30) also notes the connections between the trickster and the clown. Thus, the trickster figure and genre have especially expansive powers to incorporate new material and themes. This is the one relatively traditional genre of Native American narrative that easily expands to include Euro-American individuals, themes, and encounters. It can be understood as an intertextual bridge between the more traditional and the more contemporary themes in oral narratives.

Among the Northern Arapaho, the expansive power of the trickster genre resonates or echoes through many other stories and genres. Not only do crazy guy stories in the Henry Snake vein echo the trickster, but so do believe-it-or-not stories. The traditional trickster is always fascinated by new powers: he sees a small bird that can throw its eyes up into the tops of trees to see for great distances, for example, and immediately seeks to replicate—and misunderstands and abuses—that power. Protagonists in believe-it-or-not stories likewise show a fascination with new powers, as well as a tendency to misunderstand how those powers work, with a naiveté appropriate to the trickster. The main difference is that while in trickster stories this trait turns out disastrously for the trickster (his eyes end up stuck at the top of a tree, for example), in the believe-it-or-not stories, things accidentally work out okay somehow or other. Indeed, both believe-it-or-not and crazy guy stories actually seem to be parodies of trickster stories, rather than direct parallels to them.

Old folks stories and John Plume stories echo another aspect of the trickster's character—he is constantly finding himself a victim of circumstances beyond his control and ending up in ridiculous situations. The key difference is that in the former instances, the victims are hapless innocents, whereas the trickster constantly goes too far and gets himself into his own predicaments. Even Strong Bear stories have a vague resonance with trickster stories: Strong Bear is notable for his extreme confidence—one might even say overconfidence. He refuses to fight the world boxing champion not because he is afraid to do so, but because he is absolutely sure he would hurt him badly. His tagline to other Arapahos is, "Gee, you should be able to do that! It's nothing!" One can easily imagine the trickster saying exactly the same things. The difference is that Strong Bear's confidence is actually warranted. Individual storytellers can of course choose to play up or play down these potential resemblances between the genres, but the resonance is probably always there to some extent. Indeed, in chapter 5, one teller called a story a "trickster" story, even though the characters involved were just "a man" and a bear, and the story seemed to be more generally a comical or believe-it-or-not story. Echoes of the trickster seem always to be lurking behind Arapaho comicals—examples of what Mirjam Hirch refers to as a broader "tricksterish spirit" (Taylor 2005, 112) that is characteristic of Native American humor. Again, it is probably best to think of the more recently emerging comical stories as parodies of the trickster: the main character ends up actually learning his or her lesson; actually being reintegrated back into the group; or actually exercising the crucial degree of wisdom, insight, and self-control that the trickster himself always seem to lack—or at least showing the self-awareness that the trickster so often fails to attain. The characters in comicals manage to rise above a trickster-like state or fate, in a moment that combines humor with social harmonization. They then retell these moments in ways that subtly play with numerous tropes of trickster stories, so that their performative mastery echoes their comic behavioral mastery.

8

Story Sequence C

Riverton, Wyoming (2015)

This story sequence arose from a meeting between Bill and Roger. Bill's wife was temporarily in the Riverton, Wyoming, rehabilitation and retirement center after an operation, and he was going to go visit her. Roger was a permanent resident of the rehabilitation center. He was a friend and relation of Bill's, so Bill suggested that he and I visit Roger, and that Bill and Roger could tell stories that I could record. This was therefore a session requested and arranged by one of the participants himself. Roger had often worked with me before, so both men were comfortable with each other as well as with me, though we did not check with Roger ahead of time on the arrangements.

Upon arrival, everyone was agreeable, so we found an empty room, and I set up the video camera. The two men sat down, arranging their chairs, and then Bill initiated the session by telling Roger that the two of them would tell each other stories, with a focus on the old days and the way things were different in the old days compared to today. After some banter in Arapaho, Roger told an old couple story, about a named husband and wife, which involved the husband being scared of ghosts and the dark, to the amusement of his wife—a story quite similar to the one told by Robert in chapter 4. The protagonist of the story was Tommy Brown (real name). This led Bill to follow up by noting that Tommy Brown had told him many stories. He then told one particularly comic one about "bringing home the bacon," in which the English idiom was played off against a literal situation in which the bacon was brought home. The story did not fall into any particular genre other than that of an extended cross-linguistic pun, although puns themselves could be considered a genre of Arapaho comical stories. Bill then proceeded to tell a second story, also attributed to Tommy Brown, in which a Euro-American anthropologist is mocked for asking too many questions—also what could be considered an extended joke story. He followed that with a third story, of the crazy guy genre, in which Tommy Brown accidentally got his hand stuck in the lock of a door.

This chain then dissolved back into general conversation about the Brown family and the way of life back when they were around (primarily the 1940s and early 1950s). Bill then explicitly urged Roger to tell a story about those times (Video 128b, 6:06):

Bill: wootii hini'iitiino, hinee teexco' howoo hini'iitiino, heinoonin ci' neinoo, nih- noonohco'oo-3i'.

For example, those ones, those ones also long ago, our mother and my mother, they took part in all that.

'oh hini'iit heinoo, hi3oowo' nih-tebinesee-t.

And your mother, remember, she was missing a hand.

Roger: Yeah.

Yeah.

Bill: Nih-tebinesee-t, yeah.

She was missing her hand and lower arm, yeah.

Wohei heetniini . . .

Well, I am going to [run to the restroom].

Nuh'uuno hoo3itoon-inee.

Tell him about these things.

'oh heet-woniini he3ebiini hihcei'ihcehi-noo.

I am going to go there and lift a leg real quick.[1]

[[2 sec.]]
I'll be right back.

I'll be right back.

[[1.5 sec.]]
He's gonna tell . . . , heetn-oo3itoon-ein.

He's [Roger's] going to tell you [Cowell] a story.
[[13 sec.]]

((Roger is hesitant to begin the story without Bill being present, but then goes ahead and starts.))

Henry Snake and the "Young Woman"

((Henry Snake, also Henry Gunnison, was this man's real name. Snake is described in chapter 7.))

Chuck: <u>Wohei nehe' nihii Gunnison</u> nih-co'on-woteekoohu-t.[2]
Well this, uh, Gunnison was always driving to town.

Nohtou toh-co'on-woteekoohu-n? nih-'ii3-eit nehe' Monica-huho'.
"Why are you always driving to town?" the mother of the family he lived with, Monica (real name), said to him.

Ne'iini, he-ihoowP husei nii-cih'ini nii-no'o3onohei-t, nih-'ii-t.
Then, "There is a young woman who writes to me a lot," he said.

'iiheihoo.
"Gee whiz!" [Monica said].

Hiikoot no'o3-ceesi-n houwo, nih-'ii3-eit.
"What's more, you are buying a lot of blankets," she said to him.

Hee, heet-no'koohu-t.
"Yes, she will come here."

Noh nihii, nuhu' hoonou3ooni-', keet-won-nii3i-niibei'i?
"And, uh, this Christmas, are you going to join the singing?"

Hiiko, hiiko, heet-won-nouxon-o' ne'=nih-'ii'P ne'P nehe' neeneinkoohuu3ei-t, nih-'ii-t.
"No, no, I'm going to go meet that passenger bus," he said.

Heet-won-nouxon-o'.
"I will go meet her at the station."

Heet-no'koohu-t hiiwoonhehe', nih-'ii-t.
"She will come here today," he said.

'oh teecxo' ne'=nih-'ii'-cih-wo3onohowuun-o'.

"A long time ago I wrote her a message about coming here to meet me."

((Video 128c, 0:00))

Roger: Henry-hihe', Henry T.-hihe'.

   "So Henry , Henry T. . . ." [real name]

   Wohei heetP heet-no'koohu-t. [[gesture: indicating someone arriving here]]

   "Well, he will arrive too."

   No'kooh-ehk, heet-wonouxon-einoo, nih-'ii-t. [[gesture: someone arriving]] [[gesture: going to a place to meet someone]]

   "When he gets here, he will meet me," he said.

   Ne'-won-nouxon-oot. [[gesture: pointing to the place where he goes to meet the person]]

   Then Gunnison went to meet the bus.

   Nehe' nihii heso'oonotii, ne'-noo'oekoohu-3i' hiit. [[gesture: pointing to the bus]] [[gesture: bus arriving here]]

   This, uh, train [intended 'bus'], then it turned around here.

   Ne'-cih-'oonoowusee-3i'. [[gesture: people getting off the bus]]

   Then the passengers got down off the bus.

   Yeh, nesihoo!

   "Hey, uncle!" Henry T. said.

   Heeyou hei-toyoohoo3oo, nih-'ii-t. [[PSL gesture: "what?"]]

   "What are you waiting for?" he said

   Hei'ooP husei. [[gesture: pointing at someone]]

   "A woman."

   Teco'on-no'oto3onohowuun-einoo. [[gesture: writing a letter]]

   "She always writes a lot to me."

Beebei'on neentoo-t, nih-'ii-t. [[gesture: pointing at somewhere far away]]

"She lives way far away," he said.

Yehei, nih-'ii3-eit.

"Gee," Henry T. said to him.

Nooxeihi', nooxeihi' niiP, nooxeihi' nii-teco'on-toyoohow-ot. [[gesture: pointing at someone]]

"Maybe you are always waiting for her."

Hee, seesiihi-noo, nih-'ii-t.[3]

"Yes, I'm eager," he said.

Henee3nee-sesiihi-noo, nih-'ii-t.

"I am really eager," he said.

Nii-beet-nouxon-o'. [[gesture: person arriving here]]

"I want to meet her."

Nii-beet-iniini-noo. [[PSL gesture: "marriage," "two together"]]

"I want to have a wife."

Nii-beet-niiseekuu-ni', nih-'ii-t. [[PSL gesture: "marriage"]]

"We want to get married," he said.

Hee, heet-ni'itoo-n, nih-'ii3-eit. [[PSL gesture: "marriage"]]

"Yes, that would be good," [Henry T.] said to him.

Ne'iini, ne'P ne'-eh-ce3ei'oo-t nehe' Henry. [[gesture: indicating someone leaving]]

Then Henry left.

Ne'-cih-ce'-ko'eisi-'.

Then he turned back around this way.

Wohei nesihoo, nih-'ii3-oot.

"Well, uncle," he said to him.

Heeyou? nih-'ii-t, heeyou?
"What," he said, "what?"

He'ii3ou'u heetn-ei'towuun-e3en.
"I will tell you something."

wohei, cih-'ei'towuun-i.
"Okay, tell me."

Neneeninoo, nii-co'on-wo3onohowuun-e3en. [[gesture: points at self]] [[gesture: putting letters in the mail]][4]
"I'm the one who always writes to you."

Yehei, henee3nee-3iikoniini-n, nih-'ii3-oot. [[gesture: pointing at an addressee, shaking hand reprovingly]]
"Gee, you are a real ghost," he said to Henry.[5]

Henee3nee-woxeihi-n. [[gesture: pointing at an addressee, shaking hand reprovingly]]
"You are really bad."

Heet-noxowuh-i3en. [[gesture: hitting someone on the head]]
"I'm going to knock you out."

Sii=heet-noxowuh-i3en, nih-'ii3-oot. [[gesture: hitting someone on the head]]
"I'm really going to knock you out," he said to him.

Ne'iini, neneeninoo, nih-'ii-t, yeheihoo, heet-ce'eeckoohu-noo. [[gesture: throwing hand up in exasperation, indicating departure]]
Then, "me," he said, "gee whiz, I'm going back home."

Ne'P ne'-ce'eeckoohu-t. [[gesture: pointing at someone departing]]
Then he went back home.

Noh huu3e', hit-o'oowu-u', noonouukuutii-t nuhu' hit-ouwo, heenei'isiihi'. [[gesture: pointing at house over there]] [[gesture: throwing down blankets]][6]

And over there, at his house, he threw out all the blankets and various things.

'iiheihoo! nih-'ii3-eit Monica-huho'.
"Gee whiz!" Monica said to him.

Hot-ouwo, niini'ou-'u. [[gesture: pointing at things on the ground]]
"Your blankets, they are good."

Wonooyou-'u. [[gesture: pointing at things on the ground]]
"They are new."

Hei-beex-ce'-wo'ten. [[gesture: pointing at things on the ground]][7]
"You should pick them back up."

Hiiko, hiiko. [[PSL gesture: "no"]]
"No, no."

Woow heet-konoh-nooh'-owoo. [[gesture: flames rising up]]
"Now I will set them all on fire, burn them."

He-etne-ihoowuuni.
"You won't do that."

He-etne-ihoow-nooho', nih-'ii3-eit.
"You're not going to set them on fire, burn them," she said to him.

Hoohookeeni-n, nih-'ii3-eit, toh-'oonotoonoot-ow.
"You're crazy," she said to him, "because you bought all of them."

Nih-'owoto'oo-noo," nih-'ii-t.
"I woke up," he said.

Yehei, ne-ihoow-ooh-'ohookeen, nih-'ii-t.
"Gee, I'm not crazy anymore," he said.

Nehe' ne-ih-no'o3o3onohowuun-eiit, honoh'oe he'ih-neen; teecxo'. [[gesture: pointing at someone]]

"The one who wrote to me so much, it was apparently a young man; a long time that went on."

Henee3neeP henee3neen-esinih-einoo hiiwoonhehe', nih-'ii-t.

"He really has made me angry now," he said.

Woowuuno, ne-etne-ihoow-niiniibei'i, nih-'ii-t. [[PSL gesture: "no more"]]

"Now I'm not going to sing/take part in the Christmas ceremonies," he said.

Ne'P ne'iini won-nokohu-t.

Then he went to go to sleep.

Ne'-ce'-woteesee-t nuhu'.

Then he drove back to town.

Ne'iini won-3iiyouhu-t. [[gesture: pointing to braids]]

Then he went and got a haircut.

Nih-kou'usi-ni'i nuhu'. [[gesture: cutting off hair]][8]

He had his braids cut off.

Nih-'ii-cih-kou'usi-ni'i. [[gesture: cutting off braids on both sides of head]]

They were cut off here.

Nohtou toh-nee'eestoo-n, nih-'ii3-eit.

"Why did you do that?" Monica said to him.

((Bill returns from the restroom. Roger stops his account midway, engages with Bill, then restarts the narrative.))

Roger: <u>Koo-he-e'inon-oo nehe' nihii Gunnison?[9]</u>

    Do you know this, uh, Gunnison?

Bill: Hee, 'oh nei-how3o'-uni . . . , koh'-nih'oo3ouni-t.

    Yes, but I never . . . , he was half white.

Roger: [Hee.
           Yes.

Bill: [XXX . . . koh'-nih'oo3ouni-t.
           ??? He was half white.

           [[2 sec.]]
           Wootii . . .
           Like/I guess . . .

Roger: NihP . . . nih-co'on-woteekoohu-t.[10]
           He was . . . he was always driving to town.

Bill: Uhm-hmm.
           Uhm-hmm.

Roger: Nih-won-nouxon-oot neeneinkoohuu3ei-ni3. [[gesture:
           pointing to a location over there]]
           He went to meet the passenger bus.

Bill: Uhm-hmm.
           Uhm-hmm.

Roger: 'oh nehe' nihii Henry, he'ih-neen,
           nih-co'on-cih-wo3onohowuun-oot.
           *But this, uh, Henry T., he was apparently the one, he always
           wrote him letters.*

           Nih-'eenei'towuun-oot, I love you.
           He was telling him, "I love you."

           Nee3nee-ni'eeneb-e3en.
           "I really like you."

           Heet-niiseekuu-no'.
           "We are going to get married."

           Heetniini cih-niisxoo-ni'.
           "We will be a couple."

Yeheihoo, nih-'ii-t.
"Gee whiz!" he said.

Noxowe-esnonee-t.
He was really angry after he found out.

Sii=heet-noxowuh-i3en. [[gesture of shaking finger or fist at someone]]
"I'm really going to pound you."

SiiP siiyeihP . . . [[gesture: shaking finger or fist at someone]]
I'm really going to . . ."

Ciibeh-cih-neyei3itii, nih-'ii3-oot. [[gesture: pushing or throwing something away]]
"Don't you try that again," he said to Henry T.

Bill: Hmm.
Hmm.

Roger: Het-eh . . . neh-ce3ei'oo. [[gesture of sending someone away]]
"You must . . . you better get on out of here."

Noonouukuutii-t nuhu' hit-ouwo, heenei'isiihi'. [[gesture: throwing something away]]
He threw out his blankets and so forth.

Monica-huho' nih-'ii3-eit, 'iiheihoo, huut ce'-wo'ten!"
Monica said to him, "Gee, you must pick those back up!"

Hetiini ce'-iiyoo3-ciinen. [[gesture: pointing at things lying about]]
"You must put them back in their proper place."

Hiiko, woow benee3tii-noo, nih-'ii-t. [[gesture: refusing or dismissing something]]
"No, now I'm done with that," he said.

Heneenesinih-einoo, nih-'ii-t.
"He has gotten me real mad," he said.

Nehe', nehe' honoh'oe, nih-'ii-t, woowuuno beneebee3too-no'. [[PSL gesture: "no more"]]
"This, this young man," he said, "now we are all finished as friends."

Ne-etne-ihoow-ooh-niiniibei'i, nih-'ii-t. [[PSL gesture of 'no more']]
"I'm not going to sing anymore either," he said.

'oh tohuuP, tohuu-nii3ootee'ei-t, [[gesture, pointing to braids]]
And his braids,

Bill: Uhm-hmm.
Uhm-hmm.

Roger: Nih-won-kou'usi-ni'i. [[gesture: braids cut off short on both sides]]
He went and had them cut off.

Yeheihoo, nohtou toh-nee'eestoo-n?
"Gee, why do you do that?"

Yeheihoo, nii-beet-ce'-wooneihi-noo, nih-'ii-t.
"Gee, I want to be young again," he said.

Ne-ihoow-beh'eihehiin, nih-'ii-t.
"I'm not an old man," he said.

'ine tous, toon-heeneestoo-noni, nih-'ii3-eit.
"Okay, then, whatever you want," she said to him.

[[2.5 sec.]]

Henry Snake and the "Devil"

<u>Roger:</u>   <u>Noh ne'iini</u> nuhu' hoonou3oo nih-no'uxoo-'.

And then Christmas arrived.

<u>Nehe' Simon</u> nih-'ii-3ebiinisee-t. [[gesture: pointing to a distant person or place]]

Simon [real name] was wandering around out there, outside the house.

Nih-ceene'eini-t nehe' Gunnison. [[gesture: sitting bent over with head down]]

Gunnison was sitting with his head down.

Nih-ceene'eini-t. [[gesture: sitting bent over with head down]]

He was sitting with his head down.

Yeheihoo, 'oh ne'-ihce'eini-t. [[gesture: raising head to look up]]

"Gee!," and then he raised his head.

Simon was wandering around out there, outside the house.

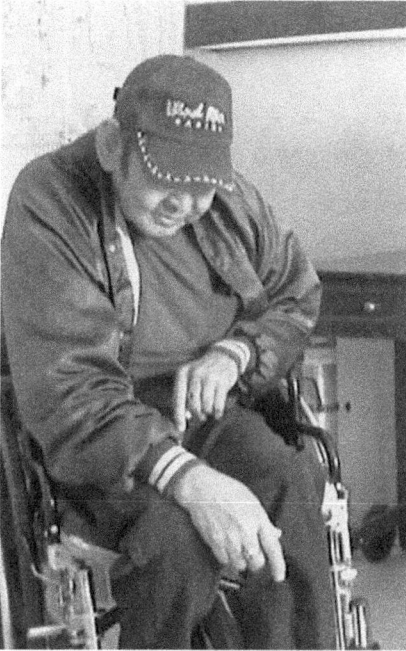

Gunnison was sitting with his head down.

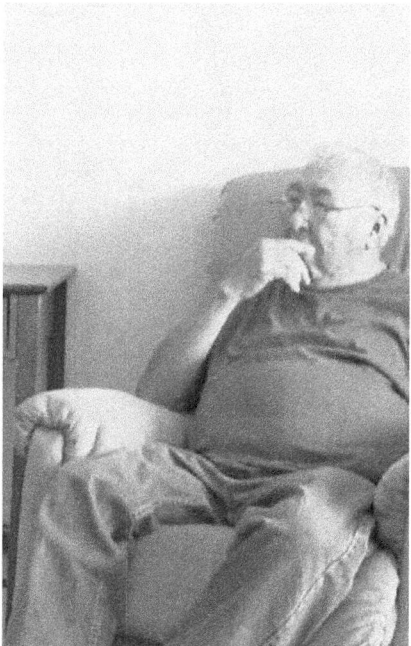

"Gee!," and then he raised his head.

'oh ne'P 'oh nehe' Simon nih-cii3-nei'ooku'oo-t. [[gesture: looking in through a window]]

And then, Simon was looking inside there at him.

Hey, hey, hey, nih-'ii-t. [[gesture: seeing something scary or surprising]]

"Hey, hey, hey," he said.

Hih-no'o3-be'e3eino'ono'. [[gesture: picking things up and throwing them on a fire]]

He grabbed a lot of cedar.

Noh henee3nee-be'e3eino'o, nih-3eiikuu3-oot. [[gesture: throwing something on a fire]]

And a lot of cedar, he threw it into the stove.

Hesitee, nih-'ee3nee-xouu'eyei'i-t. [[gesture: smoke rising]]

He made the fire all smoky.

And then, Simon was looking inside there at him.

And a lot of cedar, he threw it into the stove.

He made the fire all smoky.

Kooteeyei-t.
He made a lot of smoke.

Ne'=nih-'ii'-no'koohu-t hi'in Monica.
Then Monica came running there.

'iiheihoo, heeyou?
"Gee whiz, what is it?"

Hei-toustoo? nih-'ii3-eit.
"What are you doing?" she said to him.

Yeheihoo nih-noohow-o'.
"Gee, I saw him!"

Hoocoo nih-cih-nei'oohob-einoo. [[gesture: pointing to devil outside]]
"The devil was looking at me in here."

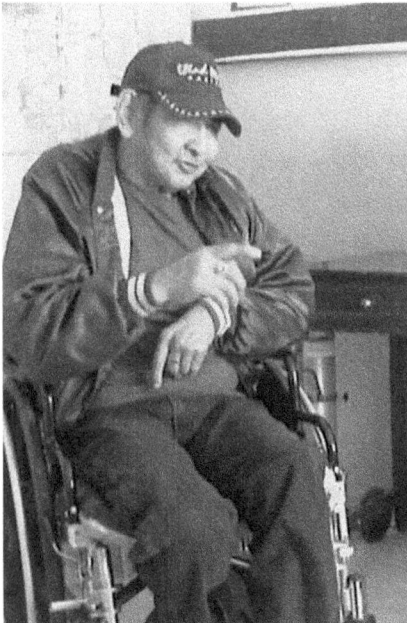

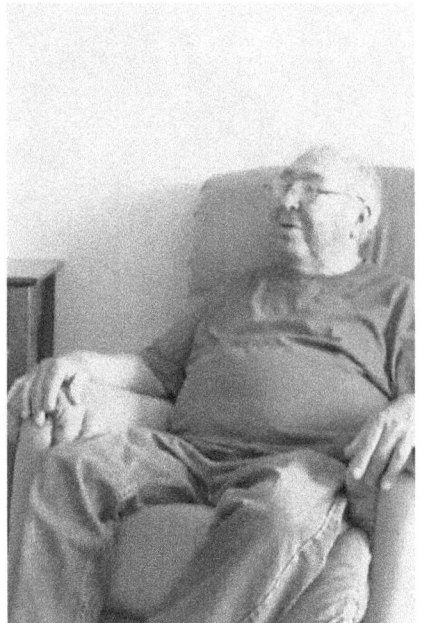

"The devil was looking at me in here."

[[laughter]]

[[laughter]]
Yehei, hoowuuni, nih-'ii3-eit. [[PSL gesture: "no"]]
"Gee, that's not true," she said to him.

Hiiko, hiiko, nih-'ii-t.
"No, no, it's true," he said.

3eb-ce'eeckoohu hot-o'oowu-u', nih-'ii-t. [[gesture: pointing somewhere over there]]
"Go back to your house," she said to Gunnison.

Nih-'e-e3eb-ce'-yihoo-t. [[gesture: pointing somewhere over there]]
Then Gunnison was going back over there.

Ne'-yihoo-t nehe' Simon.
Then Simon went back there too.

Ciitei-t.

He went in.

((Roger leaps ahead in the story, to G's reaction to Simon's words.))

Ce'-no'oehi, nih-'ii3-oot. [[gesture: dismissing someone from one's presence]]

"Go back outside," Gunnison said to Simon.

Heesinih-in; heet-noxowuh-i3en, nih-'ii3-oot. [[gesture: hitting someone]]

"You have made me really mad: I'm going to knock you flat," he said to him.

[[laughter]]

HeetniiP . . .

"I'm going to. . . ."

((Roger circles back to when Simon enters, and provides his words.))

Ne'=nih-'ii3P . . .

That was what/how . . .

wohei nesihoo, nih-'ii-t,

"Well, uncle," Simon said to him,

Heetn-ei'towuun-e3en.

"I will tell you about it."

Nih-neeninoo tohuu-cih-nei'oohob-e3en, nuhu' noh'eihoon-e', nih-'ii-t.

"I was the one who was looking at you through the window."

Yeheihoo, nih-'ii-t.

"Gee whiz," he said.

Nih-'ee3nee-woxeihi-n, nih-'ii3-oot.

"You were really bad," Gunnison said to him.

Ciibeh-cih-neih-i.
"Don't scare me!"

Ciibeh-'ooh-cih-ciitei not-o'oowu-u', nih-'ii-t.
"Don't ever come in my house again," he said.

Beebeet nih-neeneih-in.
"You just scared me badly."

<u>Wohei.</u>
Well, that's it.[11]

[[chuckles]]
[[5.0 sec.]]

((Video 128d, 0:00))

Anecdote about Joe White Owl

((At this point, Bill, who listened to the first two stories, takes over as narrator, telling a story of Joe White Owl (real name).))

Bill: <u>Simon Blackman, Simon Blackman, koo-neen,</u>
nih-'iis-nei'ooku'oo-t.
Simon Blackman, Simon Blackman [real name], was he the one looking around in the story you just told?

Roger: Yeah.
Yeah.

Bill: Simon Blackman, yeah.
Simon Blackman, yeah.

Roger: Simon, neneenit [nih-cii3-nei'ooku'oo-t.
Simon, he was the one who was looking in the house.

Bill: [Yeah, nih-cii3-nei'ooku'oo-t, yeah.
Yeah, he looked inside there, yeah.

Cee3-ciitei-t <u>ceesey neh'eeno</u>, woP uhm hees-ii-tousihi', hees-ii-tousihi', 'oh niine'eehek neh'eeno Gunnison?

One time this guy inadvertently came in, uh, what was his name, what was his name, this here Gunnison?

Hinono'einiihi' koo-he-esP <u>koo-he-e'inobeen-oo</u>?

Do you know what his Arapaho name was?

[[4 sec.; no response]]
Nih-'e-e'inobeenoon-o',

I knew his name.

Nii-coon-bii'eenowuskuutii-noo hiiwoonhehe'.

I can't think of it real quick right now.

[[4 sec.]]
<u>Uhm</u>, nih-cih-cee3-ciitei-t niiyou <u>nuh'uuno</u> heenees-3i'okuutooni-'.

He inadvertently walked in where people were sitting.

'oh hini'iit nih-biito'oku-3i' heenoo.

And they customarily sat on the ground.

'oh hini'iitiino, <u>hi3oowo'</u>, nih-'eneihi-t. [[gesture: indicating a tall person]]

And remember that guy who was tall.

Nih-'eneihi-t.

He was tall.

Nooku-bee3ei, ne'=nih-'iis-cebih'i-t.

White Owl, that was his last name.

Nooku-bee3ei neneenit.

He was called Joe White Owl.

Wootii hiwoP hi-wo'ohno, wootii nihP nihtesP, hini'iitiino nih-tes-beesoo-ni'i, hi-wo'ohno. [[gesture: indicating long feet or shoes]]

*I guess his shoes, I guess they were very, they were very big,
his shoes.*

Nih-'owoooteihi-t.
He was disabled.

Wootii niiyou nuh'uuno, niiyou nuh'uuno, wootii nih-
'esowobeihi-t, niiyou nuhu' noxowP noxow-uyowobe3e'eihiit.
*I guess these ones, these ones, I guess he was sick, with this
arthritis.*

Hi3oowo' hi'in tohP hi3oowo' nuhu'. . . .
Remember that . . . remember this. . . .

'oh 'oh nih-'ee3neene-eneihi-t.
And he was very tall.

'oh nuhu' toh-3i'oku-3i, 'oh biitobeiP biito'oku-t.
*And whenever he was sitting down, he always sat on the
ground.*

Co'on-biito'oku-t.
He always sat on the floor.

'oh niiyou nuhu', niiyou nuhu' ce'iiteyei-no' huutiino.
[[gesture: knees high on each side of a person]]
*And there were these, there were his knees that came up real
high next to him.*

Noh heneebees nih-noohow-oot niine'eehek neh'eeno.
[[gesture: pointing at a person]] [[gesture: indicating eyes/
seeing]]
And Gunnison happened to see him sitting there.

Nei'oohow-oot.
He looked at him.

Yeheihoo, nih-'ii-t.
"Gee whiz," he said.

Yeheihoowun, nii-3i'okuuP 3ee3i'okuutooni-', <u>he'ih</u>-'ii.
"Gee, there are people sitting here," they say he said.

Huut 3i'okuutooni-'.
"There are people sitting here."

Nih'etP het-cih-3i'okuutooni-', heesi3ecoo-noo, nih-'ii-t.
"I thought there were people sitting there," he said.

Noh neh'eeno huutiino neehii3ei' 3ii'oku-t, neehtiih-o',
nih-'ii-t. [[gesture: pointing at someone over there]]
"And I recognize this one sitting in the middle," he said.

Neehtiih-o' nehe' neehii3ei' 3ii'oku-t. [[gesture: pointing at
someone over there]]
"I recognize the one sitting in the middle."

'oh nuhu' heeneitonoku-ni3i, 'oh neiP neih'oow-nehtiih-
oono', nihP nih-'ii-t. [[gesture: knees high on both sides of a
person]]
*"But these sitting on both sides, I didn't recognize them," he
said.*

<u>He'</u>=nee'eesi-nihii3-eit.
I guess that's what Gunnison said to him.

Yeheihoo, nih-'ii3-oohok. [[gesture: knees high on both sides
of a person]]
"Gee whiz," Joe said back to him.

Hini'iitiino, 'oh hoowP hoow-3i'okuutoon. [[gesture: knees
high on both sides of a person]]
"There is no one sitting there."

Ce'iiteyei-no nenee-ni3i, nohP toh-noohow-oti. [[gesture:
knees high on both sides of a person]]
"My knees, that is what you see on either side."

[[chuckles]]

[[4 sec.]]

Wox uhh, heesih'P, ni'i3ecooP

Bear, uh, what was his name . . .

Nii-coon-bii'eeneetebee-noo hi-niisih'iit neh'eeno.

I can't remember his Arapaho name.

Henry Snake, ne'=nih-'iisih'i-t nih'oo3ouniihi'.

Henry Snake, that was his English name.

Henry Snake, Henry Gunnison, nih-'ii3-oo3i'.

Henry Snake, Henry Gunnison, they called him.

Henry Snake Tries Calf-Roping

Bill: Anyway, heenoo nihP, totoonee nihP nih-co'on-iin-ceitee-t.

Anyway, his custom was that he would, he would always go around everywhere visiting people.

Nih-co'on-iin-ceitee-t hi3oowo', neh'eeno.

Remember, he would always go around visiting people.

Hini'iitiino ahh, GuP ahh, GuP ahh. . . . kooP koo-he-e'inon-oo hini'iitiino. . . . henii'eesee-t?

Did you know that. . . . Noisy Walker? [real name, aka Royce Lone Bear]

[[1.5 sec.; no response]]

Henii'eesee-t, 'oh nih-co'on-neeP nee-niitokuw-oot.

Noisy Walker always rode around with him in his car.

Hi3oowo' nihP bisiihi' nih-'iwookeciibiitooni-'.

Remember, everyone had cows.

Bisiihi' nih-'iwookeciibiitooni-'.

Everyone had cows.

Hini'iitiino ceesey nih-woo3ee-3i' woxhooxeb-ii.
At that time there were a lot of horses, too.

Noh koo-<u>neh'eeno, neh'eeno nehe'</u> beh'eihehi' . . .
And was it this one, this old man . . . ?

Huu3e' ne'P ne'iini hoo'eiso'oetiini-' hinee, nih-'iisixoh-oo3i'
hi'in wookec-ii
*Over there then, they herded those cattle, where they took
those cattle to.*

'oh ne'-cih-yih'oon-oo3i'.
And then they chased the cattle this way.

Yih'oon-oo3i'.
They were chasing the cattle.

'oh, toh-yih'oon-ooP . . .
And when they were chasing them . . .

Heenoo nih-beet-woonikobee-t, nehe' beh'eihehi'.[12]
*The way he was, this old man always wanted to act like he
was young.*

He'iicxooyeiniiihi' 'oh ne'P ne'iini ceese' ceese' wookec, 'oh
ne'-ce3kuhnee-t.
After some time, then one of the cows, they, it got away.

Noh ne'i-i3kuu3-oot niixoo nuhu' hi-seenookuuw. [[gesture:
trying to rope an animal]]
And then he grabbed his rope.

Noh XXX, ne'-yih'oon-oot. [[gesture: trying to rope an
animal]]
And then he was chasing the cow, twirling his lariat.

Ne'P ne'-yih'oon-oot. [[gesture: trying to rope an animal]]
Then he went chasing after it.

Woow, woow, woow nonoonoo'oekuu3-oot. [[gesture: trying to rope an animal]]
Now he is twirling his lariat around.

Noonoo'oekuu3-oot. [[gesture: trying to rope an animal]]
He was twirling the rope around.

Noh heet-beexuuni 3i'ookuuhcehit. [[gesture: pointing to a foot in a stirrup]]
Now he was going to stand up in the saddle a little bit.

Heet-ne'-cesiskuu3-oot hinit. [[gesture: throwing a lariat]]
Then he was going to throw that rope.

'oh toh-3i'ookuu-t, hini' censib-eit, nih-'ii3-oo3i'. [[gesture: being thrown from a horse]]
But because he was standing, he was thrown off his horse, they said about him.

[[laughter]]
CihP cihP censib-eit, nuhu'.
The horse threw him off.

Ne'P ne'-won-nehyonih-oo3i' nuh'uuno.
Then the other guys went to check up on him.

Nih-cihP cih-ce'-3owoten-oo3i'. [[gesture: grabbing someone to stand the person up]]
They stood him back up.

Hee, nih-'ii-t, nih'et-niise'eikuu3P het-niise'eikuu3-o', nih-'ii-t.
"Yeah," he said, "I was just about to lasso it," he said.

Ne'=nih-'ii'-iici3inoo'oo-noo.
"Then I got a cramp."

Ne'-oow-ceno'oo-noo, nih-'ii-t. [[gesture: falling head over heels]]
"Then I jumped off," he said.

'oh nih-'iiP he'P he'ih-censib-e'.
But in reality they say the horse threw him off.

[[laughter]]
[[2 sec.]]

Roger: Yehei!
          Gee!

[[laughter]]
[[5.5 sec.]]

Henry Snake Can't Keep His Mouth Shut

Bill: <u>Wohei hini'iitiino</u>, ne'-no'o'koohu-3i', [[gesture: pointing to distant location]]
         Well, those guys, then they drove out in the hills.

'oh hini'iitiino hoow-uunoo'oetiin.
But at that time of year, there was no hunting permitted.

Hoow-uunoo'oetiin.
There was no hunting.

Ne'P ne'P ne'ini, huu3e' ne'iini nooku-ho, nooku-ho nih-cee-cob-oo3i' nooku-ho.
Then over there, then rabbits, they were shooting rabbits.[13]

'oh ne'-noohow-oo3i' niine'ee-no nuhu'P nuh'uuno cenee-no.
And then they saw some sage chickens.

Yehei, noohob-e', cenee-no'.
"Hey, sage chickens!"

Henee3nee-ni'ceihi-3i'.
"They really taste good."

'oh hoowP hoowu-ni'-cebeihi-no'.
"But they are not to be shot at this time."

Nooxeihi' nehe' henii'eesee-t, 'oh ne'-ceeP coocob-oot.
[[gesture: pumping a trigger and shooting a gun]]
And then, maybe Noisy Walking [Royce Lone Bear], then he shot some.

Ne'P ne'iini ce'-teesen-oo3i'.
Then they put them back in the car.

Ne'-ce3koohu-3i'.
Then they drove off.

'oh hei'P heetP heet-ce'-woteiihcehi-3i' hini'iit heetP heenoo booo.
And they were going to get back on the main road.

Ne'-3ii-3i'ookuu-t hini'iitiino. [[gesture: indicating a car parked alongside a road]]
And then someone was parked there.

Nuhu' uhh, noonoyoohow-oot nuhu' cese'ehii-ho, nuhu' nih-3i'ookuu-t woow touku3eihii.
Uh, a game warden, a game warden was parked there.

BehP ciibeh-kohtowu-nihii-', nih-'ii3-eihok niine'ee-n neh'eeno henii'eesee-ni3.
"Don't say anything," Noisy Walking said to the others.

Ne'iini cih-too'usee-t.
Then Noisy Walking came to a stop.

Ne'P hei-toustoo-be?
"What are you guys doing?" the warden asked them.

Kookon niinkoohu-'.
"We're just driving around."

Nii-noo-notooxebei-ni', he'ih-'ii3-ee nehe' henii'eesee-t
"We're looking for horses," I guess Noisy Walking said to him.

Koo-heP koo-heP koo-he-ciini coo-cob-oobe?
"Are you guys shooting anything?"

Nee'eeP ne'-cih-'eenetiikoohu-t neh'eeno.
This Henry Snake spoke up real quick before Royce could stop him.

Hee, nih-'ii-t, nookuho', nookuho' neh'-ee3i'.
"Yes," he said, "we got some rabbits."

NoP noP nookuho' nih-no'o3-neh'-ee3i', nih-'ii-t.
"We killed a lot of rabbits," he said.

Uhm, heetn-oonokouhu-ni', he'ih-'ii3-ee.
"We're going to cook them for ourselves," I guess he said to the warden.

KooP koo-beebeet, koo-beebeet nookuho'?
"Only rabbits?"

Hiiko, nih-'ii-t.
"No," he said.

Hiiko, ceneeno' ci' nih-neh'-ee3i'! nih-'ii-t.
"No, we got some sage chickens too!" he said.

[[laughter]]
[[3.5 sec.]]
Hi3oowo' nihP hi3oowo' nih-yoh-woowo'oo3eti-t.
Remember, he was constantly bragging on himself.

Nih-co'oniini.
He always did that.

Heenoo, heenoo [ne'=nih-'iistoo-t.
That's what he just always had to do.

Roger: ['ihee.
                          Oh yeah!

Bill: Yeah, nihP
          Yeah, he would. . . .

          [[1.3 sec.]]

Roger: Nihco'onwo'oo3etit.
          He always bragged on himself.

Bill: Nih-co'on-wo'oo3eti-t.
          He always bragged on himself.

          [[1 sec.]]

General History and Remarks on Henry Snake

Bill: Noh hini'iitiino. . . .
          And that guy.

          [[1.5 sec.]]
          Nih-'iis-cih-'e'inobeenoon-o', Wox Niiseih.
          The way I knew him was as Lone Bear.

          'oh hoowuuP hoowuuP heP he'inobeenoon-o' hi-niisih'iit.
          No, it wasn't Lone Bear, but anyway, I knew his name.

          'oh hini'iit, niine'eeno', nii-cooniini, hiiwoonhehe' nii-coon-
          beebii'eeneet-owoo 3eboosei3iihi' nih-'eeneisih'i-3i'.
          *Those guys, these ones, I can't, today I can't think of what
          their names were back in the past.*

          [[1.2 sec.]]
          'oh nee'ee3P nee'ee3e'inon-o' niine'eehek neh'eeno,
          niine'eehek nehe' heih-'eenetiitoon-in, Siisiiyei.
          *Anyway, that's what I know about this guy, the one we have
          been talking about, Henry Snake.*

          'oh neeyou huu3e' tih-toune'etiitooni-' huu3e', hinee uhh,
          hi3oowo', hi3oowo', tih-noowukuhnee-3i'.
          *And it was over there, when they were being held captive
          over there at Fort Robinson, with the Sioux under Red*

Cloud, remember, when they escaped from being sent to the south?

Heet-won-no'uukoh-ei3i'.

They were going to have to ride down to the south and join the Southern Arapahos.

'oh ne'-cih-ce3kuhnee-3i'.

But then they escaped.

Bill: [Ne'P

then . . .

Roger: [hee.

Yes.

Bill: Yeah huu3e' nehe' nootinei ceitee, 'oh ne'-touneihi-3i'.
[[gesture: thumb pointing behind him]]

Yeah, over there with the Sioux, on this side of the Fort Robinson area, that's where they were held.

'oh tohP toh-touneihi-3i', 'oh hini'iitiino, hini'iit hoo3oo'o', nooxeihi' hini'iitiino beniiinen-no', nooxeihi' hini'iit nih-'eenee3iten-oo3i' hini'iit hinono'usei-no.

And when they were being held there, some of those others, maybe those soldiers, maybe they got a hold of some of the Arapaho women.

'oh nee'eeteihi-t neh'eeno, he-ih-'eenetiitoon-in.

And that's where Henry Snake came from, the one we're talking about.

Koh'-nih'oo3oo.

He was half white.

[[1.5 sec.]]

Noh hi3oowo' hi3oowo' nih-no'otP teesiini nookoxonee-t.
[[gesture: a person's face]]

And remember, he had a very white complexion.

Hisiiseii 'oh ci', ci', ci'=cee-ceneeteenooP [[gesture: eyes blinking]]

His eyes, they were green/blue too.

Ceeceneeteenooku-t.

He had bluish/green eyes.

Neneenit, neneenit, neneenit no'usP beebeet hini'iitiino hini'iit heenoo wootii wootii nih-'oonobee-' nih-'eeneisiine'etii-t.

He just lived a happy-go-lucky way of life.

Nih-cee-ceitee-t.

He visited around.

Wootii wootii nih-co'on-oon-oxootowoo-3i', tohuu-woowo'oo3eti-t.

Remember, people always laughed to themselves because he always bragged about himself.

Roger: Hee.

Yes.

[[2 sec.]]

Bill: Ne'P ne'=nih-'iisiini, hi3oowo' nuhu' toh-co'on-ceitoonetiitooni-' heenoo, heenoo, heeyow-uusiini-'i.

And that was how, remember, people visited each other every day.

Bisiihi', wootii nih-bis-e'inonetiitooni-'.

It was like they all knew each other.

Wootii hini'iitiino, wootii hini'iitP nii-bi'-3ookut-ou'u hiiwoonhehe'.

I feel like those people of the past, well, today they just talk about that time.

Wootii hini'iitiino, wootii hini'iitP nii-bi'-3ookuP nuhu' nuhu' nuhu' ni'-eeneti-3i'.

It seems like they just talk about that time but don't live it anymore.

Nii-ni'-eeneti-3i' wootii hini'iitiino tohuuP tohuu-niiteheibeti-3i'.
They talk all about those times, when people helped each other out.

Hini'iit tih-'ee3neeP hee3neene-entou'u hini'iitiino hononeenebetiit.
About those times when that protective thinking was here.

Wootii nih-bis-oonoyoohobetiitooni-'.
They all watched out for each other.

'oh hiiwoonhehe' hoowuuni.
But today they don't do that.

Hoow-ooh-nee'eesoo.
It's no longer like that.

Roger: [Hoowuuni.
          It's not . . .

Bill: [Kookon siiP, kookon neyeiniihi', kookon niiyou hees-iine'etiin-o'.
          It's really not . . . just going apart, that's just how we live.

          Nee'eeneesoo-'.
          That's how it is.

          [[1 sec.]]
          'oh nohuusoho'.
          That's it.

((At this point Bill tries to elicit a story from Roger, but fails:))

Bill: Neneenin, 'oh, 'oh koo-he-e'inobeenoon-oo hini'iit ne-ih-'eenetiit, nuhu' nih-'enixonoehi-t?

Well, you, do you know about that guy I was talking about,
the tall one?

Nooku-bee3ei, ne'=nih-'iis-cebih'i-t.
White Owl, that was his last name.

Joe White Owl.
Joe White Owl.

[[3 sec.]]
Koo-heih-cooP coo3itoo3-oo?
Do you ever tell stories about him?

[[1 sec.]]
Roger: Uhm!
Uhm!
[[7.5 sec.]]

((Bill now goes ahead and tells a story about Joe White Owl and a nephew
of his. The nephew gets drunk and threatens Joe White Owl. Joe runs
away, but because he was disabled, he is described as running like a
loping camel. But the nephew is both drunk and shirtless, and Joe gets
the best of the situation by not only escaping, but telling the story later,
describing the nephew as left standing at the house with an enormous
white belly sticking out. The last line of the story is as follows:))

Bill: Sii=hiiwoonhehe' heet-noxowone3eih-e3en
hot-o'oowuu'nih-'ii3-eit

I'm going to knock you and your house flat!" the nephew said
to him.

[[laughter]]
((Video 128e, 0:00))

Henry Snake and the Sweat Lodge

((Bill and Roger discuss Joe White Owl further, remembering how he
occupied a prominent position in the Sun Dance. As an old man, he
became sick. The white doctors wanted to give him a shot, but he said

that as a Sun Dance priest, he could not undergo such treatment. He died as a result of refusing the treatment. This leads to general discussion of the old way they used to live and how things changed after World War II. That discussion concludes as transcribed next, leading into the next story. Bill proposes quite a detailed topic for Roger to talk about next. Roger largely ignores the suggestion, however (though he does, in fact, know many stories about raising cattle and has shared them extensively with me). Instead, he uses the suggested topic as a way to transition to another comic story about Henry Snake. (Video 128e, 3:04).))

Bill: 'oh niiyou, 'oh hiiwoonhehe' ,'oh nuhu' hees-iine'etii-no', hiP hoowoohP hoowooh-'e'inoneihiinoo.

But now, the way we live today, this old way is no longer known about.

Hoowooh-nee'eeneestoo.

One no longer does that kind of thing.

[[3 sec.]]

<u>Wohei cih-'oo3itoon-oo he'ii3ou'u!</u>

Well, tell a story about something!

<u>kooP Koo-hei-cee'in</u> hini'iitiino toh-'oo'eixP toh-'oonoo'eiso'on-oo3i' hini'iit uhm wookec-ii?

Do you know about those times when they herded all the cows together/rounded them up?

TohP tohuuP hinee <u>hi3oowo'</u> huut ne'P neeyou hinee uhh, hini'iit nih-'et-no'eso'on-oo3i';

That time of year, remember, there was that place, they were going to drive the cattle there;

Hini'iit huut hoowuniihiihi', 'oh hinee konouutosei-3i',

Those Indian cattlemen from downstream here around Arapahoe would drive them to Burgess, and those cattlemen from Ethete would drive them to Trout Creek.

'oh hinee cihnee ceese', hinee hoh'eni' cihnee, ne'=nih-'ii'-ce3eso'onP bebei3i'P wootii beenii'owuuni-'i.

And that other place over here, that mountain over here, that's when they would drive them over there, when the spring came.

Ne'P ne'=nih-'ii'-cee-censi-'i hini'iitiino wookeciisoo-no', hi3oowo'.
That was when the calves were born.

Wootii ne'=nih-'iitini hoonoyoohow-oo3i'.
I guess that was where they watched over them calves.

Koo-he-cii-woo-wonoote'in?
Do you happen to remember all that?

Nehe' he-ih-'eenetiit, nehe' Monica, Sherman, 'oh nihP nih-woo3ee-ni3i hi-wookeciib-inoo.
The ones you were talking about, Monica, Sherman, they had a lot of cattle.

[[1.5 sec.]]

Roger: 'ihee
Oh sure, of course!

Bill: Yeah
Yeah.

[[2.5 sec.]]

Roger: Nehe' nihii Sherman, nih-'iitoo-3i', huu3e', [[gesture: points over there]]
This, uh, Sherman, where they stayed over there,

Wohei, nih-'ii-t, nehe' Sherman, huu3e' heet-won-ciibe-no', nih-'ii-t.
"Okay," this Sherman said, "we're going to have a sweat over there," he said.

'oh nehe', nehe' beh'eihehi', nih-'ee3nee-sesiihi-t.[14]
And this old man Gunnison, he was really eager.

Wohei, wohei, heetn-iiP heetn-eeneise'enou'u-noo, nih-'ii-t.
"Okay, okay, I will get ready," he said.

Simon hiikoot nih-'ii3-oot, uhh hiit hetkouskuutii nuhu' nec,
nih-'ii-t. [[gesture: throwing water on rocks]]
*To Simon, "also," he said to him, "uh, here you must pour [a
lot] of this water [on the hot rocks]," Gunnison said.*

Hee, nih-'ii-t.
"Okay," Simon said.

'oh nehe' beh'eihehi', nih-woowo'oo3eti-t.
And this old man, he was bragging on himself.

Yeheihoo, hoowuu-hesitee, nih-'ii-t, huut heet-ciibe-no'.
*"Gee whiz, it's not even hot," he said, "in here where we're
sweating."*

Nih-'esinih-oot nehe' Simon-iho'.
He got Simon angry.

Ne'-nookohei-t. [[gesture: going to fetch water]]
Then Simon fetched the water.

Beneesou-'u nuhu'. [[gesture: indicating a big bucket]]
These buckets were big.

Nih-'e3eb-kouskuutii-t rocks. [[gesture: throwing water on
rocks]]
He threw all the water on the rocks.

Nih-'ee3nee-hesitee-'. [[gesture: steam rising up]]
It was very hot.

Bill: Uhm.
          Uhm.

Roger: Hey, hey hiihoowuh-'esitee-', hiihoowuh-'esitee-'!
          "Hey, hey, it's too hot!"

3eb-nouu-3ebkoohu-t back-iine' niicib-e' . . . [[gesture: running out a door]]

Gunnison ran out the back of the lodge, in back of the lodge . . .

Ne'-eh-cii3ihcehi-t. [[gesture: jumping into water]]

Then he jumped in the ditch.

Hini' heet-cebinoo'oo-', nuhu' koh'owuuhee ne'-3eii-ceno'oot. [[gesture: indicating irrigation ditch]] [[gesture: jumping into water]]

Where the water runs by, in the irrigation ditch, he jumped in there.[15]

Nih-'ii-3i'oku-t.

He was sitting in there.

Yeheihoo, nih-woowo'oo3eti-n, nih-'ii3-eit.

"Gee whiz, you were bragging on yourself!" they said to him.

[[laughter]]

Nih-cii-hiten-ow.

"You couldn't take it."

Hi3oowo' nono'oteihi-noo, nih-'ii-t.

"Remember, I'm tough," he had always said.

Nono'oteihi-noo ciibeet, nih-'ii-t.

"I'm really good at sweating," he had said.

Bill: Uhm-hmm.

Uhm-hmm.

Roger: 'oh nohtou tih-nouuhcehi-n?

"Then why did you run outside?"

Hih'oowuh-'esitee-', hih'oowuh-'esitee-', nih-'ii-t.

"It was too hot, it was too hot," he said.

Nih-'ee3nee-hescoowu-'; nih-'oonoxoen-i3i', nih-'ii-t.
"It was really hot steam; they got back at me," he said.

[[laughter]]
Hookoh nii-nihiit-ow, nih-'ii3-eit, Simon-iho'.
*"I did it because you said you wanted more water," Simon
said to him.*

Nee'ee-kouskuutii-noo.
"I poured it like you said!"

Ciibeh-'ooh-nee'eestoo!
"Don't do that anymore!" Gunnison said to him.

Ciibeh-'ooh-nee'eestoo!
"Don't do that anymore!"

Hi-ihoow-nee'eestootiin.
"You don't do that."

Neneenin neisie, nih-'ii-t
"You are my grandson," he said to Simon.

Het-ii-cih-ceh'e3ton, nih-'ii-t.
"You must listen to me," he said.

Heetih-cih-ceh'e3ton-in hiiwoonhehe', nih-'ii-t.
"I'm asking you to listen to me now," he said.

Nii-bi'-een-ei'towuun-e3en,
"I am just telling you about this."

Hi-ihoow-ooh-nee'eestootiin.
"You don't do that anymore."

Ciibeh-'ii-kouskuutii nuhu' nec.
"Don't pour this water like that."

[[laughter]]

Nuhu' nih-'iit-esitee-' hih'oowuhP, nih-'iihoowuh-'esitee'-, nih-'ii-t.

"Where the heat was, it was too hot," he said.

Bill: Hmm!

Hmm!

Roger: Ne'P nehe' Monica, 'iiheihoo, nehe' beh'eihehi', nih-'ee3neeP, ne'-tokohu-t huut. [[gesture: indicating someone fleeing]]

Then Monica [said], "Gee whiz! This old man, then he really, then he ran off scared here."

Siiyei=nih-ceno'oot nuhu' heet-toyoobee-ni', nih-'ii-t.

"He really jumped in there where it's cool," she said.

Hei-beex-ce'ixoh-oobe. [[gesture: bringing someone back]]

"You should go bring him back."

Ce'-ciiten-e'.

"Take him back inside [the lodge]," Monica says to the young men.

Hiiko, hiiko ne-ihoowu-uneniin.

"No, no, I'm not man enough," Henry said.

Ne-ihoowu-uneniin."

"I'm not man enough."

Woow benee3tii-noo, nih-'ii-t.

"Now I'm finished with this," he said.

[[laughter]]

Neetne-ihoow-ooh-'uni.

"I'm not going to do it anymore."

Neetne-ihoow-ooh-'uni ciib, nih-'ii-t.

"I'm not going to sweat anymore," he said.

[[2.5 sec.]]
<u>Ne'-ce'</u>-niitowoot-o' nuhu',
But then he heard about it again,

Huut heet-ciibe-no', nuhu' nih-'iit-ciibe-no'.
"We are going to have a sweat here, where we sweated before."

Ce'iihi' wohei, wohei, heetn-eeneise'enou'u-noo, nih-'ii-t.
Then again, "Okay, okay, I will get all ready," he said.

Neetne-ihoow-nouu-tokoh, nih-'ii-t.
"I won't run out scared anymore," he said.

Heet-nee'ee3i'oku-noo, nih-'ii-t.
"I will sit right in there," he said.

Wohei, nih-'ii3-eit nuhu' beh'eihoh'o, cih-nee, teiitoonoku.
[[gesture: pointing to the place where he is to sit]]
"Okay," the old men said to him, "come here and sit still."

Nuhu' niicib-e', ceebeh-'e3eb-nouuhcehi! [[gesture: pointing to the back of a place]]
"Out the back, don't you run outside over there to the ditch!"

Yehei, neetne-ihoow-nouuhceh, nih-'ii-t.
"Gee, I won't run outside," he said.

[[laughter]]
'oh neneenit, niito' nouuhcehi-t. [[gesture: someone running outside]]
But the first thing, he ran outside.

[[laughter]]
Nih-'ee3neeP nih-'ee3nee-nihi'koohut, [[gesture: someone running away]]
He ran really fast.

'oh hih-'oow-uusiiten-e'.
And they couldn't catch him.

Nih-coon-eteb-eit.
They couldn't catch up to him.

[[chuckles]]
Beebeet nih-'e-eso'oo-t.
He was just running too fast.

Koo-ko3eihtee-t, hiikoot.
He had his shoes on the wrong feet, too.

Hih'oowuuni
He didn't do it again.

Ahh, ne-ihoow-beet-ce'-ciitei.
"Ahh, I don't want to go in there again."

Hiihoowuh-'esitee-' ciitoowuu', nih-'ii-t.
"It's too hot inside there," he said.

Bill: Uhm-hmm.
          Uhm-hmm.

Roger: Hee, ciibeh-'ooh-woowo'oo3eti, nih-'ii3-eit Monica-huho'.
          "Yes, don't brag on yourself anymore," Monica said to him.

          Niiyou nuhu' nec,
          "Here is the water,"

          'oh neene'eeno' hinee, nih-'ii-t, hoh'onookee-no'.
          "And there are the rocks," she said.

          Nii-hesitee-' nuhu' nec.
          "This water [steam] is hot."

          Hee'in-owoo woow, nih-'ii-t.
          "I know that now," he said.

          Woow, woow hee'in-owoo.
          "Now, now I know it."

Bill: Uhm-hmm.
         Uhm-hmm.

Roger: Neetne-ihoow-oohP neetne-ihoow-ooh-woowo'oo3et,
         nih-'ii-t.
         "I won't, I won't brag on myself anymore," he said.

         [[laughter]]
         Hih-'oow-ooh-ciitei nuhu'.
         He never went in this sweat lodge again.

((Following this story, Bill takes over the lead again in the discussion, going into a long series of ethnographic-type remarks on sweat ceremonies, changes in these over time, and noting that things are quite different today. He concludes with the following line (Video 128f, 4:56).))

Bill: Beebeet ne'P beebeet ne'P nee'eesoo' hiiwoonhehe'.
         That's just how it is now.

         ((Video 129a, 0:00))
         [[3+ sec.]] ((pause to put a new videotape in the camera))

Henry Snake Tries to Ride a Bronco

Roger: Nuhu' Simon nih-'ii-cii-cih'ohuseee-t.
         This Simon was chopping wood.

Bill: Uhm-hmm.
         Uhm-hmm.

Roger: Henee3neeP nih-noxoneihi-t.
         He was really fast at it.

         Yeheihoo, henee3nee-noon-oxoneihi-n, nih-'ii3-eit nehe'
         beh'eihehiho'
         "Gee whiz, you are really fast at that," this old man said to him.

         Yeh, nih-'ii-t, noosou-wooneihi-noo, nih-'ii-t.
         "Yeah," Simon said, "I am still young," he said.

Howoo neneeninoo, beh'eihehiini-noo, nih-'ii-t nehe'
Gunnison;
"Well as for me, I'm an old man," this Henry Gunnison said;

Hiit noosou-neyeito'ei-noo.
"But I still ride broncos."

Neneeninoo, nii-teesisee-noo xonou nuhu' woxhooxeb-ii.
"Me, I jump right on these horses."

Hee, nih-'ii-t, nih-'ii3-eit nuhu' Simon-iho', heetP heet-cih-
'iixoohoo3ih-in, nih-'ii-t.
*"Yes," Simon said to him, "you're going to show me," he
said to him.*

Wohei, heet-no'koohu-noo.
"Well, okay, I will come over and show you."

Wohei, nih-'ii-t.
"Okay," Simon said.

Ne'-ciino'on-woo3ee-ni3i no'uxoh-oot.
Then Simon brought over a number of horses.

"Wohei won-teesisee niiseihi-t." [[gesture: pointing to
someone over there]]
"Well, go get on one of them," Simon said to him.

Ne'-e3eb-koxo'uuni yihoo-t.
Then Henry went over there slowly.

Nih-neyeih-'oxow-oot. [[gesture: feeding a horse]]
He was trying to feed them to see which one was gentle.

Ne'-cih-koxo'-no'usee-t nuhu' woxhoox.
Then one of the horses slowly walked over to him.

Tii-tii'en-oot. [[gesture: stroking a horse]]
He patted it a few times.

Wohei ne'-teexokuut-[o'] nuhu' hooku'oox. [[gesture: putting a saddle on a horse]]
Well then he set the saddle on the horse.

Ne'-too-toukutii-t. [[gesture: tightening a saddle cinch]]
Then he tightened it.

Ne'iini, wohei nooxeihi' niih'oo-', nih-'ii-t.
Then, "Okay I guess it's tight," he said.

Heet-teesisee-noo.
"I'm going to get on."

Heetn-iixoohoo3ih-e3en.
"I'm going to show you."

[[chuckles]]
Ne-ihoow-uux-oono', nih-'ii-t.
"I'm not afraid of them," he said.

'oh ne'-teesisee-t. [[gesture: mounting a horse]]
And then he got on.

Beneex-3eii'ohookutii-t.
He got his hand under the tied-on rope a little bit.

[Ne'P, ne'ee3ebP
Then over there . . .

Bill: [KooP[16]
Is. . . .

koo-cii-hooxei hesnee?
Was his Arapaho name Hungry Wolf?

Hooxei hesnee?
Hungry Wolf

Roger: Yeah.
Yeah.

Bill: Yeah.
Yeah.

Hoonii benii'eeneetobeenoon-o' hi-niisih'iit, nehe' Henry Snake.
I finally remembered his Arapaho name, this Henry Snake.

Hooxei hesnee.
Hungry Wolf.

Hi3oowo', ne'=nih-'iisih'i-t hinono'einiihi', neneenit
heih-i'-eenetiit.
*Remember, that's what he was called in Arapaho, the one
you're talking about.*

[[1 sec.]]

Roger: Nuhu' nihii, nuh'uuno,
These, uh, these guys watching,

Heetn-iixoohoo3ih-e3enee.
"I'm going to show you," Henry Snake said to them.

Heet-teesisee-noo.
"I'm going to get on."

Heet-nei'oku-noo, nih-'ii-t.
"I'm going to stay on there when it bucks," he said.

Wohei, nih-'ii3-eit.
"Okay," they said to him.

Ne'-teesisee-t.
Then he got on.

Teesisee-t.
He got on.

Ne'-3eb-nouukuu3-oot nehe' Simon. [[gesture: pushing an animal out of a chute]]

Then Simon drove the horse out of the chute.

Too-to'ow-oot. [[gesture: striking horse on the rear several times]]

He gave it several blows.

Woo-woxuhcehi-t nehe' woxhoox. [[gesture: horse bucking repeatedly]]

This horse was bucking all over.

Hey, 'eiyo' 'eiyo' 'eiyo' 'eiyo', heet-censine-noo.

"Hey, watch out, watch out, I'm going to fall!"

Cih-'iisiiten-i, cih-'iisiiten-i, neisie! nih-'ii3-oot.

"Grab me, catch hold of me, grandson!" he said to Simon.

Hiiko, nih-'ii3-eit.

"No," Simon said to him.

Nei'oku, nih-'ii3-eit.

"Stay on there," he said to him.

Hiiko, hiiko. Woow neneinoo'oo-noo, nih-'ii-t.

"No, no. Now I'm getting scared," he said.

Yeheihoo, nih-'ii3-eit, noh nih-'ii-cih-'ei'towuun-in toh-'uneniini-n.

"Gee whiz," Simon said to him, "you were telling me that you were a man."

Heet-nei'oku-n, nih-'ii3-eit.

"You're going to stay on there," he said to him.

Hiiko, niix-ou'u woxhooxeb-ii.

"No, I'm afraid of horses."

[[laughter]]
Niix-ou'u.
"I'm afraid of them."

Ne-ihoow-beet-teexok, nih-'ii-t, sii=hoowuuni.
"I don't like to ride them," he said, "I really don't."

Ne-ihoow-beetP ne-ihoow-beet-neeheyeisee, nih-'ii-t, nuhu'
woxhooxeb-ii, tohuu-to'oxowoo-3i', nih-'ii-t.
*"I don't want to get close to them," he said, "because they
kick," he said.*

[[laughter]]
Yehei, he-ihoowP he-ihoowuuni, nih-'ii-t, nih-'ii3-eit.
"Gee whiz, you can't be afraid of them," Simon said to him.

Hiikoot, nii-toyo'ee-3i'.
"And they bite too."

Hoowuuni, nih-'ii3-eit.
"They don't do that," Simon said to him.

'oh nuhu', nuhu' nii'-3ouuyetee-3i', neneeni-ni' nii-toyo'oe-
ni3i. [[gesture: horse's ears standing upright]] [[gesture:
horse biting a person's arm]]
*But these horses, when they have their ears up, that's when
they bite.*

Bill: Uhm-hmm.
Uhm-hmm.

Roger: Ne'-3eiisee-t. [[gesture: going inside something]]
Then Henry Snake went inside there one time.

Nih-'iis-tee-teeseyei'i-t, ne'-toyob-eit. [[gesture: putting
things on a horse]] [[gesture: horse biting a person's arm]]
As he was putting things on the horse, then it bit him.

[[chuckles]]
'o'xu'. Nih-toyob-einoo nehe' woxhoox. [[gesture: pointing to arm where horse bit him]]
"Ouch! This horse bit me."

Nih-teexoho'oe-n nehe' donkey. [[gesture: points at addressee]]
Remember, you put your hand on this donkey one time?

Bill: Yeah.
         Yeah.

Roger: Ne'P ne'-toyob-ein. [[gesture: being bitten on the arm]]
         Then it bit you.

Bill: Uhm.
         Uhm.

Roger: Yeheihoo, toyob-einoo. [[gesture: holding arm where bitten]]
         "Gee, it bit me," Henry Snake said.

         Henee3nee-hesowoxuh'u-', nih-'ii-t. [[gesture: holding arm where bitten]]
         "It really burns," he said.

         [[laughter]]
         Ne-etne-ihoow-ooh-'uni neeheyeisee.
         "I'm not going to get near one anymore."

         Hoowuuni, nih-'ii-t.
         "I'm not," he said.

         Yeheihoo, nih-'ii3-eit Simon-iho', ceeboh-'ooh-cih-woowo'oo3eti!
         "Gee whiz," Simon said to him, "don't brag about yourself anymore!"

         [[laughter]]
         He-ihoow-touhooniin, nih-'ii3-eit.
         "You're not a cowboy," he said to him.

Nuhu' hunee touhoowo'oh-no, het-oseikuutii. [[gesture: points to boots]] [[gesture: throwing boots away]]
"These cowboy boots, you should throw them away."

"Hee, noosou-wooyou-'u," nih-'ii-t.[17]
Well, they are still new, Gunnison said.

[[laughter]]
Het-eh-won-i'otoonee.
"You should go sell them back."

Huu3e' het-won-i'otoonee.
"You should go over there and sell them back."

Ne'=nih-'ii'-ee3neen-esnonee-t.
Then Henry was really angry.

Henee3neen-esnonee-t.
He is really angry now.

Bill: Uhm.
        Uhm.

Roger: Ne'-nouuten-o'.
        Then he took the boots out of the corral.

        [[laughter]]
        Ne'-no'o'kuutii-t.
        Then he threw them as far away as he could.

        [[laughter]]
        Koo-woow hei-huuxowooteih? nih-'ii3-oot, Simon-iho'.
        "Are you satisfied now?" he said to Simon.

Bill: Uhm.
        Uhm.

Roger: Sherman-iho',
        Sherman said,

Bill: Yeah.
        Yeah.

Roger: Yehei, ciiwoh-'ooh-'ohookeeni!
        "Gee, don't be crazy anymore!"

        Teebe nih-ceesenowuun-een nuhu' touhoowo'oh-no.
        "We just now got these boots for you."

Bill: Hmm!
        Hmm!

Roger: Yehei, wonooyou-'u, nih-'ii3-eit.
        "Gee, they're new," Sherman said to him.[18]

        Hee, ne-etne-ihoow-ooh-neyeito'ei, nih-'ii3-eit, nih-'ii3-oot.
        "I'm never going to try and ride a bronco again," Henry said to him.

        [[laughter]]
        Ne-etne-ihoow-ooh-neyeito'ei.
        "I'm not going to try and ride a bronco again."

        Niix-ou'u woxhooxeb-ii.
        "I'm afraid of horses."

        Woow ne-etne-ihoow-ooh-neeheyeisee, nih'iit.
        "I'm not going to go near them anymore," he said.

        Yehei, nii-woowo'oo3eti-n neeneistP niiP neeneistoo-n, nih-'ii3-eit.
        "Gee, you brag about all the things you do," Simon said to him.

        Hee, ne-etne-ihoow-ooh-nee'eestoo, nih-'ii-t.
        "Well, I won't do that anymore," Henry said.

        Woow benee3too-noo, nih-'ii-t.
        "Now I'm done with that," he said.

[[2.5 sec.]]

<u>Wohei.</u>

Okay.

Bill: Yeah hini'iitiino, woow, <u>woow hee'inobeeno'</u> neh'eeno
          he'=hi-niisih'iit, hesnP, uhh hihtousinihiitP Hooxei Hesnee.

          *Yeah, that guy, now, now I know his Arapaho name, what he
          was called, Hungry Wolf.*

((At this point the speakers shift to talking generally about telling stories
in the old days, visiting with each other, and the way these things are no
longer done at present. The storytelling part of the conversation ends at
this point, and they begin discussing Roger's treatment schedule in the
rehabilitation center.))

This story sequence offers a number of additional examples of the Henry
Snake cycle of stories and, more generally, of the crazy guy genre of
comical stories. In some ways the cycle may resemble old folks stories,
as Henry Snake's older age is invoked on several occasions. But Henry
is never presented as physically debilitated or as pitiful. The key feature of his character as presented in the stories is rather his braggadocio,
overconfidence, quickness to anger when things go wrong, petulance,
and general emotional and social immaturity. His age is used simply to
underline the absurdity of his behavior, which someone his age should
long ago have overcome. Anyone familiar with Native American trickster
figures will immediately see ways the Henry Snake character resembles
the trickster.

It is difficult to tell exactly where actual behaviors end and embellished, exaggerated accounts begin, but Henry Snake clearly seems to
have actually done some of the crazy things reported in the stories. In
addition, as the double-voiced tellings of Bill indicate, Henry Snake also
seems to have enjoyed reporting on his crazy doings, while at the same
time no doubt embellishing them for the sake of entertaining his audience. The stories have now passed into general circulation, as Roger's
direct, single-voiced versions show. Thus, Henry Snake is a complicated
narrative persona: part the object of narrations, part narrator of action,
part crazy guy performer, part performative narrator of his own craziness. Even aside from his complexity as self-narrator, his actions themselves are still complex: both craziness, and also performed *as* craziness
in an apparently highly self-aware manner. A parallel might be the persona of Buffalo Bill—someone who engaged in spectacular actions, but

then described his own actions for the public in a highly manipulative manner. By allowing those descriptions to pass into the public record, then continuing to engage in spectacular actions that were at the same time conscious performances and enhancements of the existing public narratives, he produced a complex feedback loop of reflexivity and performativity that finally resulted in pure showmanship. Henry Snake represents a somewhat similar example within Arapaho society. Of course, the differences between Euro-American mass media and Arapaho oral tradition are immense. More fundamentally, Henry Snake also seems to have thought of himself primarily as a social healer and moderator through performance (somewhat like the way that Earl described performing comical stories as an aspect of medical healing in chapter 5). Henry's aim was tribal and social harmony, not self-promotion and profit. This is certainly the way that he is presented in the story sequence here and in external ethnographic comments.

The sequence itself is interesting as a collaborative accomplishment, because in fact it seems less collaborative than the other sequences presented in this book. As we have seen in chapter 5, Earl uses a request for a comical story to steer the conversation in a somewhat different direction, but the result is still a highly collaborative comical sequence. Similarly, in chapter 4 we see that Roger is interested in a certain ("high-minded") type of storytelling session, but his friend Carl resists Roger's attempts on at least one occasion, steering the sequence in a different direction, specifically by deploying a comical story at a key moment. Nevertheless, that sequence (only part of which is reproduced in this book) remains quite collaborative overall as well. In the sequences in this chapter, however, Roger repeatedly steers the conversation in a direction away from the high-minded, ethnographic one Bill proposes—again, through the deployment of comical stories. Bill begins by proposing to talk about old-timers, where they lived, what their names were, and details of the old way of life. Yet, Roger responds with a comical old couple story. Bill then responds in kind with three more comical stories that slot nicely into the sequence and develop it, based on the thematic fulcrum of Tommy Brown, who is either the subject or original narrator of all the stories. But then Bill moves into ethnography and the history of the Brown family, urging Roger to add a story in this vein. Roger instead provides a crazy guy story about Henry Snake—a story that is indeed about the time period in question but has little direct ethnographic or historical focus.

For a second time, Bill takes up Roger's lead, as the narrators exchange a series of crazy guy and old folks stories. Bill then again takes the lead in the conversation, focusing on Arapaho ranching in the days before commodities and per-capita payments largely ended these activities (in the late 1950s). He very explicitly asks Roger to talk further about ranching, though he links the request to two specific individuals who appeared in the earlier crazy guy stories as secondary characters. Roger resists for a third time, however, launching into another comical about sweating—though it is indeed about the characters Bill has mentioned. Bill then uses this comical to lead into a general historical and ethnographic discussion of sweating practices on the reservation. He concludes this discussion, and then, perhaps having accepted the fact that Roger has his own ideas about what kinds of stories he wants to tell, does not provide any further explicit suggestions for topics. Nevertheless, the fact that he has talked for several minutes about sweat ceremonies at least implies that a historical or ethnographic story would be appropriate as a follow-up. But for the fourth time, Roger chooses to present a comical story, about trying to ride a bronco. The story is certainly not wildly irrelevant; in fact, it jumps back to one of the characters Bill himself had earlier proposed as a potential focus of narration, Simon. It also is about cowboys and the ranching life, which accords with Bill's earlier request for stories of this type. Thus, while the story shows Roger's stubborn insistence on continuing to tell Henry Snake stories, it is also a conciliatory gesture in terms of Roger's choice of content out of the range of Henry Snake stories he could have told.

Nevertheless, this sequence does not come across as nearly the collaborative *artistic* achievement of the Arapahoe School sequence, or the Estes Park sequence either, for that matter. One of the participants, Bill, does most of the collaborative work, consistently responding to Roger's sequential moves with the appropriate genre or topic. Another way to look at the sequence is to see the two participants as more like narrator and commentator, with Bill building off Roger's comicals by adding interesting ethnographic and historical context and commentary. If viewed in this way, the sequence is certainly a successful *documentation* session of Northern Arapaho language and culture—indeed, one of the most interesting I have recorded. This documentation goal was in fact explicitly stated by Bill prior to the meeting, and this sequence was the least spontaneous and most arranged of those presented in this book. Consequently, it was the chain least oriented toward purely *hoonoxoeheti3i'* 'making each other laugh,' and building social solidarity—though certainly plenty of laughter occurred, and social solidarity among two elders with very similar personal backgrounds and experiences was maintained.

The contrasts in content are also reflected in the contrasting story styles. Note that Roger often tells his stories almost entirely as dialogue, in a way that is highly engaging but can also be hard to follow at times, as it can be momentarily unclear who is talking. He also uses virtually no formal stylistic features. He clearly treats both the stories and the occasion in a very casual way, and shows little concern for telling his stories in a way that would be easily comprehensible to other future audiences at future times. Bill, in contrast, presents his stories with a great deal of ethnographic detail, even internally to the narrative. This detail further illustrates his orientation toward a documentary context, even as he also seeks to enjoy a visit with a friend. On the other hand, Roger's stories tend to have quite explicit moments of (often painful) lesson learning and moralizing, which are largely lacking in Bill's stories, so this too reflects a different orientation among the speakers.

Just as every story is its own unique version of some more general plot and characters, every sequence of stories is its own unique event. Different goals may be involved and different outcomes may be reached. Some sequences are more fully collaborative than others, and the relative degree of cooperation in the joint social accomplishments may be asymmetrical, with more work falling to some participants than others. There is always a delicate balance between creating social solidarity and displaying individual performative virtuosity. Some sequences are more self-consciously documentary than others, especially in the context of language documentation and language shift. Perhaps the most interesting takeaway from the sequence in this chapter is that although it contains the least amount of overt construction of either social solidarity or joint artistic accomplishment, it features the longest and most fully told stories of any of the sequences. This fact echoes Richard Bauman's observation (with regard to individual narratives) that the longest and most elaborated versions are often told for formal, captive audiences (the researcher in this case), while the shortest versions may occur with intimate friends around a campfire (1986, 78–106). Most fundamentally, the sequence shows how a researcher's goal of fully documenting narratives (in the classic language documentation sense) may be in substantial tension with the goal of documenting social interaction and social work done by means of narratives and narration. Still, the social work of negotiating what topics to cover and what stories to tell in this documentary-oriented context is itself an interesting type of meta-social work. This tension is, of course, exactly why in this book I have alternated between chapters that attempt to extensively document narratives and narrative genres and chapters that focus more heavily on social interaction through narration.

9

Conclusion

I began this book by invoking the Arapaho practice known as *hoonoxoe-heti3i'* 'they are making each other laugh.' This is a very broad notion, but it can be characterized in terms of a few social goals. First, the people present are seeking to enjoy themselves in a group, in particular through humor (though not everything has to be humorous, and many socially and morally important points may also be made). Second, they are seeking to build social solidarity and relationships among themselves, while committing to a collaborative effort to help *others* enjoy themselves. Third, they are seeking to build their personal stock of social knowledge and stories. And finally, the narrators have the opportunity to display that stock of knowledge and stories and their storytelling skills, and thus gain distinction.

Within this very general social practice, both conversation and storytelling occur. The latter can encompass both everyday stories, such as recent amusing personal anecdotes or life-history moments, as well as more institutionalized "stories." These institutionalized stories can be from a number of genres, or in quite a few cases, may not fall into any particular genre. Often, a story emerges, is told, and then general conversation reasserts itself. But these occasions fairly commonly develop into sequences of stories. The structure of the sequences tends to be well ordered and guided by a set of expectations concerning story genres as well as themes. In fact, we can draw a broad analogy to the study of conversation generally. For decades in linguistics, conversation was largely an ignored practice, as it was considered too chaotic and disorganized to be formally studied and described. Yet, over the last few decades, the field of conversation analysis has shown that this is far from the case. Instead, there are rules, expectations, and structures that govern much of conversation quite clearly, and that explain the sequential development of interaction. Most importantly, every utterance must be examined in terms of this sequential, interactive process and its place in that sequence. This is the basis of the mutual construction of meaning (see Schegloff 2007, for example). I argue that the same is true of story sequences. Not only do they often emerge from conversation, but like conversation, the ways in which the stories are chained together can be understood as well ordered, guided by rules and expectations that ultimately relate to the mutual construction of meaning and the maintenance and negotiation of human relationships. Any given "story utterance," so to speak, must be understood in terms of its place in the sequence of stories, its interaction with the generalized sequence of conversation that surrounds or intermingles with the stories, and the paradigmatic alternative possibilities available to the speaker.

This is the reason I have focused not on the practice of "making each other laugh" generally, but rather on institutionalized stories in some key genres, and especially on chains of stories, as collaborative achievements in verbal artistry as well as relationship building among the Northern Arapaho people. There are certainly some potential internal meanings of various stories, outside of any context, just as linguistic words and phrases have denotative meanings. But my focus has been on how the story meanings interact with the surrounding conversational context as well as other stories in the chain—not just to produce "story meanings," but to accomplish social work. I have also considered how the stories are enriched and more fully understandable through a knowledge of their genres. Just as a speaker has a choice of what exact words to use in formulating a response to a preceding utterance, storytellers have choices of which exact story from a given genre to use in formulating their narrative response. Thus stories, like conversation, are always both sequential and syntagmatic but also governed by paradigmatic considerations of alternative framings and choices.

Within conversation analysis, a key concept is preferred response. When one asks for help, the preferred response is "yes" rather than "no," for example. If a dispreferred "no" response is to be given, it typically involves a more elaborate linguistic formulation than the preferred "yes" response. We could draw a parallel to story sequences. Preferred story responses involve continuing in the same genre as the preceding story, and ideally with a story from that genre that carries forward some key theme or topic of the preceding story. Failing this, a narrator may at least stick either with the same genre, or with the same themes and topics but using a different genre. But in the latter case, the narrator often takes extra trouble to reframe the genre in question as more cohesive with the preceding sequence than it might otherwise first appear, as happened in the Estes Park sequence (see Rühlemann 2013, 30–34, on "recipient design" in storytelling). Alternatively, the narrator may give a dispreferred response, switching genres, as Roger does in the Riverton sequence. But in this case, it is preferable at least to continue with the same theme or topic, as Roger does. And, as in conversation, storytellers can accommodate to such perhaps less-than-ideal responses in ways that maintain relationship and harmony, as Bill does in the Riverton sequence. All of these features are quite familiar from the sociological study of narrative within conversation, where stories are almost always "small stories" of the everyday, personal, anecdotal variety (Ochs and Kapps 2001; Langelier and Peterson 2004; De Fina and Georgakopoulou 2012; Rühlemann 2013). But I have found little work that examines more formalized Native American institutionalized stories and their sequential telling from a similar perspective. Indeed, as I noted in chapter 1, studies or collections of such stories themselves, even ones devoid of any sequential context, are uncommon. We can now at least better appreciate why these types of stories—especially as they occur in natural story sequences—are difficult to anthologize: their meanings depend heavily on their syntagmatic position in a given story chain, as well as their paradigmatic resonance with their broader genres; and they are most fundamentally used for the purpose of sequential, mutual construction of meaning and relationship. As Margaret Feld nicely puts it, "traditional stories may be viewed as forms of linguistic structure, or interactional strategies, through which identity is discursively produced" (Feld 2012, 115).[1] The one thing they are most clearly not intended for is decontextualization as individual, stand-alone narratives in an anthology. The need to focus on human *relationships* in the documentation of both language and narratives, rather than focusing exclusively on language or narrative per se as objects, has been a consistent theme in recent linguistic anthropology (Debenport 2015, 117; Nevins 2013, 2; Cowell 2018, 263–69; Carr and Meek 2015, 181).

I would like to return now to another issue raised in chapter 1—the "story" status of these stories. From a formal perspective, the stories are often differentiated from traditional narratives, as already noted. Use of the formal quotative verbs *heeh-* (intransitive) and *hee3-* (transitive) with subjunctive inflection to indicate 's/he said' is typically rare or absent from the stories. Many of them are told using everyday Arapaho past tense grammar (past *nih-*; sequential *ne'-* 'and then, next'), though in some cases more formal narrative past tense is used (*he'ih-*, with non-affirmative inflections, 'it is reported that . . . '; sequential *he'ne'-* 'and then, next'). Notably, the believe-it-or-not stories, which have the most formalized generic label, also tend to have the most formalized style, with Strong Bear stories being the second most formalized in this regard.

Another important formal difference concerns code-switching. In Arapaho formal traditional narratives (as well as prayers, speeches, formal welcomings, announcing, formalized traditional histories, and other "high" genres) code-switching has historically been avoided wherever possible. People who do not have the linguistic ability to speak entirely in Arapaho either do not take on the responsibility of performing in one of these genres, or they work with a fluent speaker to memorize a prepared version of the genre ahead of time (see Jackson 2013, 72, for discussion of the same dynamic among the Yuchi). In contrast, code-switching is quite acceptable in comical, *hoonoxoeheti3i'* situations, and it shows up in a number of the stories documented here. In some cases, it occurs because speakers cannot quickly produce some sentences entirely in Arapaho or can't recall an Arapaho word. Because nonfluent speakers are largely restricted from high genres, these types of relatively informal and comical storytelling sessions are important occasions for them to participate collaboratively in a social and artistic performance, which helps maintain solidarity between older speakers even when some are less fluent than others. For this reason, settings such as the Arapahoe school gathering (described in chapter 6) or language immersion camps are among the most common places to see such story chains develop—not just because multiple fluent speakers are present, but because everyone seeks to create a sense of good feeling and inclusivity at these occasions (see King in Taylor 2005, 171–81, for more on the "inclusive" and "community-building" nature of Native humor).

In other cases, however, code-switching is precisely the point of the story. Cross-linguistic jokes and puns (and misunderstandings) are not a feature of traditional narratives, but they are a common topic of comicals and a common plot device as well, as in the story of the old ladies and the anthropologist (see Cunningham 1992 for many similar Navajo examples). More generally, cultural encounter with Euro-Americans is not a theme of most traditional narratives, but it is a central theme of these stories, and thus language differences can become a key focus. The code-switching in the "Strong Bear Shakes Hands" story is clearly central to the message, as it occurs in all three versions documented in this book. The code-mixed utterance from Strong Bear, *heet-chief-hiihe3en* ('I will chief you'), combining an English noun with Arapaho verbal morphology, is not just a joke, but also a symbolic representation of the way that Arapaho people seek to encapsulate and contain Euro-American cultural influences more generally by manipulating them on their own terms (see Fowler 1986 for much more on this concept). Code-switching is fundamental to this story of cultural encounter.

Another formal difference from traditional narratives is the relative lack of repetition, parallelism, and similar devices that abound in many high genres—see, for example, the text and accompanying discussion of "The Shade Trees" in Cowell and Moss (2005, 335–49). On a broader level, the informal and comical stories often lack any clear division into sections (and especially avoid any formal marking of such divisions). This is a relative feature, of course—some stories in this book do have segmentation. But the comicals typically lack the complex series of resonances and echoes that hold lengthy, traditional narratives together across various sections; see, for example, the discussion of "The Scouts" and "The Eagles" in Cowell and Moss (2005, 101–3 and 67–69, respectively) and the example of "Tangled Hair" in Cowell, Moss, and C'Hair (2014, 241–91).

A difference that is simultaneously formal and thematic is the lack of organization into groupings of four in the stories—either on a line-by-line level or in terms of sections. Four is the sacred number in Arapaho culture, and ceremonial or other important activities almost always are done four times. This fact is not only mentioned in traditional narratives, but those texts actually perform the narration four different times, as if the narrative is itself a ritual act that recapitulates in its form the actions being described; see, for example, "The Scouts" and "The Forks" (Cowell and Moss 2005, 101–35 and 313–33, respectively), where the four-part sequences are clearly presented in the texts. These four-part sequences are related to the fact that such stories not only depict rituals and the employment of more-than-human power, but their very telling is itself ritual in nature. The informal and comical stories do not engage with ritual or ceremonial more-than-human power, and they are therefore not ritualized in their form or telling. Virtually nothing happens four times in the stories in this book.

All these distinctions show that comical stories have a different ontological status than the high genres. The lack of the complex, formal structures found in traditional narratives is itself an index of the different ontological status. When Art comments during the Estes Park chain that the traditional narratives "take a long time to tell" while the comicals are "short stories," this is really a shorthand way of referring to the elaborate formal structures—both micro and macro—that characterize the traditional narratives, and also a way of indexing the different ontological status of the less serious comicals. As a result of this distinction, general "making each other laugh" sessions rarely seem to mix the two types of narratives—though in both the Estes Park session and in one referenced (but not presented here) between Carl and Roger, a trickster story is added at one point during the proceedings. As we have already seen, trickster stories are the traditional genre that has the most in common with genres such as old folks or crazy guy stories, so this is not a surprising mixture. But even this is rare in actual narrative sequences that occur within more generalized conversational sessions, at least that I have witnessed.

The preceding paragraphs have emphasized differences between modern, comical narratives and the comparatively traditional, formal narratives. But another key claim of this study has been that the narratives presented here are institutionalized stories that can be considered shared cultural resources. As such, they also differ from the "small stories" that dominate much of everyday conversation, and which are purely personal or anecdotal. As we have seen, they make use of a number of markers to establish the speaker's right to hold the floor and engage in an extended conversational turn. Some of these are similar to what Wagner (2021) reports for the initiation of small stories in Arapaho, including uses of self-repair-type utterances such as *nihii* 'well' or the use of temporal markers such as *teecxo'* 'long ago' or *ceesey* 'one time.' Others, however, are much more formalized, including explicit requests for or at least mentions of a particular story genre, and indications of "it's your turn" or "so-and-so used to tell the story about. . . ."

The relatively structured nature of story turn-taking found here fits to some extent with the findings of Rühlemann and Gries (2015) that conversational storytelling has different rules related to turns than does conversation in general, and that turn order is not in fact always "locally" controlled in the moment-by-moment turns (as is normally the case), but instead can be "globally" controlled based on the activity itself (2015, 171). Rühlemann and Gries's work focuses on small-story personal narratives, however, and thus their findings in relation to turns are not always relevant to the more formalized procedures occurring in the Arapaho sequences here. In particular, while many studies of small stories point to the frequency of co-narration and mutual construction of the narrative— and the same certainly occurs in informal Arapaho storytelling and conversation—the narratives in the sequences recorded in this book are quite striking for the lack of such co-narration. This feature indicates that the narratives already exist in a more-or-less fixed form—their details do not need to be negotiated and elaborated in the moment, unlike an attempt to reconstruct a personal or mutually shared experience.

A number of comical and informal stories seem to have begun life simply as funny personal anecdotes about the narrator or someone else, so it is not surprising that they lack the high ontological status of a traditional narrative. But another key point of this book is to show that some narratives have risen above the status of mere anecdotes, while others have the potential to do so or are in the process of doing so. In this sense they are very similar to certain Navajo comical stories discussed by Keith Cunningham (see Cunningham 1992, 133–36). Those stories all focus on the fact that 'grandfather' and 'toad' are the same word in Navajo, leading to comical misunderstandings ("Grandma, Grandpa got run over in the road!"). In each telling the stories are presented as true, and they are all told in the first person. But in reality, the joke and the stories surrounding it have clearly become institutionalized and proverbial, as shown by the existence of numerous different yet very similar versions. And, like similar Arapaho stories, no actual individual is typically named in the Navajo stories as the victim of either the cars or the misunderstandings.

The complex double-voicing that often occurs with the Arapaho stories is another key index of this special, more-than-anecdotal status. Although they are sometimes personalized to a named individual, either protagonist or narrator or both (as in Strong Bear stories or Wox Betebi stories), that identification serves primarily simply as an indicator of genre status—as a guide to what to expect from the story and how to interpret it, or what has been called in literary theory the "horizon of expectations."

Notably, when anyone is actually named in these stories, that person has always passed on, sometimes decades or even perhaps more than a century ago. For Strong Bear and believe-it-or-not stories in particular, tellers rarely either claim a personal or familial relationship with the narrator or protagonist, or suggest that such relationships in any way motivate the telling. Unlike stories about a beloved (or goofy) grandmother or grandfather, they are not typically told in single-family groups or gatherings, as a kind of "family history"—though John Plume and Henry Snake stories are perhaps somewhat less institutionalized than other genres in this regard. As the early chapters of this book show, stories about supposed individuals, whether Strong Bear or Henry Snake, are not just random accounts that people happen to remember about the person. Rather, the stories coalesce into a genre about a type of persona, in which personal characteristics and typical situations become highly predictable. The personal characteristics are stripped down to the most salient essentials, and the events are almost certainly embellished to highlight those essentials. In no sense are the stories intended to be biographical or ethnohistoric, with all the randomness of individual experience that such terms imply. While John Plume and Henry Snake retain connections to particular families, Strong Bear could be seen as well on the way to becoming not just a folk hero, but a mythical character of the traditional type—with narratives such as William C'Hair's unique account of his acquisition of special powers through fasting serving to speed up that transition.

The stories have now become a cultural stockpile available to—and typically widely known to—the community as a whole, which is a key distinction between the personal anecdote and the story. Earl's instrumentalist view of the stories as resources for talking, or "telling," a medical patient back to health is one index of this fact. Alonzo Moss's comment that serves as the opening epigraph to this book is another: he sees the stories as belonging to the community as a whole and as a commodity of value to the community. The documentary focus that motivated Bill in the Riverton series (chapter 8) is another indication of this status.

But despite his interest in documentation, Bill had also arranged for that documentation to happen with a friend and relation who earlier had experienced a stroke and was now a permanent resident of the rehabilitation center. The context of health and healing arises once again. In fact, a key unifying feature of the story sequences in this book is the concept of healing, broadly conceived (compare Kroskrity 2012, 3–6, including the excerpt of a poem by Leslie Marmon Silko that he quotes there). In some cases the stories themselves are literally about healing and doctors. In other cases, the overall humor is designed to make one or more members of the audience feel better or get well: the stories are a healing treatment (see Teuton 2012, 174–79, on laughter as medicine among the Cherokee; and Toelken 1987, 390–94, on narrative as medicine and the use of images of healing in narratives among the Navajo). In other cases, physical challenges (such as R.'s burned legs) are turned into a source of healing comedy. In other contexts threats to social face (such as social mistakes or awkward moments) or old age and its challenges are acknowledged and resolved through the comic stories. A comic narrator/subject, such as Henry Snake, may use both his own behavior and his stories about that behavior to make people feel better and more at ease, thereby serving as a social mediator and harmonizer. More generally, the traumas of colonialism are addressed, reflected on, and in some ways remediated by these stories. Arapaho loss of agency, for example, may be "healed" through storytelling sessions. The narrators and participants in the Estes Park story sequence were all well aware they had returned to historically Arapaho lands, retracing the footsteps of earlier Arapaho visitors from nearly a century before. Deciding to tell stories in Estes Park was itself a decolonial, healing act, bringing Arapaho language and performance back to a place from which it had long been absent. The Strong Bear stories generally, as well as the stories focused on Euro-American technologies, are also often understandable as healing responses to historical trauma or cognitive dissonance.

On a meta-narrative level, the very act of telling the stories again in places such as the school at Arapahoe and Estes Park can become moments not only of having fun in the present, but also of re-enacting past times when Arapaho language and cultural practices were more pervasive than they seem to be now. One gets the sense—indeed, the participants explicitly say so through their metanarrative commentary—that the narrators and listeners are making each other laugh on a basic level, but also on a secondary level *performing* the way that such sessions used to occur and enjoying this remembrance. The sessions seem to be simultaneously enactments or accomplishments of social solidarity and *re-enactments* of such events, in part for purposes of documentation, in part for the pleasure of nostalgia and memory, and in part as acts of decolonization. Just as the individual stories are often double-voiced, at least some audience members may perceive the entire story sequence as double-voiced: a performance of stories but also a re-creation of the old-time performance of storytelling.

Probably all ritualistic human activities partake of this dual nature as both act and re-enactment to some degree, from Thanksgiving dinner to family night around the television. The re-enactment element becomes increasingly salient however in the context of language shift and loss of oral traditions, which the Northern Arapaho community is both undergoing and resisting. Awareness of language loss heightens nostalgia and a desire for documentation. The important point here is that the very awareness of re-enactment marks comicals and other informal narrative genres and *hoonoxoeheti3i'* as especially salient forms of performance, as institutionalized cultural resources and events that community members can draw on repeatedly over time to build and maintain community. As Cunningham (1992, 156) says about the Navajo comicals, they "are funny largely because they acknowledge confusion but also assert the power of *hozho* or harmony. . . . These very jokes assert people's world view and deal with the tensions disharmony brings." In this function of community-building at least, the stories are not so different from traditional narratives. As Vine Deloria said long ago about comedy specifically, "When a people can laugh at themselves and laugh at others and hold all aspects of life together without letting anybody drive them to extremes, then it seems to me that that people can survive" (Deloria 1988, 167). Whereas traditional narratives are widely appreciated, documented, and anthologized, modern stories—both the narratives themselves and, especially, the emergent sequences that are created with them—deserve far more attention than they have thus far received in Native American studies, linguistics, and anthropology. In particular, they need to be seen as more than just "jokes" or "Indian humor," but rather as a key aspect of indigenous verbal art and community.

Appendix

Grammatical Affixes and Function Words Commonly Used in the Stories

NOTE: The symbol V indicates that there is a vowel in this position in a prefix but that vowel assimilates to the vowel of the following (vowel-initial) form. Where a prefix has a final -Ci-, the last -i- typically drops unless it receives stress.

Template (Affirmative)
Proclitic + tense + instrumental + aspect + lexical prefix(es) + verb + inflections
Example:
ne'=nih-i'-ii-co'on-niistoo-3i' .
that=PST-INSTR-IMPF-always-what.do-3P
'that is what they always did with it'

Template (Non-affirmative)
Neg/interr proclitic + person marker + tense +instrumental + aspect + neg/quest prefix + lexical prefix(es) + verb + inflection markers
Examples:
sii=ne-ih-'oow-beet-nee'eestoo-be.
EMPH=1S-PST-NEG-want.to-do.that-1P
'we really didn't want to do that'

he-ih-i'-ii-toustoo-be?
2S-PST-INSTR-IMPF-what.do-2P
'what would you all (habitually) do with it?'

Common Function Words
See the Arapaho Lexical Database at https://verbs.colorado.edu/arapaho/public/view_search for access to a large online dictionary/database of the

Arapaho language. All words and lexical affixes found in this book are included there.

beebeet	just, only, limited to
hee	yes
hiiko	no
hiiwoonhehe'	now, today
hoowuuni	no, not
kookon	for no reason or purpose, just anyhow, any way, anything
hinee	that, that one
hini', hi'in	that, that one (already mentioned)
nehe'	this, this one (animate singular proximate only)
nenee'	that's it, that's the one, that's the thing
nihii	uh . . .
noh	and
nuhu'	this, these, this one, these ones
wohei	okay, yes; so, now then; well, then
wootii	like, as if; I guess, apparently
woow	now, already, right now
wo'ei3	or
'oh	and, but

Common Prefixes and Proclitics

beet(oh)-	want to do s.t.
beneet(oh)-	IC form of *beet(oh)-*
beni'i-	IC form of *bi'i-*
beisi-	IC form of *bisi-*
bisi-	all
bi'i-	just, only
cee'i-	IC form of *ce'i-*
ce'i-	back, again
cih-	to here, toward the speaker
cii-	negation (in subordinate clauses)
ci'=	too, also
cooni-	unable to do s.t.
co'oni-	always
heetih-	so that, in order to
hei'i-	once, when, after (background to main event)
koo=	interrogation (yes/no questions)
keet-	interrogation + 2S + future tense

kei-	interrogation + 2S
keih-	interrogation + 2S + past tense
he'i=	I guess, maybe, I wonder (dubitative)
he-/ho-	you, your (2S)
heet(nV)-	future tense
heetnii-	future tense ongoing or habitual
heh=	emphatic
hei'i-	*when, once, after (background to main event)*
heni'i-	IC form of *(h)i'i-*
he'ih-	narrative past tense; hearsay evidential marker
he'ih'ii-	narrative past tense ongoing or habitual
he'ne'i-	then, next (in more formal narrative style)
he'ne'i=	that (in more formal narrative style)
hi-	he, she, him, her, his, hers (3S)
nih-	past tense
(i)hoowV-	negation
(h)i'i-	with, by means of (instrumental)
ne-/no-	I, me, my (1S)
nee'eesi-	that is what, how, thus
nee'eet-	that is where
nee'ei'i-	that is when
ne'i-	then, next
ne'i=	that
nih'ii-/nih'V-	past tense ongoing or habitual
nii-	habitual aspect
niisi-	what, how (habitual or future)
niit-	where (habitual or future)
nii'i-	when (habitual or future)
ni'i-	able to do s.t.
senii=	IC form of sii=
sii=	emphatic
tih-	when (background to main event, without causal connection)
toh-	when, after, because (background to main event, with causal connection)
woni-	go to do s.t. (allative)
-'ii-	habitual or ongoing aspect
-'iisi-	what, how (past)
-'iit-	where (past)
-'ii'i-	when (past)

Common Suffixes

Since the suffixes are entirely inflectional, I present them in inflection tables. Arapaho inflections are extremely complex, so I make no effort to account for all inflections occurring in this book but only present some basic inflections. For full information on Arapaho inflections, see Cowell and Moss (2008).

Verb Inflections

	Affirm., Intransitive	Non-Affirm., Intransitive	Affirm., Trans., Inan. Obj.
1S, I, me	*-noo*	*ne-*	*-owoo*
2S, you	*-n*	*he-*	*-ow*
3S, he, she, him, her	*-t, -'*	*(hi-)*	*-o'*
3S.OBV	*-ni3*	*(hi-) -n*	*-owuni3*
3S.INAN, it	*-'*	*(hi-)*	*N/A*
3S.INAN.OBV	*-ni'*	*(hi-) -n*	*N/A*
1P, we, us (excl.)	*-ni'*	*ne- -be*	*-owuni'*
1P, we, us (incl.)	*-no'*	*he- -n*	*-owuno'*
2P, you all	*-nee*	*he- -be*	*-owunee*
3P, they, them	*-3i', -'i*	*(hi-) -no'*	*-ou'u*
3P.OBV	*-ni3i*	*(hi-) -no, -nino*	*-owuni3i*
3P.INAN, they, them	*-'i*	*(hi-) -no*	*N/A*
3P.INAN.OBV	*-ni'i*	*(hi-) -nino*	*N/A*

Full Linguistic Analysis of a Story

("Raising the Ridgepole for a House or Barn" from chapter 2)

Heet-noh'P,	hi'in . . .	hini'iit	tih-'ii-ini . . .
FUT-up-	that	that.one	when-IMPF-DETACH

[They] will raise, that . . . that one [they use] when [they] are . . .

Wohei. . .	hee . . .
okay	yes

Well . . . yes . . .

Nih-'o'oobei'i-3i'	beh'eihoho'.
PST-build.house-3P	old.man.P

Some old men were building a house.

Hee.
yes
Yes.

Hini'iit   ridgepole,   he'ih-'ii-coon-noh'en-eeno'.
that.one   ridgepole   NPST-IMPF-unable-raise.s.o.-3P/3.OBV
That ridgepole, they couldn't raise it.

Hee.
yes
Yes.

He'ih-'oo3onoxuuheti-no'.
NPST-fail.despite.effort-3P.NON-AFF
They weren't getting anywhere with all their efforts.

Hee.
yes
Yes.

Woow Tei'ox   he'ne'-no'usee-t;
now   Strong.Bear   then-arrive-3S
Now then Strong Bear arrived;

Yeah.
yeah
"Hee, nii-coon-noh'en-eet   nehe',"   he'ih-'ii3-eeno'
yes   IMPF-unable-raise.s.o.-1P/3S   this.one   NPST-say.to-3P/3.OBV
Tei'ox.
Strong.Bear
"Yeah, we can't lift it up," they said to Strong Bear.

"'osteihoow-un!"
reproach-EMPH
"You should be able to do that!" [he said to them].

Nuhu' he'ih-'eeneiten-ee.
this.one NPST-hold.in.multiple.places-3S/3.OBV
Then he got a good hold on it.

Ne'-bi'-tees-tou'u-t.
then-just-on.top-strike/hit-3S
Then he just tossed it up there.

" 'osteihoo, hi-ihoowu-uhei3."
reproach 3S-NEG-heavy
"Gee whiz, it's not heavy!"

"Nih-'oo3onoxuuheti-nee," he'ih-'ii3-ee.
PST-fail.despite.effort-2P NPST-say.to.-3S/3.OBV
"You guys weren't getting anywhere with your efforts," he said to them.

Note: Additional stories with full linguistic analysis can be found in Cowell and Moss (2005) and Cowell, C'Hair, and Moss (2014). Abbreviations used in the appendix and notes are: 1 = first person; 2 = second person; 3 = third person; DETACH = suffix that detaches a prefix from a stem; EMPH = emphatic; FUT = future tense; IC = initial change (indicating present ongoing tense and aspect); IMPF = imperfective; INAN = inanimate noun or subject; INCHOAT = inchoative; INDEF = indefinite; INSTR = instrumental marker; NEG = negative; NON-AFF = non-affirmative inflection; NPAST = narrative past tense; OBV = obviative; P = plural; PST = past tense; RECIP = reciprocal; REDUP = reduplication; S = singular.

Notes

Chapter 1

1. See Greg Sarris's observation (Sarris 1993, 188) that there is a consistent tendency to decontextualize, formalize, autonomize, analyze, and depersonalize Native American texts, a point echoed by Cruickshank (1998, 64) among many others. See also Nima-chia Howe's point that scholarship often fails even to analyze a full story, much less sequences of stories, and that the type and order of stories recorded are often products of outside collection practices (Howe 2019, xi, 10, 101–3). Sarris (1993, 24) likewise comments on the problem of outside questioners trying to "manage" contents and contexts. My book presents types and sequences of stories that are maximally controlled by the tellers themselves, especially in the chapters focused on sequences.

2. See Carr and Meek (2015, 187) for a very similar discussion of the importance of inter-textuality, the historicity of performance, and the importance of performative sequence.

3. Brian Swann's anthologies serve as examples. Swann (2005) focused on Algon-quian oral literatures, including only a single example of a contemporary narrative (ironically, contributed by me); Swann (2004), which is continental in focus, includes Maliseet examples of folk-hero-type stories, but is otherwise entirely traditional in focus; Swann (1994), also continental in focus, is somewhat more diverse, including nineteenth-century stories of encounters with Euro-Americans, but has very little material representing a twentieth-century context. Kozak (2013) is a notable anthology focused on the southwestern United States, but again is strongly traditionalist in content.

4. Some notable tribe- or language-specific anthologies include Dauenhauer and Dauenhauer (1987) for Tlingit; Thompson and Egesdal (2008) for Salish; Thompson (2007) for Upper Coquille Athabaskan; Parks (1991) for Arikara; Brockie and Cowell (2017) for Gros Ventre; Leman (1987) for Cheyenne; Feeling, Pulte, and Pulte (2018) for Cherokee; Brightman (2007) for Rock Cree; LeSourd (2007) and Newell and Leavitt (2020) for Passamaquoddy and Maliseet; and Treuer (2001) for Ojibwe. Treuer (2001) is notably more diverse than many of the other collections and contains a number of contemporary comical stories (see pp. 37–39, 53, 61–65, 69, 171–73, 201). Newell and Leavitt (2020) focus mostly on fairly contemporary stories. Feeling, Pulte, and Pulte (2018) include ghost stories beginning on pages 33 and 41 (another very common con-temporary Arapaho genre which there is not space to cover in this book) and offer a nice comical story beginning on page 214 involving cross-linguistic and cross-cultural mis-understanding similar to several in the present book. Teuton (2012) reproduces several good comical stories (see pp. 129–31, 169–70, 177–79). Brightman (2007) has some good

cross-cultural encounter comical stories with a religious focus (pp. 141–44) and several comicals as well (pp. 159–66). For some very good English-language versions of comicals, see Taylor (2005, 47–48, 48, 82–83, 120, 122, 144). Cunningham (1992, 129–56) has excellent examples of Navajo comical stories. Finally, Deloria (1988, 146–67) contains many examples of jokes and comical stories; most are brief jokes, but some are developed more fully into short vignettes.

5. Isaacs's focus differs from mine, however. She looks especially at "lesser-known intergenerational stories" shared within families that show "how life and land . . . have changed since the European invasion" and "how the Cherokees have adapted" (2019, 7). As such, the stories serve as "countermemory" and "alternative history" (6), and are especially used for early childhood education. I would maintain that the Arapaho comicals that are the focus of this book perform many of the same functions, but in a more indirect way that is targeted more toward adult audiences. See also Ballinger's division of Comanche oral narratives into four types. Type three is "predicaments in circumstances involving white people," and type four is "attempts to manage twentieth-century problems" (2004, 12). See also Jackson (2013, esp. p. 22) about Yuchi stories as countermemory and alternative history.

6. Compare Jackson (2013, 47) on the "compressed, self-evident" style often used in Yuchi storytelling and, more generally, Hymes (1996, 112–16) on the difference between "elaborated" and "restricted" narratives, with the latter being especially characteristic of well-established indigenous traditions. See also Cruickshank (1998, 28) on stories as "points of reference."

7. See Sarris (1993, 21) on the same feature in the Kashaya Pomo stories of Mabel McKay.

Chapter 2

1. It is worth noting that one of the Arapaho scouts who participated in expeditions with General Crook in the 1870s was named Strong Bear (Fowler 1986).

2. See also the comments of Jarold Ramsay (1999, 170–76) on non-mythological hero stories in Native America, which begin with a historical event and, though they develop "literary" features, never undergo transformation to "mythical" status.

3. Questions about "do you know so-and-so" are common in Arapaho as a way of initiating stories, since the question serves both to indicate the forthcoming topic and also to ask permission to proceed with that topic. See further discussion of this practice at the end of chapter 5.

4. This is an uncommon word that could be translated most literally as 'fail to achieve one's goals, despite strenuous effort.'

5. This exclamation can occur as *'ostei*, *'osteihoo*, or *'osteihoowun*. The last form (used here) is the most emphatic—and thus the most comical in this situation. More loosely, the translation could be "what a pathetic bunch of wimps!"

6. Note the use of exactly same verb, *noh'en-*, in talking about lifting the ridgepole (previous story) and getting the horse out of the mud here. Combined with the repeated use of the roots for 'fail' (*hoo3on-*) and 'unable' (*coon-*), and the repeated use of *'osteihoo(wun)*, the overall effect here is somewhat comic-book-like or superhero-like, in that Strong Bear and Strong Bear stories acquire a kind of iconic vocabulary.

7. Note again the terms 'heavy' or 'not heavy', which were used in reference to the ridgepole earlier. Implicitly, the wagon, the horses (previous story), and Strong Bear

himself are also heavy—or not. The concept of heaviness comes up repeatedly in the stories.

8. Literally 'knocking holes in their heads.' Combined with the use of *kookon* 'just anyhow, just anyway, without rhyme or reason' the overall sentence suggests Strong Bear is so strong that he knocks them all cuckoo almost by accident, as he defends himself.

9. This is an unusual and highly specific verb, meaning 'bend s.t. belonging to s.o.,' with the possessor (the Swede) being the object marked on the verb. Thus the focus is still on the (no doubt befuddled) Swede, not the rifle.

10. Note that the initial part of this verb (*tone'ei-*) again refers to knocking a hole in someone's head, echoing the verb used earlier about the men he was fighting against.

11. This verb, like the previous *tone'eisiiton-* and *beeyooneenebeen-*, are secondarily derived applicative verbs. They all focus on the owners (of the rifle, the horses), rather than the objects owned, and thus function to keep the Swedes as the focus of the victim-hood, while also emphasizing their lack of agency or ability to respond to the situation as all their possessions are destroyed. This is a key part of the humor of the stories, at least in Arapaho.

12. The base form of this verb is *hiisiw-* 'lie down to sleep, go to bed,' which is redu-plicated here to indicate an extended process. The verb is incongruous because of the added ending *-o'oo-*. This ending typically indicates non-volitional motion (used with verbs like 'float, sink, roll'). It is discordant with the fact that the Swede is using all his strength to try and crush Strong Bear's hand—yet it is he who is slowly sinking to the ground despite himself, exhausted by his fruitless efforts.

13. This verb is very funny in Arapaho. The word 'chief' is embedded in an Arap-aho grammatical framework of prefixes and suffixes, which makes the expression quite amusing.

14. Note once again the use of an applicative verb in relation to the victim of Strong Bear's strength. In contrast, two and three sentences earlier, when the Swede tries to act on Strong Bear, basic transitive verbs are used, with the hand rather than Strong Bear being the referent. This subtly reflects the fact that Strong Bear cannot be affected by the Swede's actions—in contrast to the effect Strong Bear has on the Swede.

15. This is just a sound invented by the narrator, not an actual word.

16. 'Chief' is inserted into an extremely complex agglutinated construction here, which makes the presence of the English morpheme all the more amusing.

17. This is an admonitive exclamation, often used in a somewhat comical manner, as in when someone piles way too much food on their plate, and the response is "that's way too much!" Here the expression is used in reference to his excessively loud singing. Although Strong Bear is greatly admired in the stories, there is also an element of humor about him, in that he sometimes doesn't seem to know his own strength.

18. The humor in this line lies in the understatement. Strong Bears says *wohoe'-et-wonoo3-iine'etii*, I don't know/maybe-3S.FUT-continue/still-live, which could be more loosely translated as 'I don't know whether or not he would still be living.' The line also resonates with Strong Bear's tendency (see earlier note) not to recognize his own strength sometimes.

19. As noted earlier, applicative verb constructions are often used to emphasize both the agency of an actor and the victimhood of an undergoer in Strong Bear stories. Up to this point in the story, such verbs have been used both when talking about Strong Bear, and when talking about the Swede (and what he does to the other Arapahos). At this point

however, a basic transitive verb is used, focused on Strong Bear's hand, not Strong Bear himself—just at the moment when the Swede's agency fails.

20. *Ho'wohoe-* 'close one's hand.' The verb lacks any connotation of force, quickness, etc., and makes no reference to squeezing or some other strong effort. The humor (like with *ce3ei'oo-* in note 22) lies in the casualness of the verb in comparison to the effect caused by the action.

21. Note the contrast between the white man's volubility in his greeting and the very prosaic response from Strong Bear. Note also the way Strong Bear cuts the white man off.

22. The verb here is *ce3ei'oo-,* which means simply 'depart, leave' (without any trouble), which produces the humor of the line—he walks away as if completely unencumbered, casually carrying something (*nohk-*) along, as if it were a sack or bag or small item.

23. Field notes, May–June 2018.

24. Field notes, May–June 2018.

25. These stories can be compared to Cherokee doctoring stories about the contemporary Cherokee healer John Little Bear, reported by Robert Conley (2005). In particular, the stories on pp. 106–17 of Conley's book include some examples of humorous or quite nonceremonial uses of medicinal power, such as using four cigarettes to procure a $12,000 loan (107) or chasing someone out of a sweat lodge by making it too hot (109).

26. This exact repetition of the preceding speaker's verb is a nice example of expressing approval of a proposed narrative (indicated by the use of *teecxo'* 'long ago').

27. The double question here makes John Plume appear not just unaware of Beaver Dodge's power (as emphasized earlier) but also a little too eager to drink. The first question uses the slangy verb *hitookohei-* 'get water,' which is normally used to mean 'get alcohol.'

28. *Si'ih'ebi-* 'too eager to drink, overdrink.' Notice the many different expressions used to emphasize John Plume's excessive eagerness for another drink.

29. *Nootookohei-* 'fetch water.' This is another example of a slangy verb used in reference specifically to alcohol rather than water. The language of the entire story is an amusing mix of formal narrative features with highly informal, even slangy language (as might be expected in a bar).

30. The speaker may have been intending to say *houuneenoo'* here—see the use of this word a few lines later.

31. The actual word is *hónohúbe',* which means literally 'to/on the other side, in the other direction.'

32. In August 2008, Alonzo Moss Sr. called Strong Bear "the Arapaho Samson" (field notes).

33. A notable difference between the story cycles, however, is that the Tom LaPorte stories are not claimed to be true, and indeed, are placed in eras centuries apart (LeSourd 2007, xx).

34. See Basso (1979, 51) for similar remarks about the ways Western Apaches perceive and parody the white hand-shaking style.

Chapter 3

1. From Alfred Kroeber, notebook 1, ms. 2560a, p. 45 (1899), National Anthropological Archives.

2. The plot of this story corresponds generally to Navajo stories about a coyote that is surprised by the presence of a human. When the human suddenly talks and reveals his presence, the coyote falls over dead (see Cunningham 1992, 131).

3. 2003, CD #50, Center for the Study of Indigenous Languages, University of Colorado, Boulder.

4. 2003, CD #50, Center for the Study of Indigenous Languages, University of Colorado, Boulder.

5. Joe Goggles, 2002, CD #180, Center for the Study of Indigenous Languages, University of Colorado, Boulder.

6. 1998, analog cassette tape #4, Center for the Study of Indigenous Languages, University of Colorado, Boulder.

7. This line and the preceding are especially amusing together due to the contrasting attitudes of thought. The first line contains a long, agglutinated form: *wohoe'=henei=cii-tokooxuu'oot-owoo* = maybe/I wonder=potentially=negative-jump.across.it-1S. There are two different hedging proclitics and a negative marker attached to the base verb, suggesting long and careful thought. But then in the second line, the particle *noonoko'* 'oh well, what the heck, why not' (basically, a shrug of the shoulders) negates the serious attitude. The devil-may-care attitude of this line is comical in relation to the careful thought and hedging of the previous one.

8. The verb is *ne'-eh-ce'iin-no'-oxuuheti-t* = then-from.there-back.around-arrive-through.great.effort-3S. This is an unusual, complex, and expressive verb, translatable as 'and then he managed with much effort to get himself back to where he started from.' The base form *no'oxuuheti-* means 'to get oneself to a place with effort/struggle/difficulty' and often implies that it took a long time to arrive, due to the effort. The verb is therefore especially funny and incongruous in a situation where, in reality, the protagonist has nothing but air to work against, and not much time to do so!

9. Note the speaker actually says *wooxe* 'knife', perhaps thinking of *woosoo3* 'arrowhead.'

10. Field notes, October 2010.

11. Richard Bauman (1986, 77) has pointed out that the humorous anecdote differs from the joke in at least one fundamental way: the joke is typically decontextualized in space, time, and character identity, and thus fairly abstract. In that sense, these Arapaho stories are really extended narrative jokes. Cunningham (1992) categorizes similar Navajo stories as "jokes" as well, although I think the term undervalues the genre.

12. Many of these stories remind me of the Wile E. Coyote and Roadrunner cartoons. Roadrunner often does "reasonable" but impossible things by extending an analogy, much as the Arapaho characters in the stories do, then Wile E. Coyote tries to do the same thing, but discovers the reality (impossibility) of the feat, to his chagrin.

13. The teller also suggested that Wox Betebi is "the Arapaho 007" (James Bond).

14. As Toelken and Scott note, "Sometimes an attitude may be accurately communicated in a statement that is technically false but uses humor as a vehicle" (1997, 96). Or, as Toelken puts it elsewhere, the stories can be seen as "the absolute truth being expressed in clever hyperbole" (Toelken 1996, 145). Here we see a full genre devoted to this purpose.

Chapter 4

1. One older man was asked to become part of the Arapaho ceremonial elders group called the Four Old Men. His comical response was, "No, I'm still horny."

2. The proclitic *konoo'=* means 'anyway, nevertheless' and implies a lack of choice or lack of alternative ideas. Notice how often the narrator uses it from this point to the end of the story. It becomes iconic of the entire scene, which involves confusion, lack of choice, lack of understanding, and bad decisions.

3. The use of reduplication here is especially funny, as it implies 'thinking something over repeatedly,' but in a context where rapid action and desperation are needed or predominant. The reduplication is then ironically echoed in the way the woman 'tumbles over and over' (*tee-teco'oo-t*) in the following moments.

4. Between Hudson and Lander, Wyoming.

5. Recording mp3-17, 0:00, Center for the Study of Indigenous Languages, University of Colorado, Boulder.

6. Robert literally says 'I told about it,' but he must have intended *niitobee-noo* 'I heard about it.'

7. This particular line is especially comical because of the verb *nee3nee-oonoxoni-i3eti-*. *-i3eti-* means 'nice, good.' *nee3nee-* means 'very, really'. This would be a common thing to say in Arapaho. But the narrator goes over the top by adding *hoxon-*, in its reduplicated form *hoonoxon-*. This root is often used to mean 'fast, quickly, hard' or 'decisively, suddenly' (*hoonoxonisee-* would mean 'get up and walk out very suddenly and quickly,' 'hit the road'). Its use with stative expressions such as here is very unusual. One might translate this as 'strikingly good.'

8. The narrator again goes over the top with this verb. Rather than the normal verb for 'long' (*heyoo-*), he uses *no'o3iici3oo-*, meaning something like 'powerfully long' or even 'frightfully long' (*no'o3-* 'powerful, frightful').

9. In this opening line, the narrator uses topic-initiation *wohei*, uses a definite marker to indicate referents of future interest, and uses a self-repair device—all despite the fact that the story is elicited, so holding the floor is not at stake.

10. The narrator uses the narrative past tense marker *he'ih-* on several occasions, along with the narrative sequential marker *he'ne'-* on occasion, which gives his narrative a more formal feel than many others reproduced in this book. Note that he alternates between these forms and their everyday equivalents *nih-* and *ne'-* however, and sometimes uses the non-affirmative inflections required by *he'ih-* but without actually using the prefix (another fairly informal choice).

11. This line is funny because in Arapaho *hineniini-* 'be a man' is primarily used in contexts of saying, 'I'm no longer a child, I'm a man now,' or in situations such as, 'We need a man to do it,' and evokes younger men who are physically in their prime. Thus, the use of the vocative form 'old man!' is comically jarring.

12. This is a spontaneously invented sound, not an actual Arapaho word, though it bears a resemblance to *yeheihoo*, which can mean 'yikes!' and can indicate surprise.

13. *toon=hei'-ce'-beex-een-e'in-oo'oo-t* = INDEF-when-again-a.little-REDUP-know-INCHOAT-3S. This long agglutinated form could be loosely glossed as 'whenever it was that he was just starting to regain a little of his senses again,' all expressed in a single word. The length and detail of the verb are symbolic of the man's slow process of recovering from his faint. This makes the following verb, especially the root *noxow-* 'very near; very intense; very hard,' comically contrastive.

14. The word here is *yehei*, indicating surprise.

Chapter 5

1. Such stories of linguistic mishaps are no doubt common around the world. See Cunningham (1992, 141) for a Navajo example.

2. Note in both this and the next story, the narrator uses the narrative past tense *he'ih-*, not the simple past tense *nih-*. This gives the story a more traditional feel. He does not however use the narrative citational verbs.

3. An area of the Wind River Reservation west of Arapahoe, Wyoming, where the road across the reservation crosses the Little Wind River.

4. The same narrator told me this story again in March 2006 as we were doing language work together. In that version, he explicitly mentioned the slaughterhouse near Riverton, Wyoming, as the source of the guts.

5. A quite similar story for Navajo is reported by Cunningham (1992, 147). The story involves an old couple and animal intestines, but in this case it is the old Navajo lady who thinks her son has lost all his intestines. Another (148) again involves intestines, and this time it is a white man who is not only shocked, but shocked to death by the scene.

6. North of Riverton, Wyoming, along the Wind River.

7. Note that the first narrator continued using the narrative past tense in his third story, and now the new narrator begins with the narrative past tense as well.

8. Although this story is comical in nature, this small scene has an interesting resonance with the Arapaho creation story. In that story, the animals go on all fours, but people are eventually set upright by the creator, leading to the name *3owo3nenitee* ('Indian,' literally 'upright person'). Here, ironically, it is the animal that "creates" the person by raising him upright (*3owoto'oo-*).

9. This scene also has faint mythological resonances. In the Arapaho story of so-called Devil's Tower, a bear chases seven sisters up the tower, trying to catch them. It fails, falls backwards, breaks its back, and dies when it hits the ground. Meanwhile, the sisters have escaped into the sky. In one version of the story, they remain there as the stars that make up the Broken Back Bear (i.e., the Big Dipper). Thus, the story could be seen as a kind of amusing parody of serious Arapaho myths.

10. I do not know the particular significance of the left side here.

11. This is perhaps the key line of the story. *Konoo'=nih-'iis-cih-koxo'-ceenoho'oe-t* = anyway=PST-manage-to.here-slowly-lower.hand-3S 'since he didn't have any better idea, he managed to slowly work his hand back down here.' The highly descriptive verb, through its very length, iconically captures the slow nature of the process described. It is also presented from the point of view of the bear (*cih-* 'to here, to where the bear is'), who is behind the man.

12. Note that this story was told in Estes Park, Colorado, very near the location where the same story was told in 1914 (see chapter 3).

13. This is an unusually complex expression. *Ne'=nih-'iis-een-eeceh-eteeb-eti-3i'* = that=PST-how-REDUP-recover.strength-speak.to.-RECIP-3P.

14. Art told me the same story in March 2006 as we were doing language work together.

15. The doctoring here is being done by sucking—in particular, sucking some harmful foreign object out of the body.

16. This line is especially funny for two reasons. First, the word *'oohoohei* is exactly what John Plume. says in another story—though in that case, he is looking at his own private parts (see chapter 7)! Second, the 'how . . . !' construction is both rare and comical in Arapaho. It is also used in the story of "The Good Garden" (chapter 4).

17. Literally, 'put his hand out of sight someplace,' which is a much more comical way of saying it.

18. In March 2007, Art said that this story was sometimes told by R. He noted that R.'s version included the specific comment to watch out and make sure you didn't see both of the doctor's hands. He also noted that Robert's version (see chapter 7) does not include this detail.

19. A common teasing greeting, especially from older men to younger ones. Since kidney is eaten raw, young men are compared to it since they, too, are "raw" socially.

20. The verb *nih'ko'usi-* means 'turned on, running' and usually refers to a machine. *Niihen-* means 'by oneself, by itself', as if the machine turns itself on. *Hee3nee-* means 'truly, really.' The overall image is of some kind of machine running on a regular cycle, on its own, without any volition, perhaps like pistons pumping up and down.

Chapter 6

1. Black Coal (c. 1840–93) was one of the two principal chiefs of the Northern Arapaho at the time they moved to the Wind River Reservation. In particular, he was the head of the band that settled in what later became known as the community of Arapahoe (where the story presented here was being told). This story is thus an account of the founding of the community of Arapahoe, and it attributes sacred or medicinal power to Chief Black Coal, as his lance is converted into the trees that will shade the future residents. The story also marks the firm Arapaho claim to this land, on what had been up to that point a Shoshone-only reservation.

2. This story can be compared to a Cherokee story about an especially astute raccoon (Teuton 2012, 169–70), which though presented as a true story, is also presented as something that nobody else believes when it's told. It seems to be a Cherokee version of a believe-it-or-not story, though one based in the realm of at least the extremely implausible, rather than the impossible, as many of the Arapaho stories are. The Arapaho narrator commented later to me that the story has a serious moral lesson for Arapaho people: don't hurt me, and I won't hurt you. In this instance, the moral message seems clearly secondary to the performative placement of the story as it provides a link to the thematic relationship with the preceding one.

3. It is common in Arapaho to refer to telling comical tales as "telling lies."

4. For interesting parallels to elements of this story, see Brightman (2007, 137–45), who presents an entire chapter on the Rock Cree genre of stories about first encounters with Catholicism and the misunderstandings that often resulted. One of these stories explicitly describes someone acting as if he is being crucified (137) and another describes someone wanting to act like Jesus (138), which can be compared to the man acting like Saint Francis in the Arapaho story here.

5. An interesting parallel to this story can be found in a Rock Cree narrative (Brightman 2007, 143), which describes some Cree people expecting to get supplies miraculously from heaven after the Christian religion was introduced, without having to do any work. Brightman says the story "suggests parallels with certain aspects of Melanesian cargo movements" that grew up after the world wars (143). The Arapaho story here does not evoke any specific religious connections (though the same speaker previously told the pseudo–Saint Francis story), but it does capture some of the wonder that commodity culture may have produced among earlier Arapaho people.

Chapter 7

1. This very long, descriptive structure is hilarious in Arapaho. *Hei'-iis-eh-ce'-koxceinee-n-etoho'oe-t* = when/after-manage-from.here-back-sticky.noise-remove.hand. from.container-3S. The scene is described from the point of view of John Plume. (*neh-* 'from here to there'), and more particularly, from the point of view of his rear end (even though in reality John cannot see any of this). The root *koxceinee-* is typically used to describe the sound of being stuck in mud or pulling something out of sticky mud (with a

sucking sound then a popping sound). The base verb *hetoho'oe-* 'remove one's hand from a container' is especially graphic and incongruous. When I described the verb and its meaning to my wife (without describing the context) she said, "You mean like Winnie-the-Pooh with his hand in the honey jar?" Not quite.

2. Told in English by Art in March 2007, among other occasions.

3. See Kenneth Lincoln's *Indi'n Humor* for an extended discussion of the *heyoka* figure, including John Lame Deer (Lincoln 1993, 5–6, 58–67, 76). See Fire and Erdoes (1972) for a biography of Lame Deer.

Chapter 8

1. Arapaho men's slang for urinating (like a male dog).

2. Hearing this first line, it is hard not to think of traditional trickster stories, which commonly open with a description of the trickster as always restlessly traveling somewhere.

3. This line echoes the classic sexual over-eagerness of the trickster.

4. A classic element of Arapaho trickster stories is that the trickster is himself tricked into thinking various other characters are desirable young women, but they turn out to be coyotes, foxes, succubi, or some other disappointment.

5. Calling someone a ghost is a strong insult in Arapaho, as close to "cussing someone out" as one can express in the language

6. This line makes me think of the traditional story of the trickster and the rolling skull, where the trickster throws away his blanket in disgust, only to regret it later (Cowell, Moss, and C'Hair 2014, 102–9).

7. This theme of throwing away perfectly good things in anger, and being scolded for it, will be repeated in a later story where he tries to ride a bucking bronco.

8. This scene echoes situations where the trickster gets his hair cut, to the consternation of others in his family, in similar contexts of pursuing young women (see Cowell, Moss, and C'Hair 2014, 73–84).

9. As already seen in chapter 4, questions about "do you know so-and-so" often work metapragmatically to indicate the theme and genre of the forthcoming story, as well as to ask permission to proceed with a story in that theme and genre.

10. Note the speaker is careful to restate this line, reinforcing its importance (refer to n. 2).

11. See Cunningham (1992, 149) for a Navajo example of a grandson tormenting his grandfather in a way very similar to the two stories told here. The Navajo story is especially similar to the second Arapaho story: a grandson flashes a flashlight at his grandfather in the dark outside, then hits him on the rear with the flashlight, and the grandfather rushes inside thinking he has been hit by lightning.

12. Recall that the same theme of wanting to be young arises earlier, when Henry Snake cuts off his braids.

13. There was no season for hunting rabbits; they could be shot at any time.

14. Note the recurrent use of the verb *sesiihi-* 'eager,' also used earlier in relation to his feelings for the young person who was going to arrive on the bus to visit him. More generally, as with the Strong Bear stories, the narrators here repeat the same specific words, phrases, and reactions with regard to Henry Gunnison/Snake, turning him into an iconic character with iconic characteristics.

15. Several classic trickster stories involve trickster jumping into a stream (looking for plums, which are actually only reflected in the water) or falling into a stream (with

his head stuck in a skull, wandering blindly). The scene here, of Henry sitting in an irrigation ditch, strikes me as an ironic parody of trickster stories, and also a commentary on the differences between the old world of trickster days and tamer reservation times.

16. This interruption by Bill, to verify an ethnohistorical fact, is an excellent indication that the stories being told here are clearly considered informal in nature, as such an interruption would virtually never occur in a traditional narrative.

17. Notice how this scene involving new cowboy boots, which have been purchased but hardly ever or never used, echoes the earlier story in which blankets have been bought but never used (and Henry Snake wants to throw them away in disgust).

18. Notice the very active back-channeling from Bill that has occurred during the preceding few lines, as well as the laughter. Not only did both participants enjoy the episode of throwing away the brand-new boots, but a different consultant, who was helping me check the story, also commented that this was "the funniest part of the whole thing."

Chapter 9

1. See also Eleanor and Thomas Nevins's work, including many illustrations of how stories are fundamentally about relationships and relationship building (Nevins and Nevins 2012, 131–37, for example) and Cruickshank (1998, 41–43) on stories as a social activity, as opposed to a reified product.

Bibliography

Allen, Chadwick. 2014. "Decolonizing Comparison: Toward a Trans-Indigenous Literary Studies." In *The Oxford Handbook of Indigenous American Literature*, edited by James H. Cox and Daniel Heath Justice, 377–94. Oxford: Oxford University Press.

Ballinger, Franchot. 2004. *Living Sideways: Tricksters in American Indian Oral Traditions.* Norman: University of Oklahoma Press.

Barnouw, Victor. 1977. *Wisconsin Chippewa Myths and Tales, and Their Relation to Chippewa Life.* Madison: University of Wisconsin Press.

Basso, Keith H. 1979. *Portraits of 'The Whiteman': Linguistic Play and Cultural Symbols among the Western Apache.* Cambridge: Cambridge University Press.

Bauman, Richard. 1986. *Story, Performance, and Event: Contextual Studies of Oral Narrative.* Cambridge: Cambridge University Press.

Beardslee, Lois. 2003. *Lies to Live By.* East Lansing: Michigan State University Press.

Briggs, Charles L. 1988. *Competence in Performance: The Creativity of Tradition in Mexicano Verbal Art.* Philadelphia: University of Pennsylvania Press.

Briggs, Charles L., and Richard Bauman. 1992. "Genre, Intertextuality, and Social Power." *Journal of Linguistic Anthropology* 2, no. 2: 131–72.

Brightman, Robert A. ed. 2007. *Ācaðōhkīwina and ācimōwina: Traditional Narratives of the Rock Cree Indians.* Regina, SK: Canadian Plains Research Center, University of Regina.

Brockie, Terry, and Andrew Cowell, eds. and trans. 2017. *Aaniiih/Gros Ventre Stories: Told by Aaniiih/Gros Ventre Elders and/or Retold by Terry Brockie.* Regina, SK: University of Regina Press and First Nations University of Canada.

Brunvand, Jan Harold. 1976. *Folklore: A Study and Research Guide.* New York: St. Martin's Press.

Carr, Gerald R., and Barbra Meek. 2015. "The Poetics of Language Revitalization: Text, Performance, and Change." In Kroskrity and Webster 2015, 180–205.

Clements, William M. 1996. *Native American Verbal Arts: Texts and Contexts.* Tucson: University of Arizona Press.

Clifford, James. 2013. *Returns: Becoming Indigenous in the Twenty-First Century.* Cambridge, MA: Harvard University Press.

Conley, Robert J. 2005. *Cherokee Medicine Man: The Life and Work of a Modern-Day Healer.* Norman: University of Oklahoma Press.

Cowell, Andrew. 2002. "The Poetics of Arapaho Storytelling: Voice, Print, Salvage, and Performance." *Oral Tradition* 17: 18–52.

———. 2004. "Arapaho Placenames in Colorado: Indigenous Mapping, White Remaking." *Names* 52: 21–41.

———. 2018. *Naming the World: Language and Power among the Northern Arapaho.* Tucson: University of Arizona Press.

Cowell, Andrew, and Alonzo Moss Sr., eds. and trans. 2005. *Hinono'einoo3itoono/Arapaho Historical Traditions: Told by Paul Moss.* Winnipeg: University of Manitoba Press.

———. 2008. *The Arapaho Language.* Boulder: University Press of Colorado.

Cowell, Andrew, Alonzo Moss Sr., and William C'Hair, eds. 2014. *Arapaho Stories, Songs, and Prayers: A Bilingual Anthology.* Norman: University of Oklahoma Press.

Cruickshank, Julie. 1998. *The Social Life of Stories: Narrative and Knowledge in the Yukon Territory.* Lincoln: University of Nebraska Press.

Cunningham, Keith. 1992. *American Indians' Kitchen-Table Stories: Contemporary Conversations with Cherokee, Sioux, Hopi, Osage, Navajo, Zuni, and Members of Other Nations.* Little Rock, AR: August House.

Dauenhauer, Nora Marks, and Richard Dauenhauer. eds. 1987. *Haa Shaká: Tlingit Oral Narratives.* Seattle: University of Washington Press and Sealaska Heritage.

Debenport, Erin. 2015. *Fixing the Books: Secrecy, Literacy, and Perfectibility in Indigenous New Mexico.* Santa Fe, NM: School for Advanced Research Press.

De Fina, Anna, and Alexandra Georgakopoulou. 2012. *Analyzing Narrative: Discourse and Sociolinguistic Perspectives.* Cambridge: Cambridge University Press.

Deloria, Vine. 1988. *Custer Died for Your Sins: An Indian Manifesto.* Norman: University of Oklahoma Press.

Eggan, Fred. 1955. "The Cheyenne and Arapaho Kinship System." In *Social Anthropology of North American Tribes*, edited by Fred Eggan, 35–98. Chicago: University of Chicago Press.

Feeling, Durbin, William Pulte, and Gregory Pulte. 2018. *Cherokee Narratives: A Linguistic Study.* Norman: University of Oklahoma Press.

Feld, Margaret. 2012. "Kumiai Stories: Bridges between the Oral Tradition and Classroom Practice." In Kroskrity 2012.

Fire, John/Lame Deer and Richard Erdoes. 1972. *Lame Deer, Seeker of Visions.* New York: Simon and Schuster.

Fowler, Loretta. 1986. *Arapahoe Politics, 1851–1978: Shared Symbols in Crises of Authority.* Lincoln: University of Nebraska Press.

Georgakopoulou, Alexandra. 2005. "Same Old Story?: On the Interactional Dynamics of Shared Narratives." In *Narrative Interaction*, edited by Uta M. Quasthoff and Tabea Becker, 223–41. Amsterdam: John Benjamins.

Georges, Robert A., and Michael Owen Jones. 1995. *Folkloristics: An Introduction*. Bloomington: Indiana University Press.

Goodwin, Marjorie H., and Charles Goodwin. 2001. "Emotion within Situated Activity." In *Linguistic Anthropology: A Reader,* edited by Alessandro Duranti, 239–57. Malden, MA: Blackwell.

Henne-Ochoa, Richard, Emma Elliott-Groves, Barbra A. Meek, and Barbara Rogoff. 2020. "Pathways Forward for Indigenous Language Reclamation: Engaging Indigenous Epistemology and Learning by Observing and Pitching in to Family and Community Endeavors." *Modern Language Journal* 104, no. 2: 481–93.

Horse Capture, George, ed., Fred P. Gone, collector. 1980. *The Seven Visions of Bull Lodge, as Told by His Daughter, Garter Snake*. Lincoln: University of Nebraska Press.

Howe, Nimachia. 2019. *Retelling Trickster in Naapi's Language*. Louisville, CO: University Press of Colorado.

Hymes, Dell. 1981. *"In vain I tried to tell you." Essays in Native American Ethnopoetics*. Philadelphia: University of Pennsylvania Press.

———. 1987. "Anthologies and Narrators." In Swann and Krupat 1987, 41–84.

———. 1996. *Ethnography, Linguistics, Narrative Inequality: Toward an Understanding of Voice*. London: Taylor and Francis.

Isaacs, Sandra Muse. 2019. *Eastern Cherokee Stories: A Living Oral Tradition and Its Cultural Continuance*. Norman: University of Oklahoma Press.

Jackson, Jason Baird. 2013. *Yuchi Folklore: Cultural Expression in a Southeastern Native American Community*. Norman: University of Oklahoma Press.

Jauss, Hans Robert, and Elizabeth Benzinger. 1970. "Literary History as a Challenge to Literary Theory." *New Literary History* 2, no. 1: 7–37.

Killsback, Leo K. 2020. *A Sacred People: Indigenous Governance, Traditional Leadership, and the Warriors of the Cheyenne Nation*. Lubbock: Texas Tech University Press.

Kozak, David L., ed. 2013. *Inside Dazzling Mountains: Southwest Native Verbal Arts*. Lincoln: University of Nebraska Press.

Kroeber, Alfred L. 1983 [1907]. *The Arapaho*. Lincoln: University of Nebraska Press.

Kroskrity, Paul V., ed. 2012. *Telling Stories in the Face of Danger: Language Renewal in Native American Communities*. Norman: University of Oklahoma Press.

Kroskrity, Paul V., and Anthony K. Webster, eds. 2015. *The Legacy of Dell Hymes: Ethnopoetics, Narrative Inequality, and Voice*. Bloomington: Indiana University Press.

Krupat, Arnold. 1987. "Post-Structuralism and Oral Literature." In Swann and Krupat, 1987, 113–28.

Langelier, Kristin, and Eric Peterson. 2004. *Storytelling in Daily Life: Perform-ing Narrative.* Philadelphia, PA: Temple University Press.

Leman, Wayne. 1979. *Cheyenne Grammar Notes.* Lame Deer, MT: Northern Cheyenne Bilingual Education Program.

———, ed. 1987. *"Náévàhóo'òhtséme/*We Are Coming Back Home: Chey-enne History and Stories, Told by James Shoulderblade and Others." Amer-ican Philosophical Society Library website, https://diglib.amphilsoc.org/taxonomy/term/8513.

Leonard, Wesley Y. 2021. "Toward an Anti-Racist Linguistic Anthropology: An Indigenous Response to White Supremacy." *Journal of Linguistic Anthropol-ogy* 31, no. 2: 218–37.

LeSourd, Philip S. 2004. "The Legendary Tom Laporte." In *Voices from Four Directions: Contemporary Translations of the Native Literatures of North Amer-ica*, edited by Brian Swann, 546–60. Lincoln: University of Nebraska Press.

———, ed. and trans. 2007. *Tales from Maliseet Country: The Maliseet Texts of Karl V. Teeter.* Lincoln: University of Nebraska Press.

Lincoln, Kenneth. 1993. *Indi'n Humor: Bicultural Play in Native America.* New York: Oxford University Press.

Mandelbaum, Jenny. 2013. "Storytelling in Conversation." In *The Handbook of Conversation Analysis*, edited by Jack Sidnell and Tanya Stivers, 492–507. Chichester, UK: Wiley-Blackwell.

Moss, Alonzo Sr., and Andrew Cowell, eds. and trans. 2006. *Modern Arapaho Narratives/Hinono'einoo3itoono, by Richard Moss.* Boulder, CO: Center for the Study of Indigenous Languages of the West.

Nevins, M. Eleanor. 2013. *Lessons from Fort Apache: Beyond Language Endan-germent and Maintenance.* Chichester, UK: Wiley-Blackwell.

Nevins, M. Eleanor, and Thomas Nevins. 2012. "They Don't Know How to Ask: Pedagogy, Storytelling, and the Ironies of Language Endangerment on the White Mountain Apache Reservation." In Kroskrity 2012.

Newell, Wayne A., and Robert M. Leavitt, eds. 2020. *Kuhkomossonuk Akonu-tomuwinokot: Stories Our Grandmothers Told Us.* Robbinston, ME: Resolute Bear Press.

Ochs, Elinor, and Lisa Capps. 2001. *Living Narrative: Creating Lives in Every-day Storytelling.* Cambridge, MA: Harvard University Press.

Parks, Douglas R. 1991. *Traditional Narratives of the Arikara Indians.* 4 vols. Lincoln: University of Nebraska Press.

———, ed. 1996. *Myths and Traditions of the Arikara Indians.* Lincoln: Univer-sity of Nebraska Press.

Radin, Paul. 1956. *The Trickster: A Study in American Indian Mythology.* New York: Schocken Books.

Ramsay, Jarold. 1999. *Reading the Fire: The Traditional Indian Literatures of America.* Seattle: University of Washington Press.

Rorrick, Neal. 2000. *Conversational Narrative: Storytelling in Everyday Talk.* Amsterdam: John Benjamins.

Rühlemann, Christoph. 2013. *Narrative in English Conversation: A Corpus Analysis of Storytelling.* Cambridge: Cambridge University Press.

Rühlemann, Christoph, and Stefan Gries. 2015. "Turn Order and Turn Distribution in Multi-Party Storytelling." *Journal of Pragmatics* 87: 171–91.

Runstedtler, Theresa. 2012. *Jack Johnson, Rebel Sojourner: Boxing in the Shadow of the Global Color Line.* Berkeley: University of California Press.

Salzmann, Zdeněk. 1956. "Arapaho III: Additional Texts." *International Journal of American Linguistics* 22, no. 4: 266–72.

Sandoval, Rich A. 2016. "Gesture-Speech Bimodalism in Arapaho Grammar: An Interactional Approach." PhD diss., Department of Linguistics, University of Colorado, Boulder.

Sarris, Greg. 1993. *Keeping Slug Woman Alive.* Berkeley: University of California Press.

Schegloff, Emanuel A. 2007. *Sequence Organization in Interaction: A Primer in Conversation Analysis*, vol 1. Cambridge: Cambridge University Press.

Seal, Graham, and Kim Kennedy White, eds. 2016. *Folk Heroes and Heroines around the World.* 2nd ed. Santa Barbara, CA: Greenwood Press.

Simpson, Leanne Betasamosake. 2011. *Dancing on Our Turtle's Back: Stories of Nishnaabeg Recreation, Resurgence, and a New Emergence.* Winnipeg, MB: Arbeiter Ring.

Swann, Brian, ed. 1994 *Coming to Light : Contemporary Translations of the Native Literatures of North America.* New York: Random House.

———, ed. 2004. *Voices from Four Directions: Contemporary Translations of the Native Literatures of North America.* Lincoln: University of Nebraska Press.

———, ed. 2005. *Algonquian Spirit: Contemporary Translations of the Algonquian Literatures of North America.* Lincoln: University of Nebraska Press.

———, ed. 2014. *Sky Loom: Native American Myth, Story, and Song.* Lincoln: University of Nebraska Press.

Swann, Brian, and Arnold Krupat, eds. 1987. *Recovering the Word: Essays on Native American Literature.* Berkeley: University of California Press.

Taylor, Drew Hayden, ed. 2005. *Me Funny.* Vancouver, BC: Douglas and McIntyre.

Tedlock, Dennis, trans., from performances by Andrew Peynetsa and Walter Sanchez. 1972. *Finding the Center: The Narrative Poetry of the Zuñi Indians.* New York: Dial Press.

Teuton, Christopher B. 2011. "Indigenous Textuality Studies and Cherokee Traditionalism: Notes Towards a Gagota Rhetoric. *Textual Cultures* 6, no. 2: 133–41.

———. 2012. *Cherokee Stories of the Turtle Island Liars' Club.* Chapel Hill: University of North Carolina Press.

———. 2014. "Indigenous Orality and Oral Literatures." In *The Oxford Handbook of Indigenous American Literature*, edited by James H. Cox and Daniel Heath Justice, 167–74. Oxford: Oxford University Press.

Thompson, Coquelle. 2007. *Pitch Woman and Other Stories: The Oral Traditions of Coquelle Thompson, Upper Coquille Athabaskan Indian.* Edited by

William R. Seaburg, collected by Elizabeth J. Jacobs. Lincoln: University of Nebraska Press.

Thompson, M. Terry, and Steven M. Egesdal. 2008. *Salish Myths and Legends: One People's Stories.* Lincoln: University of Nebraska Press.

Toelken, Barre. 1987. "Life and Death in the Navajo Coyote Tales." In Swann and Krupat 1987, 388–401.

———. 1996. *The Dynamics of Folklore.* Logan: Utah State University Press.

Toelken, Barre, and Tacheeni Scott. 1997. "Poetic Retranslation and the 'Pretty Languages' of Yellow Man." In *Traditional Literatures of the American Indian: Texts and Interpretation,* edited by Karl Kroeber, 88–134. Lincoln: University of Nebraska Press.

Toll, Oliver W. 2003 [1962]. *Arapaho Names and Trails: A Report of a 1914 Pack Trip.* Self-published.

Trenholm, Virgina Cole. 1970. *The Arapahoes, Our People.* Norman: University of Oklahoma Press.

Treuer, Anton, ed. 2001. *Living Our Language: Ojibwe Tales and Oral Histories.* St. Paul: Minnesota Historical Society Press.

Turner, Victor. 1986. *The Anthropology of Performance.* Cambridge, MA: PAJ Publications.

Wagner, Irina A. 2021. "Conversational Storytelling in Arapaho: A Grammar of Narrative Initiations." PhD diss., Department of Linguistics, University of Colorado, Boulder.

Index

www.ingramcontent.com/pod-product-compliance
Lightning Source LLC
Chambersburg PA
CBHW020349100426
42812CB00035B/3402/J